GRACE
ABOUNDING

Dates

JAMES I 1603-1625

CHARLES I 1625-1649
- 1628 Birth of John Bunyan
  Massachusetts Bay Colony 1630
  The Long Parliament called 1640
  Beginning of Civil War 1642
  The Westminster Assembly called 1643
- 1644 Bunyan in the Parliamentary Army
- 1647 Bunyan demobilized
  Charles I executed 1649
- 1649 Bunyan married

COMMONWEALTH AND PROTECTORATE 1649-1660
  Oliver Cromwell as Protector 1653
- 1655 Bunyan a member of the Bedford congregation
  Death of Oliver Cromwell 1658
- 1658 Death of Bunyan's wife
- 1659 Bunyan married again

CHARLES II 1660-1685
  Act of Uniformity and "the Great Ejection" 1660-1662
- 1661 Bunyan imprisoned
- 1666 Grace Abounding to the Chief of Sinners published
  Bunyan released from prison for a few months
- 1672 Bunyan called to be pastor in Bedford
  Bunyan released from prison
- 1677 Bunyan again imprisoned
- 1678 The Pilgrim's Progress (Part I) published
- 1680 The Life and Death of Mr. Badman published
- 1682 The Holy War published
- 1684 The Pilgrim's Progress (Part II) published

JAMES II 1685-1688
- 1688 Death of John Bunyan

WILLIAM & MARY 1688-1702
  1689 Toleration Act
- 1691 Death of Elizabeth Bunyan

GRACE ABOUNDING

THE LIFE, BOOKS & INFLUENCE OF
JOHN BUNYAN

DAVID * B * CALHOUN

CHRISTIAN FOCUS

For my mother and in memory of my father, who introduced me to The Pilgrim's Progress *and, like Evangelist, showed me the way to the wicket gate and the Celestial City.*

Copyright © David Calhoun 2005

10 9 8 7 6 5 4 3 2 1

ISBN 1-84550-031-8

Published in 2005
by
Christian Focus Publications, Geanies House,
Fearn, Ross-shire, IV20 1TW, Scotland.

www.christianfocus.com

Cover design by Alister MacInnes

Printed and bound by
CPD, Wales

Contents

Acknowledgments

Love and appreciation to my wife and fellow pilgrim, Anne, a skillful copy editor and far more. Her little marginal notes "See me" (in the spirit of Bunyan's "Mark this") always brought greater clarity and insight to the book. She wrote the introductions for each chapter.

Also to Dorothy, and in memory of Jim, Bruce, at whose delightful Jubilee Farm in Macon, Georgia, I happily put the finishing touches on this book. Like Gaius (in the Bible and in *The Pilgrim's Progress*) are the Bruces, "whose hospitality I and the whole church enjoy" (Romans 16:23).

Thanks also to the library staff at Covenant Theological Seminary, whose pleasant and able assistance brightened many days.

And to Robert Shillaker, who made some important suggestions.

Notes

The "big picture" boxes at the beginning of each chapter serve as introductions. The boxes within the chapters contain additional information, applications, and explanations, generally from other writers.

Quotations from Bunyan are taken from the three-volume *Works of John Bunyan*, edited by George Offor, published in Glasgow in 1854, and reprinted by the Banner of Truth Trust in 1991. Parenthetical references give the volume and page numbers of these books.

Preface

I came to know and love John Bunyan's *Pilgrim's Progress* when I was five years old. My mother and father had acquired a filmstrip illustrating the scenes in the book and, for almost a year, taught a Bible class in our home using these pictures. Week by week I listened and watched, fascinated and sometimes terrified, as the story unfolded. One picture that I could not forget was that of the man with the muck rake. The poor man was looking down, searching for something of value in the dirt and muck at his feet, while an angel in shining robes stood behind him holding a golden crown. Why would the man with the muck rake not look up? Why would he not turn around and see what he was missing? At the end of the class my father gave an appeal for personal response and commitment to Christ. I had just learned to write my name, so I signed a card and put it away in my mother's cedar chest.

I have loved *The Pilgrim's Progress* ever since. I have read it over and over and have collected forty different editions, in several languages and with various illustrations. The scenes of the book, such as the one of the man with the muck rake, have shaped my picture of life. And not mine only but those of many people all over the world, from Bunyan's day to the present.

In 1890 the Reverend William Landels wrote, in an introduction to the Altemus Edition of *The Pilgrim's Progress*, that Bunyan's book was "so well known that any information concerning either it or its author seems superfluous; and our ingenuity is at a loss to know how to write an introduction for a book for which, above all others, no introduction is required."[1] Bunyan and his book are by no means forgotten today, but neither are they known and loved as they were a hundred years ago. Many readers may appreciate a new introduction.

Footnotes

[1] Introduction to *The Pilgrim's Progress* (Philadelphia: Henry Altemus, 1890).

God hath chosen the foolish things of this world to confound the wise; and God hath chosen the weak things of the world to confound the things which are mighty; and base things of the world, and things which are despised hath God chosen, yea, and things that are not, to bring to nought things that are. And why? That no flesh should glory in his presence. Perhaps, next to the first publishers of the Gospel of the blessed God, these sayings were never more strongly exemplified in any single individual . . . than in the conversion, ministry and writings of that eminent servant of Jesus Christ, Mr. John Bunyan.

George Whitefield[1]

1

The Life of John Bunyan

Studying the life of John Bunyan, we find ourselves in seventeenth-century England getting to know a person we like. The tall, redheaded John is the son of a working mechanic. He goes to school, "hangs out" with other kids, and plays sports in his small town. Later he works mending things to support his wife and children, whom he loves. He humbly opens to us his sensitive heart, which he seems to know pretty well; and his struggle with sin and guilt could be our own. We can't help being delighted as he slowly understands that God's grace has been given to him and his despair is transformed. We are sad with John when he is unfairly imprisoned for years because he will not stop preaching the grace of Christ. In his cold cell, fearing death, he misses his family and wants to care for them; but he reads his Bible, prays, preaches when he can, plays the flute he has made from a chair leg—and he writes. The preacher, weaving sermons into theological essays, discovers his vocation as a writer. With wonderful imagination and astonishing artistic skill, he creates allegories of the Christian life. The allegories tell his own story. To know Bunyan's books is to know Bunyan. To understand Bunyan is to understand his books.

Early Life

The sixty years of Bunyan's life were "the most turbulent, seditious, and factious sixty years of recorded English history."[2] When Bunyan was born in November 1628, King Charles I, who had succeeded his father, James I (James VI of Scotland), in 1625, had reluctantly accepted the Petition of Right, the first successful attempt by Parliament to limit royal power (sometimes called the second Magna Charta). Bunyan lived through the Civil War and the execution of Charles I, the Commonwealth of Oliver Cromwell, and the Restoration of 1660. He died in 1688, just before the abdication of James II, the beginning of the reign of William and Mary, "the Glorious Revolution," and the Toleration Act of 1689.

John Bunyan was born in the small village of Elstow, just south of Bedford on the London road, in south-central England. Bedford was a sleepy country town of about two thousand people. Its principal business was lace-making, introduced by Huguenot refugees during Elizabeth's reign. On November 30, 1628, the day Baby Bunyan was baptized in the parish church, the Bedford Council registered a scheme to make the River Great Ouse navigable to the sea. This project was completed the year of John Bunyan's death, establishing Bedford as a center for water communication. Tiny Elstow was set in quiet countryside of broad fields and gently rolling hills. The Bunyan family, dating back to French settlers following the Norman Conquest, had lived in this area for at least four hundred years. The Bunyans lived about a mile from Elstow, in the last house on a country lane, known as Bunyan's End. The family depended for food on produce from their small farm, fish from the nearby River Great Ouse, and occasionally a rabbit or birds from the fields. Next to their old thatched cottage was a workshop where Mr. Bunyan made and mended pots and pans. Bunyan may have exaggerated a little when he wrote that his father's house was "of that rank that is meanest and most despised of all the families in the land," but there is no doubt that he came from a poor family (1:6). John learned his father's trade, helping him in the workshop and going with him as he pushed a small wooden cart around the countryside to peddle his wares and services.

> The main source for the early life of John Bunyan is his autobiography, **Grace Abounding to the Chief of Sinners**, first published in 1666. Alexander Whyte writes that "the very title of this spiritual masterpiece . . . may very well be taken as the title of every genuine Puritan sermon; that is to say: first, sin abounding, and then grace much more abounding."[1] Rebecca Beal aptly calls **Grace Abounding** "John Bunyan's Pauline Epistle." The title reflects, she writes, "a major emphasis of Pauline epistles: salvation by grace alone."[2] In the preface, Bunyan

describes his book as "a relation of grace."[3]

Bunyan told his story with simplicity and seriousness. He wrote:"God did not play in convincing of me, the devil did not play in tempting of me, neither did I play when I sunk as into a bottomless pit, when the pangs of hell caught hold upon me; wherefore I may not play in my relating of them, but be plain and simple, and lay down the thing as it was" (1:5).

The main part of the book tells of Bunyan's difficult conversion and long struggle for assurance, a period of at least five years. Bunyan had been in prison for five or six years before he wrote **Grace Abounding** to "further edify and build up in faith and holiness" his fellow Christians (1:4).

It was a requirement in the Bedford congregation that Bunyan joined in 1655 (as well as in other Puritan churches) that new members make a public testimony of their conversion before they were admitted to full membership. Many of these accounts were recorded during the seventeenth century, and a number have survived in print.[4] **Grace Abounding** is a greatly expanded version of Bunyan's testimony to his church.

Bunyan's **Grace Abounding** leaves out many of the facts of his life but sets forth in excruciating detail the agony and uncertainty that he experienced until he found spiritual peace and assurance of his salvation. He aptly describes his book as "something of a relation of the work of God upon my own soul, even from the very first until now, wherein you may perceive my castings down, and raisings up; for he woundeth, and his hands make whole" (1:4). Bunyan's three greatest books—**Grace Abounding**, **The Pilgrim's Progress**, and **The Holy War**—owe "their brilliance and originality to the one indelible experience out of which they [were] written. Christian and Mansoul go through the same depths of affliction and conflict as Bunyan himself, and reach the same peace and reconciliation."[5]

Bunyan expanded **Grace Abounding** through six editions, sometimes giving further information about earlier events and sometimes adding material based on later happenings. Sections 306-17 were added to the fifth edition as a defense against slanderous charges about Bunyan.

Several additional sections, or pastoral letters, complete the book: "A Brief Account of the Author's Call to the Work of the Ministry," followed by "A Relation of my Imprisonment." The latter is "a series of . . . practically verbatim reports of [Bunyan's] examination before the justices. These must have been written in prison immediately after the events, and probably in the form of pastoral letters to console and fortify the Bedford congregation. There are five short narratives, each ending with an epistolary formula such as 'Farewell.'"[6]

John Bunyan was the oldest child of his father's second marriage. His childhood, he tells us, was filled with "fearful dreams" and "thoughts of the day of judgment" (1:5-6). John went to school for a short time, long enough, at least, to learn to read and write. Throughout all his writings, he never complained of his lack of education, although it was often a source of humble apology—and sometimes even of pride. He reveled in adventure stories handed down from the Middle Ages, such as the tale of St. Bevis of Southampton, who slew monsters, devils, and other villains. John's mother died on June 20, 1644, when John was sixteen, and a sad few weeks later his sister Margaret died. The next month his father remarried. He was not a godly man, for John later recalled that he did not "learn me to speak without this wicked way of swearing" (1:9). Yet John seems to have loved his father and hoped for his conversion. When the elder Bunyan died on February 7, 1676, a passage in the book John Bunyan was writing at the time may have reflected his thoughts about his father. He described how the ministering spirits or angels of Hebrews 1:14 take charge of the soul of the dying Christian and "conduct it safely into Abraham's bosom." "Neither . . . our meanness (or poverty) in the world, nor our weakness of faith" will hinder God's angels in conducting us "safely to glory" (1:341).

The Soldier

The Civil War erupted in England during the summer of 1642. Presbyterian Scotland had become incensed with the efforts of King Charles I to increase the authority of bishops in the Scottish church and to impose a modified version of the English Prayer Book. In 1638 the National Covenant asserting Scotland's ecclesiastical independence was signed by thousands all over Scotland, and an army was raised. To deal with the crisis, Charles was forced to call a parliament in April 1640, which he quickly dissolved. But with the Scottish army now in England, he had to call another parliament in November 1640—the famous "Long Parliament." This parliament's first act was to ensure that it could not be dissolved without its own consent. It soon became evident that the king and the parliament were on a collision course. Both raised armies. After two years of indecisive fighting, Oliver Cromwell gained control of Parliament's forces and created an effective New Model Army, based on a measure of religious toleration and personal ability and merit.

On or shortly before his sixteenth birthday, John Bunyan enlisted or was drafted to serve in the Parliamentary Army. He was stationed at Newport Pagnell, some fifteen miles from home. In *Grace Abounding* he makes just one brief reference to the time of his military service, as an illustration of God's providence. "When I was a soldier, I, with others, [was] drawn out to go to such a place to besiege it; but when I was just ready to go, one of the company desired to go in my [place]; to which, when I had consented, he took my place; and coming to the siege, as he stood sentinel, he was shot [in] the head with a musket bullet and died" (1:7).

Bunyan may have seen little military action, but he experienced the rough life of a soldier and came into contact with religious and political ferment of the time. Along with moderate Puritans, such as proponents of Presbyterian reform within the established church, he met radicals, many of whom outspokenly advocated separation from the Church of England. The most extreme radicals were the "Levellers," "Diggers," and "Ranters."

Levellers *wanted to establish equality and political democracy.* **Diggers** *went further, advocating economic equality as well.* **Ranters** *questioned traditional beliefs about sin, hell, and Scripture. They denied the resurrection and the day of judgment. Some espoused a pantheism in which they identified God with the universe, some a mysticism in which they identified themselves with God, and some an antinomianism marked by repudiation of the moral law. Early on, Bunyan met some Ranters who tried to convince him of their views. These Ranters, he*

> wrote, condemned him "as legal and dark; pretending that they only had
> attained to perfection that [they] could do what they would, and not sin"
> (1:11). At one time during his spiritual struggles Bunyan was tempted
> to embrace Ranter beliefs, including the teachings that "there should be
> no such thing as a day of judgment, that we should not rise again, and
> that sin was no such grievous thing" (1:25).

The parliamentary victory at Naseby in June 1645 essentially ended the war. The New Model Army purged the more conservative Presbyterians from the House of Commons in December 1648, brought Charles I to public trial and execution, abolished the House of Lords, and proclaimed England a Commonwealth with Oliver Cromwell ruling as "Protector."

In the summer of 1647 Bunyan returned to Elstow. In one of his last writings, *Good News for the Vilest of Men*, he remembers how he "infected . . . the youth of the town . . . with all manner of youthful vanities" (1:79). Although he may have exaggerated somewhat his sins, he was the "ringleader" of a group of idle young men given to swearing and breaking the strict Puritan Sabbath. "Sin and corruption . . . would as naturally bubble out of my heart as water would bubble out of a fountain," he writes (1:16).

John apprenticed with his father as a tinker until he set up on his own. He traveled the countryside mending pots and pans, sometimes carrying a sixty-pound anvil on his back. He was not much concerned with religious matters. He later wrote that he had experienced both judgments and mercy, but "neither of them did awaken my soul to righteousness; wherefore I sinned still, and grew more and more rebellious against God" (1:7).

His Marriage
Sometime in 1649 the twenty-one-year-old Bunyan married. We know almost nothing about his wife, not even her name, but we do know that Bunyan saw his marriage as an important turning point in his life. His wife's father was a devout Puritan, and she was also. She "was a model woman, and the faith from which she drew her inspiration made a direct call to Bunyan's soul. She brought him a

tender love, but it only awakened his thirst for higher joys."[9] Their first child, the blind daughter Mary, was baptized on July 20, 1650.

The young Bunyans were so poor that they did not have, as he writes, "so much household stuff as a dish or a spoon betwixt us both." They did have two books, however, inherited from Mrs. Bunyan's father: Lewis Bayly's *Practice of Piety* and Arthur Dent's *Plain Man's Pathway to Heaven*. John and his wife read these books together. They "did not reach my heart to awaken it," he writes, yet they did "beget within me some desires to religion" (1:7).

Lewis Bayly's **The Practice of Piety** *directing a Christian how to walk that he may please God (published before 1613) and Arthur Dent's* **The Plain Man's Pathway to Heaven**,*Wherein Every Man may Clearly see Whether he shall be Saved or Damned (first published in 1601) were immensely popular. Bayly's book was suppressed by Archbishop Laud and placed on the Roman Catholic Index. "It was naturally popular with Puritans," comments Christopher Hill.*[10] *Bayly was bishop of Bangor. Dent was an early Puritan minister in Essex.*

"Outward Reformation"

Bunyan began going to church twice each Sunday, and his neighbors were amazed at the change in his life from "prodigious profaneness" to "outward reformation." He became almost superstitious in his reverence for the clergy and liturgy. As he puts it, for a while he fell in "very eagerly with the religion of the times," going to church faithfully, and was devoted to "the high place, priest, clerk, vestment, service" and everything else belonging to the church (1:7). This activity seemed to appease his guilt a little, but his heart was yet like "unweldable mountain and rock."[11]

Despite his outward reform, Bunyan still indulged in Sunday sports. One Sunday he was convicted by a sermon from the parson, but he succeeded, he said, in shaking the sermon out of his mind and went on with his games. In the middle of a game of "tipcat,"[12] just as he was ready to strike a second blow, "a voice did suddenly dart from heaven into my soul, which said, 'Wilt thou leave thy sins and go to heaven, or have thy sins and go to hell?'" (1:8) He decided that he was too great a sinner to be forgiven, so he would go on in his sin. In fact, he feared that he would die before he could enjoy to the full his sinful life.

Bunyan was worried about his love of bell ringing. He became fearful that the great bells would fall on him, or even that the steeple of the church would collapse and kill him. Finally he gave up bell ringing and his Sunday sports. It was even harder for him to renounce dancing on the village green or in the Moot Hall (1:10).

Different opinions have been expressed as to whether John Bunyan's Sunday sports were an innocent pastime or a serious violation of the Sabbath. Was Bunyan extreme in his actions, or did he make proper choices in these matters? Bunyan faced a sharp conflict between popular custom and Puritan seriousness. He came to the conviction that these practices were sin, either because they were in themselves evil or because of evil associations. As Talon wisely explains it, "Only Bunyan knew why he had to stop dancing, playing bowls and ringing bells. But to anyone who knows anything about [Puritan souls], their petty renunciations, far from raising a smile, will seem like so many acts of heroism."[13]

Bunyan "went on in sin with great greediness of mind" (1:9), he says, until he was rebuked by an ungodly woman for his cursing and swearing. This silenced and shamed him and caused him to wish with all his heart that he might be a little child again so that he could learn to speak without swearing.

John was now attempting to live a moral Christian life. He gave up swearing and began to read his Bible. "[I] did set the Commandments before me for my way to heaven," he explains. Not only were his neighbors impressed; so was Bunyan. "I thought I pleased God as well as any man in England," he writes. Bunyan's "self-help phase," or "outward reformation," as he describes it, lasted for about a year; but Bunyan knew that he was "a poor painted hypocrite."[14] Yet he "loved to be talked of," he writes, "as one that was truly godly" (1:9-10). All this time he was ignorant of the fact that salvation was not to be achieved by his own righteousness but by the mercy of God in Christ.

The Women Sitting in the Sun

One day, as John worked in Bedford, he came upon "three or four poor but pious happy women" sitting at a cottage door in the

sunshine, "dexterously twisting . . . bobbins to make lace . . . while
. . . communing about the things of God" (1:i,ii). He came closer
to hear what they were saying, for he was, as he puts it, also a "brisk
talker . . . in the matters of religion." He soon realized that "they
were far above" him in spiritual matters; "for their talk was about a
new birth, the work of God on their hearts." "They spoke," Bunyan
writes, "as if joy did make them speak" (1:10). He knew that he did
not have the peace and joy of these women who could sit so happily
in the sunshine of God's love and favor. Their words went far deeper
theologically than Bunyan's external religiosity; they "enshrined key
Reformation principles" such as justification by faith.[15]

The women were members of a church in Bedford led by John
Gifford. It may be that this "separate" congregation had existed in
Bedford for some seven years, as a church of "semi-dissidents" from
the Church of England, before Gifford gave it definite shape in about
1650. Of the twelve founding members, eight were women. In 1653
Gifford moved his little congregation to the St. John's parish church
building. Calvinist in theology, and Congregational or Independent
in government, the church, as Gifford described it, was based on
"faith in Christ and holiness of life . . . by which means grace and
faith [were] encouraged, love and amity maintained, disputings and
occasion to janglings and unprofitable questions avoided, and many
that were weak in the faith confirmed in the blessings of eternal
life."[16]

The meeting with the women marked a definite change in
Bunyan's inner life. His thoughts became "fixed on eternity." He
began to look into the Bible "with new eyes" and read it as he never
had before. Indeed, as he puts it, "I was then never out of the Bible,
either by reading or meditation; still crying out to God that I might
know the truth, and the way to heaven and glory" (1:11). At home
and out in the fields he prayed.

The Spiritual Struggle
Before long, however, Bunyan was assailed by doubts. He was
troubled by two questions—"Do I have faith?" and "Am I one of
the elect?" Hours of joy and times of torment followed each other
closely. One day the idea came to him that if he were of the elect

he should be able to work miracles. As he walked on the road from Elstow to Bedford, he was tempted to try to make the puddles dry up and the dry places fill with water (1:12).

> Many have attempted to characterize Bunyan's depression and despair as reflected in his account of his spiritual and mental struggles in **Grace Abounding**. Gaius Davies, a consultant psychiatrist at King's College Hospital in London, writes convincingly of Bunyan's "obsessional disorder." In describing Bunyan's case, Davies states that one of his main aims is to show how ill Bunyan was "and yet how this illness was at the same time part of an intense and prolonged spiritual crisis which resulted in huge benefits for him and for us all, his readers."[17] Richard Greaves states that Bunyan "evinced signs of dysphoria (a generalized feeling of anxiety and restlessness, fatigue, poor self-esteem). That Bunyan should have used the insights he gained from this illness so effectively in his writings is a tribute to his literary talent," Greaves comments. "He not only survived depression, but triumphed over it by creatively utilizing his experience in his work."[18]

In a dream he saw the poor people at Bedford "on the sunny side of some high mountain, there refreshing themselves with the pleasant beams of the sun" while he was "shivering and shrinking in the cold, afflicted with frost, snow, and dark clouds" (1:12). In his dream Bunyan finally found "a narrow gap, like a little doorway in the wall" that separated him from the sunny side of the mountain. But "the passage" was "very strait and narrow" and he could not get through. (The mountain was the church; the wall, the Word of God; and the gap, Jesus Christ, writes Bunyan.) He continued to struggle until at last he succeeded and "went and sat down" in the midst of the poor people (1:12). The lesson that he drew from this dream was that "none could enter into life but those that were in downright earnest, and unless also they left this wicked world behind them; for here was only room for body and soul, but not for body and soul, and sin" (1:13).

Still he had no assurance that he was "one of that number that did sit in the sunshine" (1:13). Scriptures came to him, sometimes to comfort but often to perplex and discourage, until he was ready to sink "with faintness in [his] mind" (1:13).

Once he was so troubled that he hardly knew what to do, but the voice of Christ broke in upon his soul, saying, "And yet there is room."[19] These were "sweet words to me," Bunyan writes; "for, truly, I thought that by them I saw there was place enough in heaven for me; and, moreover, that when the Lord Jesus did speak these words, he then did think of me" (1:14). Bunyan was encouraged for a time but still faced the old temptations "to go back again."

Gifford and Luther

It is easy to think that Bunyan was making no progress. "However, the wave that comes in is less strong than the one that goes out," writes Talon; "though buffeted and sometimes submerged, our author did make progress."[20] He had never stopped seeing "those poor people in Bedford," and through them he met their pastor, John Gifford (1:15). He "was willing to be 'well' persuaded of me," Bunyan writes; "though I think but from little grounds: but he invited me to his house, where I should hear him confer with others about the dealings of God with the soul; from all [of] which I still received more conviction, and from that time began to see something of the vanity and inward wretchedness of my wicked heart." Besides Bunyan's wife, John Gifford exercised the strongest personal influence over Bunyan.

John Gifford, *a major in the king's army, was captured at a battle in Maidstone by parliamentary troops; but he escaped and came to Bedford, where he practiced medicine. He was a very worldly man until suddenly, in 1650, after heavy gambling losses, he became a Christian through reading a book by the Puritan Robert Bolton. "At last," as his church session record book puts it, "God did so plentifully discover to him the forgiveness of his sins for the sake of Christ. No sooner did John Gifford become a changed man than, like Saul of Tarsus, he openly joined himself to those whom he had hitherto persecuted and ultimately he became their beloved pastor."[21] Gifford served as minister of the Bedford congregation (which had roots from the 1630s when a Puritan group formed) from the summer of 1653 until his death on September 21, 1655. He may have ministered to his congregation of "visible saints"* *(confessing Christians who exhibited their faith in their conduct) separately from the wider body of parishioners of St. John's Church, but it is likely that they all worshiped together, at least occasionally. Gifford was buried in the churchyard of St. John's.*

Bunyan later spoke of "holy Mr. Gifford, whose doctrine, by God's grace, was much for my stability" (1:20). He paid loving tribute to his pastor in **The Pilgrim's Progress,** *in which Gifford appears as Evangelist and in the portrait on the wall of Interpreter's House. "Apart from the Bible and Luther's commentary on Galatians," Richard Greaves writes, "Gifford's sermons and pastoral counseling were almost certainly the most influential shapers of Bunyan's religious tenets."*[22]

Bunyan now understood the way of salvation. He writes, "I saw that I wanted a perfect righteousness to present me without fault before God, and this righteousness was nowhere to be found but in the person of Jesus Christ" (1:16). He continued to be troubled because he was convinced that he did not have that righteousness of Christ and never would. A sermon on Song of Solomon 4:1—"Behold, thou *art* fair, my love, behold, thou *art* fair"—moved him deeply. As he repeated the words—"thou art my love" [sic]—over and over, he found himself "between hope and fear" (1:17). "Now was my heart filled full of comfort and hope, and now I could believe that my sins should be forgiven me; yea I was now so taken with the love and mercy of God, that I remember I could not tell how to contain till I got home; I thought I could have spoken of his love, and of his mercy to me even to the very crows that sat upon the ploughed lands before me."

But this relief was followed by another period of doubt and temptation. He began to experience, to his "great confusion and astonishment," doubts even about the existence of God and Christ and the truthfulness of the Bible (1:17). He was tempted "to curse and swear, or to speak some grievous thing against God or Christ, his Son, and of the Scriptures." He thought that he was "possessed of the devil" (1:18). For about a year he remained in great despair until some relief came from various verses of Scripture, and then from Martin Luther's commentary on Galatians. The book was "so old that it was ready to fall piece from piece if I did but turn it over," Bunyan writes. After reading a little of this old book, Bunyan, as he puts it, "found my condition, in [Luther's] experience, so largely and profoundly handled as if his book had been written out of my [own] heart." He came to prefer, after the Bible, Luther's book on Galatians "before all the books that ever I have seen, as most fit for a wounded conscience" (1:22).

Luther's *Commentary on St. Paul's Epistle to the Galatians* *was composed as a course of lectures in 1531. It was first translated into English in 1575 and frequently was reprinted, including at least seven seventeenth-century editions. The book contains Luther's teaching that a person is not justified by the works of the law but by faith in Jesus Christ, as set forth in the words of Paul "the just shall live by faith." The doctrine of justification by faith alone brought great comfort to Luther, who, like Bunyan after him, had vainly attempted to satisfy God by his own accomplishments, that is, by "the works of the law." To obey the moral law as a condition of justification, for Luther, renders one accursed in God's judgment; indeed, the law and good works actually hinder justification. Bunyan, throughout his life, was greatly influenced by Luther's view of law and gospel. It centered his theology on justification by faith alone (apart from works) but at times caused people to accuse him of antinomianism (the rejection of the idea that the Christian's life is governed by the law).*

The Battle of the Texts

Bunyan's struggle, however, was far from over. Soon Satan tempted him to "sell and part with this most blessed Christ—to exchange him for the things of this life" (1:22). Sometimes the words "sell him, sell him, sell him" would churn in Bunyan's thoughts more than a hundred times until he was physically exhausted. Finally, worn out with the struggle, he gave way and felt this thought pass through his mind: "Let him go, if he will" (1:23).

"Now was the battle won [by Satan]," Bunyan writes, "and down fell I, as a bird that is shot from the top of a tree, into great guilt, and fearful despair" (1:23). He was seized with the thought that he was "bound over to eternal punishment"; and the example of

Esau, "who, for one morsel of meat, sold his birthright" (Hebrews 12:16), began to plague him. "Esau" became almost a code word for him, as he returned again and again to the words of Hebrews 12:17—"For ye know, how that afterward, when [Esau] would have inherited the blessing, he was rejected; for he found no place of repentance, though he sought it carefully with tears." These words, Bunyan writes, "were to my soul like fetters of brass to my legs" (1:23). He now believed that he had committed the unpardonable sin (Hebrews 10:26). But there were moments of relief. One day Bunyan "heard" the words "Return unto me, for I have redeemed thee." So urgent was this message that he stopped and looked back over his shoulder to see if the God of grace was following him "with a pardon in his hand" (1:27).

In his spiritual agony, Bunyan would receive some help from a Scripture verse but it lasted only a few days, or sometimes only a few hours, until another verse of Scripture would come to him to condemn him. For over two years this "battle of the texts" continued.[23] He compared his soul to a "broken vessel, driven as with the winds" (1:29). His pain was deepened by reading the life of Francis Spira, a sixteenth-century Italian who recanted his Protestantism under pressure from the Inquisition. Spira died in despair, saying that he had "denied Christ," lost all faith, and was possessed by "legions of demons."[24] In his depression Bunyan found that reading this book was like rubbing salt into a wound.

With great bitterness of soul he said to himself, "How can God comfort such a wretch as I? I had no sooner said it but this returned upon me, as an echo doth answer a voice, 'This sin is not unto death.'" Bunyan felt that he had been "raised out of a grave" (1:30). A little later, another verse—"I have loved thee with an everlasting love" (Jeremiah 31:3)—brought even more relief and hope. In those words Bunyan heard God say to him, "I loved thee whilst thou wast committing this sin, I loved thee before, I love thee still, and I will love thee forever" (1:30).

"O, Now I Know, I Know!"

Bunyan never gave up. "He was constantly seeking and was ready to grasp any vestige of hope. But even in his most miserable moments he wanted truth rather than comfort."[25]

One morning the words "My grace is sufficient" came to him. Earlier he had felt that this verse was "not large enough for me," but now "it was as if it had arms of grace so wide that it could not only enclose me, but many more besides" (1:32). For some weeks this verse and the account of Esau selling his birthright were "like a pair of scales" in his mind; "sometimes one end would be uppermost, and sometimes again the other." Bunyan still could not believe that the words "for me" applied to him. "But one day as I was in a meeting of God's people, full of sadness and terror," he writes, "these words did, with great power, suddenly break in upon me, 'My grace is sufficient for thee, my grace is sufficient for thee, my grace is sufficient for thee,' three times together; and, oh! methought that every word was a mighty word unto me. . . . It broke my heart and filled me full of joy" (1:32). At last the words and feelings about Esau's birthright began to weaken, and then vanished (for a time), and God's expression of "the sufficiency of grace prevailed with peace and joy." "The word of the law and wrath" began to give way to "the word of life and grace" (1:33).

John Bunyan's struggles were not over, but now there was more hope than despair. "He still went through hours of torment. . . . But joy beat within the sadness, and the union of these two gave his soul its characteristic note."[26] Bunyan remembered each verse and each thought as he made his way to assurance of salvation. One day when he was walking in a field, fearing that all was not right, these words came to him: "Thy righteousness is in heaven" (1:35). He was enabled to look away from his spiritual accomplishments, or lack of them, to his heavenly treasure. As he puts it, "Now I could look from myself to him, and should reckon that all those graces of God that now were green in me, were yet but like those cracked groats and fourpence—halfpennies that rich men carry in their purses, when their gold is in their trunks at home! Oh, I saw my gold was in my trunk at home! In Christ, my Lord and Saviour!" (1:36)

Still there were doubts, until one day, sitting by the fire, he "suddenly felt" this desire sound in his heart, "I must go to Jesus." "At this my former darkness and atheism fled away, and the blessed things of heaven were set within my view," he writes (1:40). He searched his mind for the biblical source of the words, and in just two or three minutes he remembered the passage in Hebrews 12:22-24. With joy he told his wife, "O now I know, I know!"

The Preacher

John Bunyan joined Gifford's church in 1655; his name stands nineteenth on its roll of members. He was baptized (even though he had been baptized as an infant a few days old in the Church of England chapel at Elstow) in the waters of the River Great Ouse, which flows through Bedford.

Shortly after Bunyan's baptism, John Burton replaced Gifford as pastor of St. John's Church, but he was frequently ill and Bunyan often preached. Bunyan moved from Elstow to Bedford to further his trade and to be closer to the church. He preached not only in Bedford but also "in the darkest places in the country." At first he could not believe that God could speak through him, still counting himself unworthy, but when his efforts were used by God to help others, he grew more confident. "For after I had been about five or six years awakened," he writes, "God had counted me worthy to understand something of his will in his holy and blessed Word, and had given me utterance, in some measure, to express what I saw to others" (1:40, 41). "I preached what I felt," he explains, "what I smartingly did feel" (1:42). For about two years, however, Bunyan was plagued with feelings of guilt and terror that accompanied him to the very door of the pulpit. At times when he prepared to preach upon "some smart and scorching portion of the Word," Satan suggested, "What, will you preach this? This condemns yourself" (1:44). Sometimes he was "violently assaulted with thoughts of blasphemy and strongly tempted to speak the words . . . before the congregation" (1:44). At first, he said, he had cried out "against men's sins, and their fearful state because of them." But then God gave him "many sweet discoveries of his blessed grace," and Bunyan set out "to hold forth Jesus Christ in all his offices, relations, and benefits unto the world" (1:42). His emphasis had shifted from guilt to grace. "For still I preached what I saw and felt," writes Bunyan, which was now "blessed grace."[27]

During 1656 Bunyan engaged in a series of rancorous debates

with Quakers. It was this dispute that caused Bunyan to first take up his pen, describing himself on the title page of *Some Gospel-Truths Opened According to the Scriptures* as an "unworthy servant of Christ and a preacher of the gospel."

> The **Quakers** *began with the preaching of George Fox in 1647. Disillusioned with the various churches, Fox heard a voice say, "There is one, even Christ Jesus, that can speak to thy condition." Christ was then revealed to him, Fox believed, in immediate direct experience. Soon Fox became the leader of a group who called themselves "Children of Light," or "Friends." They were called "Quakers" by others because they "trembled at the word of the Lord." They emphasized the inner witness of the Holy Spirit, rejected the sacraments of baptism and the Lord's Supper, and substituted Christian experience for doctrine. They sometimes went naked (except for a loincloth) as a symbolic action and disrupted religious services of other groups. They were social egalitarians, who refused to doff their hats to gentlemen or magistrates and used the familiar "thou" instead of the deferential "you" when addressing social superiors. They espoused a belligerent millenarianism and tended toward political disruption. After 1660 the Quakers moved toward pacifism, reinstated "sin and the Bible," and their earlier extreme views faded into a rather more "respectable" Quakerism.*[28] *They met in homes, where they practiced simple worship. They lived plain lives, shunning fine clothes, most amusements, and all titles of respect.*

Bunyan's next books, *A Few Sighs from Hell* (1658) and *The Doctrine of the Law and Grace Unfolded* (1659), demonstrate his compelling urgency to reach out to those who were facing eternal damnation under the covenant of works. In these books and in his sermons he held out to men and women the wonderful hope of salvation through the covenant of grace.

When Bunyan, now a popular preacher, resisted temptations toward "pride and liftings up of heart," Satan tried another way to overthrow his ministry by "slanders and reproaches" (1:44, 45). A Cambridge professor challenged the right of a tinker to preach, but a Baptist friend defended Bunyan by pointing out his ability to mend souls as well as pots and pans.[29] There then came "a long and tedious imprisonment" (1:46).

The Prisoner

After the execution of King Charles I, England became a commonwealth governed by the parliament, and then a Protectorate in 1653 led by Oliver Cromwell. Cromwell considered becoming king but eventually declined. Bunyan was one of the congregation in Bedford who signed a petition asking Cromwell to refuse the crown. Cromwell died in 1658. That same year Bunyan's wife died, leaving him with four children under ten years old, one of whom was blind. In 1659 he married Elizabeth (her surname is unknown). He was thirty-one and she was eighteen.

Richard Cromwell succeeded his father as protector. His brief and ineffective rule was followed by some months of squabbling between the generals and the remnant of the Long Parliament. On May 8, 1660, Parliament proclaimed Charles II king. Eighteen days later Charles landed at Dover, and on the 29th, his thirtieth birthday, he entered London in triumph. The new king led England into a riot of spending, splendor, pleasure, gaiety, and lasciviousness. During the Commonwealth there had been a large measure of religious freedom for most separatists, but this liberty ended in 1660 with the Restoration. Parliament now sought to reestablish a single state church controlled from above, and "preaching tinkers with undesirable views were silenced."[30] In 1662 the Act of Uniformity was passed, requiring episcopal ordination and the use of the Book of Common Prayer. That August two thousand Puritan pastors were forced out of their churches.

During the 1650s the Bedford congregation was able to remain a part of the Church of England, but after 1660 "the persecution that always attends the Word" fell upon the church. Shortly after Burton's death in 1660 the church was deprived of its use of the St. John's building by the restoration of the parish church to the Anglicans. Bunyan and his friends continued to gather for worship in private homes as they searched for another pastor.

Older people remembered the earlier suffering of the Puritans during the time of Archbishop Laud (1633-1641). Quakers and some others had suffered in the 1650s, but most of the godly had lived side by side "in argumentative peace."[31] Bunyan, who, for his outspoken views, had experienced what he described as persecution well before the restoration of the monarchy and the traditional church in 1660, now "saw what was a-coming" (1:47). He expressed his loyalty to the king at the beginning of the Restoration period: "I look upon it as my duty to behave myself under the King's government, both as becomes a man and a Christian; and if an occasion was offered me, I should willingly manifest my loyalty to my Prince both by word and deed."[32]

On November 12, 1660, Bunyan planned to preach to a group of people in Lower Samsell, Bedfordshire. A friend told him that a warrant had been issued for his arrest, charging that he had "devilishly and perniciously abstained from coming to [the parish] church to hear divine service, and [was] a common upholder of several unlawful meetings and conventicles, to the great disturbance and distraction of the good subjects of this kingdom" (1:54). He knew that he could be arrested for preaching, but he also knew that he had to preach. He even refused to move the meeting time forward to avoid arrest. He opened the meeting with prayer, and then, as he began to speak, the constable arrived and arrested him. He was charged with calling together the people and "holding unlawful meetings and conventicles" (1:47).[33]

High motives inspired Bunyan's action. He knew that by his example, as well as by his words, he could bear witness to Christ. He believed that not to preach would cause his "weak and newly converted brethren" to be discouraged (1:51). How could his faith be a living reality for his children, his friends, the people of his parish, if he did not show them that it was a living reality for *him?*

The local magistrate offered him a way out: if he would go home and not preach anymore, he would not be prosecuted. This he would not promise, so he was hauled away and locked up in the Bedford County Jail. Bunyan felt that he "was as a man who was pulling down his house upon the head of his wife and children," yet, he said, "I must do it, I must do it" (1:48). Upon hearing the news of her husband's arrest, Elizabeth Bunyan went into premature labor. Her child died at birth or shortly thereafter. John Bunyan was sentenced in January 1661 by Sir John Kelynge (or Keeling) to three months in prison, after which he would have to cease preaching and attend services in the Church of England or be banished from the realm. Should he return without the monarch's permission after being exiled, he would hang. He told the authorities, "If I [was] out of prison today I would preach the Gospel again tomorrow, by the help of God" (1:57). As he returned to prison he found comfort in Jesus' promise to give his followers "a mouth and wisdom, which all your adversaries shall not be able to gainsay nor resist" (Luke 21:15). After three months Bunyan was visited by the Clerk of the Peace, who tried in vain to persuade him to give up preaching. For most of the next twelve years Bunyan remained in the Bedford jail in filthy, overcrowded conditions, sadly separated from his wife and children, for no other crime than that of preaching. He slept on straw in a cold cell with no fireplace. There was risk of illness from other prisoners, for these were years of the contagious plague.

Why was Bunyan jailed for so long? Although many Dissenters suffered after 1660, Bunyan's imprisonment for twelve years appears unusual. He "was no plotter, no politician. But his preaching may well have been regarded by the Bedfordshire gentry as dangerous [rabble]-rousing."[34] A book he had written several years earlier, in 1658, entitled *A Few Sighs from Hell*, "carried clear messages of social protest."[35] To the gentry and their allies among the clergy, all the Puritans—especially a popular Puritan tinker-preacher—were social and political revolutionaries. The authorities did not seek to suppress Dissenters as heretics but as disturbers of law and order. Though Bunyan was cautious and restrained in his social comments, his enemies would have suspected that he held more radical ideas, such as those of the Fifth Monarchy Movement.

The Fifth Monarchy Movement *(the name is from the prophecies of Daniel) consisted of radical millenarians generally willing to embrace military force as a means of instituting the Kingdom of God and the rule of Christ, which they believed would come soon after the execution of Charles I in 1649. At first they promoted the parliamentary cause but rejected vehemently Cromwell's becoming "Lord Protector," a role they believed should be reserved for Jesus Christ. Many called for the overthrow of Cromwell so as to bring in the kingdom of God. In January 1661 they instigated a riot in London when they attempted to overthrow Charles II. The Fifth Monarchy agitators thought that the Stuart rule, and after that the Protectorate, was the continuation of the* *fourth or Roman monarchy, which was only to be ended by the advent of King Jesus, or the Fifth Monarchy. In a book he wrote near the end of his life Bunyan commented that he was once "much taken" with a sect that typically referred to Jesus as "the blessed King of Glory," a reference to the Fifth Monarchists.*

Bunyan protested his imprisonment and used all the arguments he could to convince the authorities that he should be released. But he would not promise to conform to the Church of England and give up preaching. He maintained that the powers that be are ordained by God and must be obeyed, but that neither obedience nor authority should be absolute. Sometime between April and August 1661 Elizabeth Bunyan traveled to London with a petition seeking her husband's release. The member of the House of Lords to whom she appealed advised her to petition the judges at the next assizes (sessions of the superior courts in English counties). She was articulate, resourceful and courageous and possessed a working knowledge of the law, which she learned from her husband. When it was obvious that she was not going to succeed in gaining a judicial review, she went to the Swan Chamber, where two judges sat with justices and people of the gentry. "With abashed face and a trembling heart," she threw herself on the mercy of Judge Hale. "My lord," she said, "I have four small children." This too failed, and Elizabeth told the judges (in what Christopher Hill calls a "final magnificent explosion")[36] that because her husband was "a tinker, and a poor man, therefore he [was] despised, and [could] not have justice" (1:60, 61). When one of the judges asked Elizabeth, "Will your husband leave preaching?" she answered, "He dares not leave preaching." John Brown comments, "Elizabeth Bunyan was simply an English peasant woman: could she have spoken with more dignity had she been a crowned queen?"[37]

"To Live Upon God That Is Invisible"

Two great concerns troubled Bunyan as he faced a long time in prison. The first was "how to be able to endure" (1:47). But he learned to pray to be "strengthened with all might, according to

[God's] glorious power, unto all patience and longsuffering with joyfulness." Then, he worried about "how to be able to encounter death" should that be his "portion." The answer came from two verses of Scripture. 2 Corinthians 1:9 made him understand that, like Paul, he should not trust in himself but "in God which raiseth the dead" (1:48). And 2 Corinthians 4:18 taught him, as Bunyan put it, "to live upon God that is invisible" (1:48). [38] Bunyan encouraged himself with the thought that if he should be put to death, he would be allowed some last words to people who would come to see him die. If God would convert but one soul through his last message, he wrote, he would "not count [his] life thrown away, nor lost" (1:49).

Bunyan suffered deeply in the separation from his wife and children. Parting from them, he wrote, "hath oft been to me in this place as the pulling the flesh from my bones" (1:48). He thought of "the many hardships, miseries and wants" that his poor family would face, especially his beloved blind daughter, now ten years old (1:48). His wife, Elizabeth, who had lost her first child after a premature labor brought on by her husband's arrest, was left with the care of his four children "with nothing to live on but the charity of good people," she told one of her husband's judges (1:61). God brought John comfort from the words of Jeremiah 49:11, "Leave thy fatherless children, I will preserve them alive, and let thy widows trust in me." Bunyan did all he could to support his family by making shoe laces, "many hundred gross of long tagg'd laces." [39] Elizabeth and the children could visit him in prison. His blind daughter, Mary, found her way to him, carrying soup for his supper in a little jar. When Mary died in 1663, Bunyan began the outline of a book called *The Resurrection of the Dead*.

John Bunyan did not give up his ministry. He simply moved it to the jail. He "was not altogether without hopes" that his imprisonment might be "an awakening to the saints in the country." People came to see him for counsel. Bunyan and his friends preached to one another on Sundays in their "prison chamber."

In his first prison work he recounted his recent experience and trials in five pastoral letters. He composed a collection of verse, *Profitable Meditations*, and a book on prayer called *I Will Pray with the Spirit*.

As Bunyan began what were to be twelve years of imprisonment, his church entered a period of trouble. Expelled in September 1660 from the parish church building, where it had occupied a central place in the town's religious life, the church now met in members' houses. The loss of Bunyan's regular ministry to the church was all the more serious in that the congregation was without its young pastor, Gifford's successor, John Burton, who had died in 1660. Bunyan maintained contact, however, with the church and even preached there from time to time. Seventeenth-century English jails were often casually run, and Bunyan on occasion was given "some liberty" (1:62). He used these opportunities to visit with his family and to preach in Bedford and the surrounding area—even as far afield as London. He urged sinners to repent and come to Christ and encouraged the godly to remain steadfast in their faith. He no longer "cared to meddle with things that were controverted," he tells us (1:43). "An awakening word" was what he hoped to bring to people.

Much of the time Bunyan spent studying and writing in his cell. His Bible was his treasure. He tells us that he never in all his life had "so great an inlet into the Word of God" as he did in prison; he writes that "those Scriptures that I saw nothing in before are made in this place and state to shine upon me. Jesus Christ also was never more real and apparent than now; here I have seen him and felt him indeed" (1:47). He had with him as well Foxe's *Book of Martyrs*.

*John Foxe's great book, Acts and Monuments (better known as **Foxe's Book of Martyrs**), sets forth gripping stories of Christian heroes, mainly ordinary men and women, who defended God's cause to the death with great courage and public testimony. It immediately became a bestseller and created a long-lasting impression on English Protestants. Bunyan was reading Foxe's book when he wrote **Grace Abounding**. His descriptions of Faithful's torments at Vanity Fair in **The Pilgrim's Progress** derive from Foxe's descriptions of martyrdoms—particularly the account of the burning of the Scottish preacher George Wishart in 1546.*

Puritans adjusted to the large change that the Restoration of 1660 brought. "The scriptural model for the movement was now no longer Joshua, but Job; patience was to be the exercise of saints, God's choice was to be seen imparted to His suffering servants, and, as Bunyan wrote, 'it was a mercy to suffer upon so good account.'" [40] This hope Bunyan expressed in verse in his *Prison Meditations* of 1663:

> *Just thus it is, we suffer here*
> *For him a little pain,*
> *Who, when he doth again appear,*
> *Will with him let us reign (1:65).*

"Bishop Bunyan"

Refusing to agree to the authorities' demand that he give up preaching, Bunyan anticipated exile and even death (because he intended to return to England if banished, rendering him subject to execution). In the early months of 1663, he wrote what he thought might be his final work, *Christian Behaviour; or the Fruits of True Christianity.* He sought to motivate believers to good works as a natural consequence of their divinely bestowed faith. The best way to encourage people to live true Christian lives, he believed, was "to affirm to others the doctrine of justification by grace, and to believe it ourselves" (2:550). One does not do good works to earn salvation, Bunyan asserted, but because one has already received that gift from God.

As the months passed Bunyan's spirits sank. He was worried about his wife and children, especially his blind daughter, Mary, whom he dearly loved. There were many weeks in which he was "in a very sad and low condition" (1:49). "Depression can recur," writes Richard Greaves, "and it is likely that he once again battled the illness in late 1663 and 1664 as the bleak years in prison took their toll." [41] One day, when it was Bunyan's turn to preach to his friends in their prison chamber, he found himself "so empty, spiritless, and barren" that he thought he would not be able to speak so much as five words of truth "with life and evidence." Then his eye fell on the description of the New Jerusalem in Revelation 21:11, and he preached with power upon this theme. "While distributing the truth, it did so increase in his hand" that, "of the fragments, he gathered up a basketfull," which he expanded into a book called *The Holy City* (3:395).

As time went on, Bunyan's situation began to look more hopeful. He was released from prison for a brief time during 1666, possibly owing to the threat of plague. Late in 1667 Bunyan began expanding a sermon he had preached earlier into a book called *The Heavenly Foot-Man: or, a Description of the Man That Gets to Heaven*. While he was writing this book he was inspired to write another—*The Pilgrim's Progress*. He explained in the preface of the latter work:

> And thus it was: I writing of the way
> And race of saints in this our gospel-day,
> Fell suddenly into an allegory
> About their journey, and the way to glory (3:85).

After 1668 Bunyan's imprisonment seems to have become more and more nominal. He was able to take on an increasing load of church work, culminating in his election as pastor of the Bedford congregation on December 21, 1671. In 1672 King Charles II issued a Declaration of Indulgence for both Protestant Dissenters and Roman Catholics, and in March Bunyan was released from prison. Among the few possessions he was allowed to carry home was probably an incomplete manuscript someday to be *The Pilgrim's Progress*. Bunyan set to work at his ministerial and administrative duties in the church, as well as in rebuilding his livelihood as a tinker. The Bedford church was licensed as a Congregational meeting place and bought an orchard in Mill Lane in Bedford, where a barn became its meetinghouse.

John Bunyan became a recognized leader among the dissenting churches of his part of England. Some, though most often in a jeering manner, called him "Bishop Bunyan." Bunyan ministered to his own congregation in Bedford and to other churches in Bedfordshire, Hertfordshire, Cambridgeshire, Surrey, and London, so far as it was possible in the intermittent persecution of those years. He became famous as a preacher. His "simple themes, homely anecdotes, colloquial language, and abundant repetition," as well as illustrations drawn from his own life, enabled Bunyan to hold congregations "nearly spellbound."[42] It is recorded that King Charles II once asked John Owen, the distinguished Puritan theologian and Oxford scholar, how such an educated man as he could sit and listen to a tinker. Owen replied, "I would willingly exchange my learning for the tinker's power of touching men's hearts."[43]

Bunyan's view of the church—a gathering of visible saints with congregational government—was shared by all Baptists and Congregationalists, but Bunyan refused to make baptism a requirement for membership. He insisted, following Gifford, that baptism was not necessary for church membership, provided the candidate gave a satisfactory account of his or her faith. He believed that what really mattered was baptism by the Holy Spirit, not baptism by water.

In February 1674 "a whiff of sexual scandal" played into the hands of Bunyan's enemies.[44] Bunyan was prevailed upon to give a young woman named Agnes Beaumont a lift on his horse so that she could attend a church service and Lord's Supper some seven miles away in Cambridgeshire. In those days, for an unmarried woman to be on horseback behind a married man amounted to a compromising situation. As a rule Bunyan was keenly sensitive to physical contact with women because of the possibility of scandalous rumors that could destroy his credibility as a preacher. In the later editions of *Grace Abounding*, Bunyan felt compelled to defend himself against continuing accusations of sexual impropriety (1:45-46). (He was also accused of being a Jesuit, a witch, and a highway robber!) He had not been kept from sexual sins because of any goodness in himself, Bunyan wrote, "but God has been merciful to me, and has kept me; to whom I pray that he will keep me still, not only from this, but from every evil way and work, and preserve me to his heavenly kingdom. Amen." (1:46). "However pious and gifted," Richard Greaves comments, "Bunyan was also human."[45]

Uncertainties in government policy led to inconsistency in execution of laws against Dissenters. In March 1673 the king succumbed to pressure to revoke what was portrayed as the unconstitutional Declaration of Indulgence. In January 1675 the bishops advised the king to suppress the conventicles (the religious meetings of Dissenters), and all licenses issued under the declaration were recalled. Bunyan was again imprisoned. He had not taken Communion at the parish church as required. So late in 1676 he was, as he put it, "had home to prison again" (1:47). He spent six months in jail and was released in June 1677. It was probably during his second imprisonment that he revised *Grace Abounding* for its fourth edition and completed *The Pilgrim's Progress.*[46]

Whatever Bunyan's early political views, he later expressed no interest in radical political ideas. He set forth millenarian thought (the idea that there would be a period of a thousand years during which the true church would prosper and triumph over all its enemies) in *The Holy City*, but he did not call for political or military action. He saw the suffering of the saints as a divinely sanctioned preparation for their entrance into God's presence. Antichrist (in Bunyan's view the Roman Catholic Church and/or persecuting Anglicanism) would be overthrown—of that he was certain—but meanwhile it was the saints' responsibility to suffer patiently.

When *The Pilgrim's Progress* came out in 1678 John Bunyan had already published some twenty-five books (mostly sermons expanded into book form). During the fall and winter of 1680 he wrote *Israel's Hope Encouraged* to prepare the saints for the possibility of another time of severe persecution. There was an intensifying campaign against Dissenters. The government began enforcing laws that required all officials to swear oaths of allegiance and non-resistance, repudiate the Solemn League and Covenant of 1643 (a religious covenant and civil league between the Scots and English to preserve the Presbyterian church in Scotland and establish it in England), and to take the sacrament of the Lord's Supper in the Church of England. It was against this background that Bunyan wrote *The Holy War*. Like Calvin, Bunyan opposed an insurrection of the people, but not resistance led by men of rank and authority, although it is clear that he hoped for a peaceful resolution of the crisis. Monarchs and magistrates are both ordained by God and governed by him, Bunyan believed. He drew the line, however, at the point where the state required worship that was not in accord with the Scriptures. There the Christian must "obey God rather than men" (Acts 5:29) whatever the cost. Christians must accept suffering "with patience, humility and cheerfulness, for it is a badge of the saint and evidence of one's faithfulness, not an indication that God has abandoned the elect."[47]

In his *Greatness of the Soul*, written during mid-1682, Bunyan wanted to awaken sinners from their "beds of ease, security, and pleasure" and to cast them down upon "their knees before [God], to beg of him grace, to be concerned about the salvation of [their] souls" (1:105). In *A Holy Life the Beauty of Christianity* (composed during the summer of 1683), Bunyan attempted to keep the godly focused on what is most important. "If we be reproached for evil-doing, it is our shame," Bunyan wrote; "but if for well-doing, it is our glory. If we be reproached for our sins, God cannot vindicate us; but if we be reproached for a virtuous life, God himself is concerned, will espouse our quarrel, and, in his good time, will show our foes our righteousness, and put them to shame and silence" (2:547).

Schemes and plots, associated with the Duke of Monmouth, suggested that armed intervention was necessary to force Charles II to exclude his Catholic brother from the succession. On February 6, 1685, James II succeeded Charles as king. Monmouth raised a rebellion and claimed the crown. The rebellion was crushed and Monmouth was executed. Although Dissenters probably did not compose a majority of Monmouth's army, they were among the hundreds of suspects arrested during and after the rebellion. Bunyan had distanced himself from the plotting and more fully articulated his "ethic of suffering" in *Seasonable Counsel: or, Advice to Sufferers*, published in 1684.[48] Christian suffering must be "not only for truth, but of love to truth; not only for God's word, but according to it, to wit, in that holy, humble, meek manner as the word of God requireth" (2:704).

Persecution of Dissenters, which had been flowing strongly during the 1680s, now reached a flood. The meetings of Bunyan's church ceased for the most part for over two years. Bunyan started his new book, *The Saints' Knowledge of Christ's Love*, in September 1685 to assure God's people that divine grace is more than sufficient to sustain and relieve the persecuted. God "hath set a Saviour against sin; a heaven against a hell; light against darkness; good against evil, and the breadth, and length, and depth, and height of the grace that is in himself, for my good, against all the power, and strength and force, and subtlety, of every enemy" (2:9).

On December 23, 1685, Bunyan drafted a deed of gift conveying all his property to his "well-beloved wife," Elizabeth, maybe as a safeguard against the possibility of his being arrested again.[49] With a Catholic on the throne and reports circulating about the plight of the Huguenots in France, Bunyan's thoughts once again turned to martyrdom. In *The*

Saints' Privilege and Profit he set forth the throne of grace as the place where Christians can take refuge from the fury of the wicked.

On April 4, 1687, Charles II issued a Declaration of Indulgence suspending the laws against Protestant noncomformists and Catholics. Many Protestants feared that the king's move disguised his underlying goal of imposing Catholicism on his realms. Like all noncomformists, Bunyan had to decide whether toleration was worth the price of cooperating with a Catholic ruler. Bunyan wrote *Solomon's Temple Spiritualized* (the last of three books on typology that he produced about this time) to reinforce the faithful as the church moved into an uncertain era of toleration. In *Discourse of the House of God*, a commentary in verse on most of the key subjects in *Solomon's Temple Spiritualized*, Bunyan set forth the characteristics of the gathered church, beginning with a portrayal of ministers. "Essentially, he was writing his own job description," comments Richard Greaves.[50]

Taking Revelation 22:1 as his text, Bunyan wrote *The Water of Life: or, a Discourse Showing the Richness and Glory of the Grace and Spirit of the Gospel*. Celebrating the doctrine of grace, the "keystone" of his theology, Bunyan wrote

> Grace can justify freely, when it will, who it will, from what it will. Grace can continue to pardon, favour, and save from falls, in falls, out of falls. Grace can comfort, relieve, and help those who have hurt themselves. And grace can bring the unworthy to glory. This the law cannot do, this man cannot do, this angels cannot do, this God cannot do, but only by the riches of his grace, through the redemption that is in Jesus Christ (3:549).

In *The Advocateship of Jesus Christ* Bunyan endeavoured to help "the sinking Christian" who was troubled by feelings of spiritual despondency because of undue preoccupation with his sin and depravity. Developing 1 John 2:1 ("And if any man sin, we have an advocate with the Father, Jesus Christ the righteous."), Bunyan urged his readers to ponder Christ's role as an attorney who skillfully pleads our cause before the supreme judge in the celestial court.

As the king attempted to forge an alliance of nonconformist Protestants and Catholics, Bunyan continued to write. In *Good News* he expounded Luke 24:47, in which Christ commands his disciples to preach repentance and forgiveness of sins to all nations beginning in Jerusalem. Stressing that the offer of mercy is extended first to the greatest sinners—"Jerusalem sinners"—Bunyan reflected on his own experience. He had been a great sinner himself but had obtained mercy. Still vividly remembering his own spiritual turmoil he wrote:

> *I would say to my soul, "O my soul! this is not the place of despair; this is not the time to despair in; as long as mine eyes can find a promise in the Bible, as long as there is the least mention of grace, as long as there is a moment left me of breath or life in this world, so long will I wait or look for mercy, so long will I fight against unbelief and despair" (1:92).*

The king's policy of indulgence made it possible for Bunyan to preach to large crowds. *The Pilgrim's Progress*, the tenth and eleventh editions of which appeared in 1685 and 1688, made Bunyan a celebrity. Some three thousand people came to hear him one Sunday in London, and twelve hundred turned up for a weekday sermon during the winter.

Death

Shortly after completing another book, *The Acceptable Sacrifice: or the Excellency of a Broken Heart*, an expanded sermon on Psalm 51:17, John Bunyan rode on horseback to Reading to reconcile a son and father who had quarreled. Traveling on to London, Bunyan was drenched in a heavy rain and fell sick with a violent fever. He preached on August 19 at a meetinghouse in Boar's Head Yard. His text was John 1:13—"Which were born, not of blood, nor of the will of the flesh, nor of the will of man, but of God." Toward the end of what was to be his last sermon, he said:

> *If you are the children of God, live together lovingly; if the world quarrel with you, it is no matter; but it is sad if you quarrel together; if this be amongst you, it is a sign of ill-breeding; it is not according to the rules you have in the Word of God. Dost thou see a soul that has the image of God in him? Love him, love him; say, This man and I must go to heaven one day; serve one another, do good for one another; and if any wrong you, pray to God to right you, and love the brotherhood (2:758).*

Bunyan concluded: "Consider that the holy God is your Father, and let this oblige you to live like the children of God, that you may look your Father in the face, with comfort, another day" (2:758).

That day was not far off for John Bunyan. He died on August 31, 1688. The cause of his death—influenza or possibly pneumonia—was contracted as a result of his pastoral work of family peacemaking. One of Bunyan's biographers aptly stated: "Thus one last act of love and charity put an end to a life almost entirely devoted to the good of others."[51] On September 2 the sixty-year-old John Bunyan was buried in Bunhill Fields in London. The Bedford church book records the stunned reaction of his congregation: "Wednesday the 4th of September was kept in prayer and humiliation for this heavy stroke upon us, the death of dear brother Bunyan."[52]

Elizabeth Bunyan survived her husband by only a few years. She died in 1691, "to follow her faithful pilgrim from this world to the other, whither he was gone before her" (1:65).

Footnotes

[1] George Whitefield, "The Recommendatory Preface," *The Works of John Bunyan* (London: W. Johnston, 1767), 1:iii.

[2] Christopher Hill, *A Tinker and a Poor Man: John Bunyan and His Church, 1628-1688* (New York: W. W. Norton & Co., 1988), 4.

[3] Alexander Whyte, *Bunyan Characters: Bunyan Himself as Seen in His Grace Abounding* (Edinburgh: Oliphant, Anderson & Ferrier, n.d.), 245.

[4] Rebecca S. Beal, "*Grace Abounding to the Chief of Sinners*: John Bunyan's Pauline Epistle," in *Studies in English Literature, 1500-1900* (Baltimore: Johns Hopkins University Press, 1981), 148.

[5] Bunyan's title comes from Paul's words in 1 Timothy 1:15—"This is a faithful saying, and worthy of all acceptation, that Christ Jesus came into the world to save sinners; of whom I am chief."

[6] "*Grace Abounding* is . . . the greatest of the Puritan spiritual autobiographies because its exploitation of the providences behind familiar, everyday things is never trivial." Roger Sharrock, *John Bunyan*, new and rev. ed. (London: Macmillan, 1968), 61.

[7] T. R. Glover, *Poets and Puritans* (London: Methuen, 1923), 116.

[8] John Bunyan, *Grace Abounding to the Chief of Sinners*, ed. Roger Sharrock (Oxford: Clarendon Press, 1962), xviii.

[9] Henri Talon, *John Bunyan: The Man and His Works* (Cambridge, Massachusetts: Harvard University Press, 1951), 45.

[10] Hill, *John Bunyan*, 163.

[11] Bunyan borrowed the striking image from his trade as a tinker. The passage, which occurs in *Christ a Complete Savior*, reads: "Consider, also, that he has made a beginning with thy soul to reconcile thee to God, and to that end has bestowed his justice upon thee, put his Spirit within thee, and [begun] to make the unweldable mountain and rock, thy heart, to turn towards him, and desire after him; to believe in him, and rejoice in him" (1:216).

[12] In this game a player hits a piece of wood with a stick, making it fly into the air, where he strikes it again, driving it as far as he can.

[13] Talon, *John Bunyan*, 53. Bunyan partly acknowledged that his guilt was out of proportion to his actual offences. He described himself as one of those "poor creatures . . . that though not much guilt attendeth the soul, yet they continually have a secret conclusion within them that there is no [hope] for them" (1:9).

[14] Michael Mullett, *John Bunyan in Context* (Pittsburgh: Duquesne University Press, 1996), 28.

[15] Mullett, *John Bunyan*, 30.

[16] See Mullett, *John Bunyan*, 33.

[17] See "Grace Abounding: John Bunyan (1628-1688)" in Gaius Davies, *Genius and Grace* (London: Hodder & Stoughton, 1992), 50-85. Reprinted as *Genius, Grief, and Grace: A Doctor Looks at Suffering and Success* (Geanies House, Fearn, Ross-shire: Christian Focus Publications, 2003).

[18] Richard L. Greaves, *Glimpses of Glory: John Bunyan and English Dissent* (Stanford, California: Stanford University Press, 2002), viii, 44.

[19] The words are from Jesus' parable of the great banquet in Luke 14:22— "'Sir,' the servant said, 'what you ordered has been done, but there is still room.' The master then told his servant, 'Go out to the roads and country lanes and make them come in, so that my house will be full'" (verse 23).

[20] Talon, *John Bunyan*, 63.

[21] Whyte, *Bunyan Himself*, 82.

[22] Greaves, *Glimpses of Glory*, 65.

[23] Davies, *Genius and Grace*, 64.

[24] The reading of *A Relation of the Fearful Estate of Francis Spira in the Year 1548* was almost a tradition in certain Puritan circles. Richard Baxter warned that reading this book caused or increased melancholy in many.

[25] Owen C. Watkins, "John Bunyan and His Experience," in *Puritan Papers: Volume One (1956-1959)*, ed. D. Martyn Lloyd-Jones (Phillipsburg, New Jersey: Presbyterian and Reformed Publishing Co., 2000), 134.

[26] Talon, *John Bunyan*, 72.

[27] Mullett, *John Bunyan*, 46.

[28] Hill, *John Bunyan*, 83.

[29] Richard L. Greaves, "Introduction" to John Bunyan's *The Doctrine of the Law and Grace unfolded* and *I will pray with the Spirit* (Oxford: Clarendon Press,

1976), xxxix.

[30] Hill, *John Bunyan*, 27.

[31] Hill, *John Bunyan*, 114.

[32] Mullett, *John Bunyan*, 110.

[33] New legislation had not yet been passed, but there was an old act (1593) from Elizabeth's reign forbidding conventicles, or unauthorized religious gatherings.

[34] Hill, *John Bunyan*, 106.

[35] Mullett, *John Bunyan*, 71.

[36] Hill, *John Bunyan*, 107.

[37] John Brown, *John Bunyan (1628-1688): His Life, Times, and Work* (London: Hulbert Publishing Co., 1928), 149-50.

[38] John Piper wrote, "I have not found any phrase in Bunyan's writings that captures better the key to his life than this one: 'To live upon God that is invisible.'" John Piper, *The Hidden Smile of God: the Fruit of Affliction in the Lives of John Bunyan, William Cowper, and David Brainerd* (Wheaton: Crossway Books, 2001), 43.

[39] Hill, *John Bunyan*, 121.

[40] Mullett, *John Bunyan*, 90.

[41] Greaves, *Glimpses of Glory*, 176.

[42] Greaves, *Glimpses of Glory*, 593, 595.

[43] Brown, *John Bunyan*, 366.

[44] Mullett, *John Bunyan*, 101.

[45] Greaves, *Glimpses of Glory*, 312.

[46] *The Pilgrim's Progress* is, as Bunyan makes clear, a prison writing. Christopher Hill comments that whether Bunyan wrote the work in 1660-72 or in 1676-77 "doesn't matter much, but, for what it is worth, my preference would be for the earlier period." Mullett adds that "perhaps Bunyan put finishing touches to the book in 1676-7." Hill, *John Bunyan*, 106.

[47] Greaves, *Glimpses of Glory*, 493.

[48] Greaves, *Glimpses of Glory*, 489.

[49] It is possible that drawing up his will in 1685 was more a prudent measure by a cautious man in his later years than a precaution against renewed imprisonment. The inventory of Bunyan's property after his death added up to a little more than forty pounds. Although this is more than an average tinker would leave, it suggests that most of the profits from his books had not come to Bunyan. Bunyan hid the document in their house, and Elizabeth apparently forgot about it or did not know where it was hidden. The document was not found until the nineteenth century.

[50] Greaves, *Glimpses of Glory*, 579.

[51] Talon, *John Bunyan*, 14.

[52] Greaves, *Glimpses of Glory*, 599.

I know of no book, the Bible excepted, as above all comparison, which I, according to my judgment and experience, could so safely recommend as teaching and enforcing the whole saving truth, according to the mind that was in Christ Jesus, as **The Pilgrim's Progress**.

Samuel Taylor Coleridge[1]

[Mr. Standfast] had discovered the pleasures of reading and had perfected himself in an art which he had once practised indifferently. Somehow or other he had got a **Pilgrim's Progress**, *from which he seemed to extract enormous pleasure. . . . The picture of that patient, gentle old fellow, hobbling about his compound and puzzling over his* **Pilgrim's Progress**, *a cripple for life after five months of blazing glory, would have stiffened the back of a jellyfish. . . . Soon, too, I found the* **Pilgrim's Progress** *not a duty but a delight. I discovered new jewels daily in the honest old story. . , .*

John Buchan[2]

2

The Pilgrim's Progress
Part One

> Fortunately for us, our tinker-preacher was allowed pen and paper
> during his painful isolation in Bedford Gaol. A heavenly muse joined
> him in his cell, and he created two unforgettable pilgrims, husband and
> wife, who made individual trips to the Celestial City. As they traveled
> separately, each learned about the Lord of the Hill.
>
> Bunyan explained that the Lord was the Son of the Ancient of Days,
> but He was not willing to live alone in Zion Mountain. So He abandoned
> his ancient glory, dressed Himself in "the glory of grace" (3:109), and
> became a baby, then a great warrior, in the City of Destruction. His
> courageous rescue of the doomed citizens freed them from his and their
> extreme adversary, Satan, and from the power of death. He accomplished
> this only with much loss of blood and his own death——on a cross. People
> who talked to the Lord when he was alive again and preparing to return
> to Zion Mountain heard him say that He is such a lover of poor pilgrims
> that he wants to make them princes and princesses and bring them safely
> to his home.
>
> John Bunyan, influenced by his youthful reading as well as by the
> Bible, employed the ancient concept of life as a pilgrimage in his book
> that has become a set piece of world literature. Part I describes the
> salvation and quest of Christian: lonely, exciting, sad, dangerous, but
> good. The pilgrim is rescued, tried, kept, and brought home by the Lord
> of the Hill; the pilgrimage ends with joy forever.

John Bunyan wrote at least part of *The Pilgrim's Progress* in prison.[3]
He probably started to compose his allegory in or shortly after

March 1668. He had completed three-quarters of it by September 1669, when he began enjoying what would prove to be nine months of relative freedom. This brief respite probably explains the curious break about two-thirds of the way through the first part of *The Pilgrim's Progress*, just after Christian and Hopeful visit the shepherds in the Delectable Mountains and have their first glimpse of the Celestial City. Bunyan writes, "So I awoke from my dream." Bunyan's modest liberty ended on May 15, 1670, with a renewed crackdown on Dissenters. During the ensuing ten months of close confinement, he almost certainly completed part one of *The Pilgrim's Progress.*[4] "I slept and dreamed again," he writes (3:145-6).

The Pilgrim's Progress was published in 1678 and was immediately popular. A second edition appeared that same year and a third the following year. The 1679 edition contained notable additions and was an almost complete version of the story as we know it today. There were eleven editions issued before Bunyan died in 1688, and double that number by century's end. By 1692 about one hundred thousand copies were in print in England, and the book had appeared in France, Holland, and New England. Translations were made into Welsh and Gaelic. By the turn of the nineteenth century Bunyan was probably the most popular writer among the Gaelic-speaking Presbyterians in the Highlands of Scotland. When Protestant missionaries went overseas they translated the Bible and, almost always next, *The Pilgrim's Progress* into the languages of the people to whom they ministered. In October 1847, the *John Williams*, a ship of the London Missionary Society, left Gravesend for the Pacific Islands. Its cargo included five thousand Bibles and four thousand copies of *The Pilgrim's Progress* in Tahitian.

The title *The Pilgrim's Progress* sets forth the book's theme—the "journey" that Christian and other pilgrims make from the City of Destruction to the Celestial City. Although often associated with Roman Catholic piety, the idea of life as a pilgrimage goes back to the Old and New Testaments and was frequently used in Puritan sermons and books. For true pilgrims, the "progress" is two-fold: onward toward heaven and inward toward godliness. It is true, as Kaufman points out, that "Christian's forward movement is compromised by vacillation and retreat."[5] But in fact Christian does move forward from the City of Destruction to the Celestial City. There are frequent times of suspense and uncertainty in Christian's pilgrimage, but there are also "elements of irreversibility." "Christian enters the way through a wicket gate, never to retrace that initial choice. Upon seeing the Cross his burden falls away, never to return."[6] For the true pilgrim, there are struggles, defeats, and victories; but "Christian wayfaring is not to be seen, finally, as primarily a matter of [one's] own doing."[7] Furthermore, Bunyan understands that "the Christian life is indeed at least as much a matter of rest as it is of movement."[8] But movement or progress it is, and the goal is always clearly in view, whether the pilgrim is walking or resting.

The Pilgrim's Progress is an allegory, but it can be read as much for the thrill of the story as for the sake of the idea. Although critical of the long doctrinal discussions in the book, C. S. Lewis writes that "the greater part of it is enthralling narrative or genuinely dramatic dialogue." Fortunately, according to Lewis, this "adventure story" is "visualized in terms of contemporary life that Bunyan knew." Lewis writes:

> *The garrulous neighbors; Mr Worldly-Wiseman who was so clearly (as Christian said) "a gentleman"; the bullying, foul-mouthed Justice; the field-path, seductive to footsore walkers; the sound of a dog barking as you stand knocking at a door; the fruit hanging over a wall which the children insist on eating though their mother admonishes them, "That fruit is none of ours"—these are all characteristic.*[9]

"*The Pilgrim's Progress* was woven into the warp and weft of Nonconformist experience," writes Isabel Hofmeyr. "It was not so much a book as an environment, a set of orientations, a language, and a currency shared by most evangelicals." The book was a kind of second nature that was almost impossible, Robert Blatchford said, to comment on or review: "I might as well try to criticize the Lord's Prayer."[10] Bunyan's book is no longer known and revered as it once was, but it is still read and loved by many Christians. Today *The Pilgrim's Progress* is studied by scholars who subject it to the theories of literary criticism or read between the lines to try to discover the author's political and social views. But to ignore its Christian message is to miss the heart and purpose of Bunyan's book. In the conclusion to the first part of *The Pilgrim's Progress*, Bunyan urges the reader, "Do thou the substance of my matter see" (3:167). The book sets forth orthodox Christian doctrine as found in the Bible, in the Reformers, especially Luther and Calvin, and in the teaching of many of Bunyan's Puritan contemporaries.

The names of the characters in *The Pilgrim's Progress* are important; by them, Bunyan, who is a master at this, enables us to know at once each new character as he or she appears in the book. Bunyan's personalities are not just allegorical figures with appropriate names. They are flesh-and-blood people, not abstract virtues and vices. The names are admirable, often amusing, and Bunyan must have enjoyed thinking them up. For example, there is Mr. Talkative, the son of Saywell of Prating Row, the "brisk" lad Ignorance of the County of Conceit, and the young woman whose name was Dull. In Part II we meet Great-Heart, Valiant-for-truth, and noble women in Christiana and Mercy, as well as a growing group of feeble folk with whom Bunyan deals gently—including Mr. Fearing, Mr. Despondency, and Mr. Despondency's daughter, Miss Much-afraid. Most of "the characters seldom stay long with us, but they become vivid personalities before they go, though often drawn in a few strokes with the economy of line of the great artist."[11]

Robert Louis Stevenson writes that "Bunyan was fervently in earnest; with 'his fingers in his ears, he ran on,' straight for his mark. . . . Trivial talk over a meal, the dying words of heroes, the delights of [the land of] Beulah or the Celestial City, Apollyon and my Lord Hate-Good, Great-Heart and Mr. Worldly-Wiseman, all have been imagined with the same clearness . . . and art that, for its purpose, is faultless."[12] Of course, *The Pilgrim's Progress* is a great book not simply because its author was a sincere, earnest man. As C. S. Lewis expresses it, "Sincerity, of itself, never taught anyone to write well. . . . We must attribute Bunyan's style to a perfect natural ear, a great sensibility for the idiom and cadence of popular speech, a long experience in addressing unlettered audiences, and a freedom from bad models."[13]

Bunyan's "whole outlook is biblical," and in his writings "direct or embedded quotations from Scripture" are plentiful.[14] He had so lived in the Bible that it had become his homeland, as familiar to him as the lanes of Bedfordshire. The style of *The Pilgrim's Progress*, however, is not, as sometimes stated, derived from the King James Version of the Bible. The substance of the book is biblical, but the style is the sometimes rough, sometimes elegant, almost always pungent, speech of seventeenth-century England. Lewis puts it, "The light is sharp: it never comes through stained glass."[15]

In writing *The Pilgrim's Progress*, John Bunyan read his own heart as well as his Bible. The book is the story of his soul's travels. "He had only to translate his spiritual odyssey into an allegory."[16] In *Grace Abounding*, Bunyan presents in personal testimony much of the same story that he tells in allegory in *The Pilgrim's Progess*. The state of despair in which Pilgrim finds himself at the beginning of *The Pilgrim's Progress* resembles that of Bunyan at the beginning of *Grace Abounding*. Pilgrim had a great burden upon his back; Bunyan had a "great burden" upon his spirit. Most of *Grace Abounding* is one long scramble through the Slough of Despond. "I found myself as on a miry bog that shook if I did but stir," says Bunyan (1:16); and the whole book moves forward struggling, from promise to promise. Pilgrim's fear that Mount Sinai might fall on his head parallels Bunyan's fear that the church bells or steeple might fall on him while he was ringing the bells. The blasphemies whispered to Christian by the devil in the Valley of the Shadow of Death echo those that Bunyan himself had been tempted to utter.

The Author's Apology for his Book

In his poetic "apology," Bunyan explains how he came to write *The Pilgrim's Progress*. While working on a quite different book, he writes, he fell "suddenly into an Allegory" (3:85)!

> *Thus I set pen to paper with delight,*
> *And quickly had my thoughts on black and white.*
> *For having now my method by the end,*
> *Still as I pull'd, it came. . . (3:85).*[17]

When the writer sought advice from friends concerning publishing a book of this kind, "some said, 'John, print it'; others said, 'Not so.' Some said, 'It might do good,' others said, 'No'" (3:85). Bunyan decided to print it, with sage advice to his critics that they wait and see if it proved useful.

Bunyan used an allegorical approach, not to experiment with a new literary style but more effectively to communicate the Gospel. "You see," he wrote, "the ways the fisherman doth take to catch the fish" (3:85). Sometimes ordinary means are unsuccessful, and different approaches are called for.

In answering objections that his book was "dark" and that it was "feigned" (that is, fiction), he pointed out that the Bible itself is full of "types, shadows and metaphors" (3:86). He wrote on the original title page of 1678 the words from Hosea 12:10 "I have used similitudes." Bunyan expressed his confidence that God had guided his mind and pen "for his design" and that he would therefore make "base things usher in divine" (3:87).

John Bunyan ends the long apology with an engaging invitation to his reader: "O then come hither, and lay my book, thy head, and heart together." His book, Bunyan tells us, sets before our eyes "the man that seeks the everlasting prize"; and he states that this book "will make a traveller of thee" (3:87). Indeed it has proven so for many who have laid Bunyan's book, their heads, and their hearts together.

In his great desire to communicate the Gospel in moving and memorable ways, John Bunyan became, "in spite of his Puritan self, a literary artist," writes Sharrock.[18] The opening sentences of the book are among the most memorable in English literature: **"As I walked through the wilderness of this world**, I lighted on a certain place, where was a den; and I laid me down in that place to sleep: And as I slept, I dreamed a dream" (3:89). Bunyan's first words instantly place the reader in the heart of the action that is to follow.

In his dream the author sees a man in rags with a burden on his back and a book in his hand, crying, "What shall I do?" The "pilgrim" of *The Pilgrim's Progress* is called at first simply "a man," but soon he is called **"Christian"** ("for that was his name"). Christian tells the porter of the Palace Beautiful that his name is now Christian but that at first it had been "Graceless"—before God's grace found him. *The Pilgrim's Progress* begins with a question that is just as urgent in the twenty-first century as it was in the seventeenth century: "What shall I do to be saved?"

Christian pleads with his wife and children, but they do not understand. Neither do his relatives in the City of Destruction, who think that he is mad. One day, as he is walking in the fields in confusion and fear, reading from his book, Christian meets **Evangelist**, who, as Bunyan describes in a later edition of the book, "lovingly him greets." Evangelist deals with the pilgrim in a simple, straightforward manner. He asks him some questions and points out to him a wicket gate in the distance and a shining light. Evangelist the preacher will appear again at crucial points in Christian's pilgrimage.

Hearkening to the words of Evangelist, Christian begins to run, with his fingers in his ears, to keep from hearing the cries of his wife and children. Bunyan has been accused of making his hero selfish in deserting his home and family to save his soul. But surely Christian's action is an illustration of the words of Jesus "If anyone comes to me and does not hate his father and mother, his wife and children, his brothers and sisters—yes, even his own life—he cannot be my disciple" (Luke 14:26). As Bunyan puts it in *The Doctrine of Law and Grace*, "Father, mother, husband, wife, lands, livings, nay, life and all, shall go rather than the soul will miss of Christ" (1:544). Indeed, for everyone, conversion, in a profound sense, is a solitary pilgrimage. But Bunyan did not mean that a Christian should literally abandon his family. Each father has a great work to do for God within his family circle, Bunyan writes in *Christian Behaviour* (2:555).

Two neighbors, **Obstinate** and **Pliable**, overtake Christian and try to stop him while Christian attempts to persuade them to come with him. Obstinate scorns Christian's words and his book, but Pliable is attracted to what Christian has to say. True to his name, Pliable tells Obstinate that he is beginning to "come to a point" and intends to go along with Christian. Christian shares with his companion the joys and wonders of the heavenly city to which they are bound. When Pliable asks how he can know that the words of his book are true, Christian wisely replies, "It was made by him that cannot lie." When Pliable asks how they can become sharers of all these blessings, Christian answers, "If we be truly willing to have [them], he will bestow [them] upon us freely" (3:91).

As they hurry on, they do not notice **"a very miry Slough"** until they have fallen into it.[19] Struggling to get out, Christian is perplexed and Pliable is angry. At last Pliable manages to escape the slough on the side next to his own house, and "so away he went, and Christian saw him no more" (3:92).

> *Alexander Whyte describes the sloughs that people fall into: "sloughs of all kinds of vice, open and secret; sloughs of poverty, sloughs of youthful ignorance, temptation, and transgression; sloughs of inward gloom, family disquiet and dispute; lonely grief; all manner of sloughs, deep and miry, where no man would suspect them. And how good, how like Christ Himself, and how well-pleasing to Him to lay down steps for such sliding feet, and to lift out another and another human soul upon sound and solid ground."[20]*

As Christian tries to get out of the slough on the solid bank next to the wicket gate, he cannot, because of the burden on his back, until **Help** arrives. Christian tells Help that **Fear** has followed him so closely that he has missed the steps (which are the promises of God) and so has fallen into the slough.

> *In a sermon on "Helps," Charles Haddon Spurgeon said: "Help, in* **Pilgrim's Progress**, *asked Christian why he did not look for the steps, and told him that there were good steps all the way through the mire; but Christian said he had missed them. Now you can point these poor sinking ones to the steps. Brethren, be you well acquainted with the promises of God; have them on the tip of your tongue, ready at any time."[21]*

Bunyan, in his dream, asks Help why the slough has not been filled so that poor travelers will not fall into it. He is told that it cannot be filled because it is the place where conviction of sin deposits "many fears and doubts." The King's laborers have for sixteen hundred years been at work filling the slough with "wholesome instructions," but it is "the Slough of Despond still." There are, however, as Spurgeon observes, "good and substantial steps" that have been placed through the middle of the slough (3:92).

Christian's path crosses that of a gentleman named **Mr. Worldly Wiseman**, an inhabitant of the town of Carnal Policy near Christian's own City of Destruction. He advises Christian to get rid of his burden by an easier and more pleasant solution than going to the wicket gate. He directs him to seek relief from *Mr. Legality* (or his son *Civility*), whose house stands on a high hill in the village of *Morality*. The village is nearby—not quite a mile off. Christian would learn to his sorrow that Legality and Civility might survive there, but not real Christianity.

As Christian turns out of his way toward the village of Morality, his burden seems heavier than ever and he begins to fear that the hill (out of which gust flashes of fire) will fall on him. Then he sees Evangelist coming toward him "with a severe and dreadful countenance." As Christian stands trembling, Evangelist rebukes him with Scripture and then encourages him with more Scripture and explains to him the mistake he has made in following Mr. Worldly Wiseman's advice. Evangelist reminds the pilgrim that "strait is the gate which leadeth unto life," that the way of the cross cannot be avoided, and that the way of the law of Mount Sinai cannot free him of his burden. Evangelist then kisses Christian, gives him one smile—the tender smile of a stern man, the most inspiring smile on earth—and bids him Godspeed.

Christian arrives at last at the **wicket gate**, on which he knocks repeatedly[22] until the gatekeeper **Goodwill** (one of Bunyan's names for grace) appears. (Both here and in Part II, Goodwill is called "the Lord.") When Christian asks if Goodwill is willing to let "an undeserving rebel" in, Goodwill replies, "I am willing with all my heart. We make no objection against any," says Goodwill; "notwithstanding all that they have done before they come hither. They are in no wise cast out" (3:97).

"So when Christian was stepping in, the other gave him a pull" (3:96). The *pull* given by Goodwill makes it clear: it is God—not man—who opens the gate and pulls the sinner in. Just as Goodwill was the only one who could open the gate, so God alone can bring the sinner into the covenant of grace. It is true that the sinner must knock and must step in, but the faith and repentance that are required of the sinner are the gifts of God.

"The happy, heavenly, divine disposition of the gatekeeper was such," writes Alexander Whyte, "that it overflowed from the pilgrim who stood

> *beside him and descended upon his wife and children who remained behind him in the doomed city. So full of love was the gate-keeper's heart, that it ran out upon Obstinate and Pliable also. His heart was so large and so hospitable, that he was not satisfied with one pilgrim received and assisted that day. 'How is it,' he asked, 'that you have come here alone?'"[23]*

The wicket gate represents the decisive moment that separates the course of Christian's journey into two segments, a "before" and an "after." Christian reviews his story up to this point for Goodwill, who points out the narrow way Christian now must go. He is told that he will come to a place of *Deliverance* where his burden will fall from his back (3:97).

Bunyan's handling of the wicket gate and the cross has engendered some objections, even among Bunyan's most ardent admirers. The problem is that the wicket gate (of faith and repentance) is separated from the cross where Christian is at last freed from his burden.

> *In a sermon on "Christ Crucified," C. H. Spurgeon preached: "I am a great lover of John Bunyan, but I do not believe him infallible; and the other day I met with a story about him which I think a very good one. There was a young man, in Edinburgh, who wished to be a missionary. He was a wise young man; so he thought, 'If I am to be a missionary, there is no need for me to transport myself far away from home; I may as well be a missionary in Edinburgh.' . . . Well, this young man started, and determined to speak to the first person he met. He met [a fishwife]; those of us who have seen them can never forget them, they are extraordinary women indeed. So, stepping up to her, he said, 'Here you are, coming along with your burden on your back; let me ask you if you have got another burden, a spiritual burden.' 'What!' she asked; 'do you mean that burden in John Bunyan's Pilgrim's Progress? Because, if you do, young man, I got rid of that many years ago, probably before you were born. But I went a better way to work than the pilgrim did. The evangelist that John Bunyan talks about was one of your parsons that do not preach the Gospel; for he said, "Keep that light in thine eye, and run to the wicket gate." Why man alive! that was not the place for him to run to. He should have said, "Do you see that cross? Run there at once!"*

> But, instead of that, he sent the poor pilgrim to the wicket-gate first; and much good he got by going there! He got tumbling into the slough, and was like to have been killed by it.' 'But did not you,' the young man asked, 'go through any Slough of Despond?' 'Yes, I did; but I found it a great deal easier going through with my burden off than with it on my back.' The old woman was quite right. John Bunyan put the getting rid of the burden too far off from the commencement of the pilgrimage. If he meant to show what usually happens, he was right; but if he meant to show what ought to have happened, he was wrong. We must not say to the sinner, 'Now sinner, if thou wilt be saved, go to the baptismal pool; go to the wicket gate; go to the church; do this or that.' No, the cross should be right in front of the wicket gate; and we should say to the sinner, 'Throw thyself down there, and thou art safe; but thou art not safe till thou canst cast off thy burden, and lie at the foot of the cross, and find peace in Jesus.'"[24]

One solution to the problem is to see Christian's experience at the cross not as salvation but as assurance of salvation. He had been pulled through the gate by Goodwill, he knew the way of salvation, but his conscience was still not at peace. Afterwards he came to understand the cross and receive assurance of his release from sin. That was Bunyan's own experience. Christian did not take through the wicket gate the love of sin but only the weight of sin. Like Bunyan, for a time his conscience was not at peace, until he came to the cross and was assured of release from his sin. Greaves explains: "Christian is saved from damnation only because he is brought by Goodwill (divine grace) into the new covenant, the covenant of grace. But the manner of entrance in *The Pilgrim's Progress* is more in keeping with Bunyan's experience as recorded in *Grace Abounding* than it is with Bunyan's theology as it is set forth in *Law and Grace*."[25] Theologically, the delay between Christian's entering the gate and his being relieved of his burden of sin and receiving the new clothes of Christ's imputed righteousness is intolerable, but it was Bunyan's experience. As Greaves expresses it, "The early stages of the pilgrimage do not bring unrelieved assurance."[26]

Goodwill has told Christian that he will soon come to the **House of the Interpreter**, who will show him "excellent things." When

Christian reaches the house he knocks at the door again and again. Interpreter, probably meant by Bunyan to be a picture of the Holy Spirit, is presented with reserve and with great reverence, like that of Goodwill earlier.[27] After he has invited Christian in, the host lights a candle and gives Christian a tour of the rooms of the house, showing him many things:

- *Christian sees the picture of a "very grave person" with his eyes lifted up to heaven, the best of books in his hands, the law of truth upon his lips, the world behind his back; he is pleading with men, and a crown of gold hangs over his head. This one, Christian is told, is the "only man whom the Lord of the place whither thou art going hath authorized to be thy guide in all difficult places" (3:98). Christian has already met him and will meet him again. His name is Evangelist, the faithful minister.*

- *He looks at a man sweeping a room but producing only dust, until a girl brings in water and sprinkles the room. It is not the law but the Gospel that can cleanse the heart of sin.*

- *Christian sees two little children named "Passion" and "Patience," representing people of this world, who want everything now, and people of the world to come, who are content to wait.*

- *He sees a fire in a fireplace that burns higher and hotter despite someone's throwing water on it. On the other side of the wall Christian is shown the reason: a "Man," who is Christ, is "continually with the oil of his grace" maintaining the "work already begun in the heart" (3:100).*

- *Christian observes a valiant man fight his way through many armed men and enter the door of a beautiful palace. Christian no doubt speaks for Bunyan when he smiles and says, "I think verily I know the meaning of this" (3:100).*

- *He finds a man in great despair in an iron cage, who tells him that once he too was a pilgrim ("a fair and flourishing professor"), but that he so hardened his heart that now he cannot repent. Interpreter says to Christian, "Let this man's misery be remembered by thee, and be an everlasting caution to thee" (3:101).*

• *Finally Christian sees a man rising out of bed shaking and trembling,*
who has dreamed that at the day of judgment he was left behind.

With these lessons of hope and fear in his mind, the burdened
pilgrim departs from the House of Interpreter and runs up the
highway, fenced on either side with a wall called Salvation, until
he comes to a cross and, a little below, at the bottom of the hill, a
sepulchre. What follows are some of the most unforgettable words
in the book: "So I saw in my dream, that just as Christian came up
with the cross, his burdened loosed from off his shoulders, and fell
from off his back, and began to tumble, and so continued to do, till
it came to the mouth of the sepulchre, where it fell in, and I saw it
no more. Then was Christian glad and lightsome, and said, with a
merry heart, 'He hath given me rest by his sorrow, and life by his
death'" (3:102).

Three **Shining Ones** come to Christian. The first proclaims,
"Thy sins be forgiven"; the second takes away his rags and gives him
a fresh suit of clothes; the third places a mark on his forehead and
gives him a roll with a seal upon it (which is later described as "the
assurance of his life, and acceptance at the desired haven").

"It will be remembered," writes Alexander Whyte, "that the first time we
saw this man, with whose progress to the Celestial City we are at present
occupied, he was standing in a certain place clothed with rags and with
a burden on his back. After a long journey with him, we have just seen
his burden taken off his back, and it is only after his burden is off and a
Shining One has said to him, Thy sins be forgiven, that a second Shining
One comes and strips him of his rags and clothes him with a change
of raiment. Now, why, it may be asked, has Christian had to carry his
burden so long, and why is he still kept so ragged and so miserable and
he so far on in the pilgrim's path? Surely, it will be said, John Bunyan
was dreaming indeed when he kept a truly converted man, a confessedly
true and sincere Christian, so long in bonds and in rags. Well, as to
his rags: filthy rags are only once spoken of in the Bible, and it is the
prophet Isaiah, whose experience and whose language John Bunyan had
so entirely by heart, who puts them on. And that evangelist among the
prophets not only calls his own and Israel's sins filthy rags, but Isaiah is

> *very bold, and calls their very righteousnesses by that opprobrious name."*
> *According to Whyte, then, the delay in the removal of the burden and*
> *the rags picture the Christian who comes to see that he indeed is filthy*
> *and not fit for heaven until clothed in the righteousness of Christ. It is*
> *possible to be forgiven and still burdened by guilt.*[28]

Christian soon comes upon three men sleeping with fetters clamped to their heels—**Simple, Sloth, and Presumption**. Christian tries to warn them of their danger but they cannot understand him and go back to sleep. (The marginal notation explains that none can be persuaded unless God opens their eyes [3:103].)

> *Alexander Whyte says that "it startles us not a little to come suddenly*
> *upon three pilgrims fast asleep with fetters on their heels on the upward*
> *side of the Interpreter's House, and even on the upward side of the cross*
> *and the sepulchre. We would have looked for those three miserable men*
> *somewhere in the City of Destruction or in the town of Stupidity, or, at*
> *best, somewhere still outside of the wicket-gate."*[29] *The spiritual state of*
> *the travelers we meet in the book is not indicated by where they appear*
> *on the journey, but by their names and their ultimate end. Ignorance*
> *made it all the way to the gate of the Celestial City only to be cast into*
> *hell from there. Along the way we meet hypocrites, skeptics, and evil men,*
> *as well as true pilgrims who are God's elect and come in by the gate and*
> *persevere to the end.*

Now Christian catches sight of **Formalist and Hypocrisy** climbing over the wall to the left of the narrow way. These tell Christian that they are from the land of *Vain-Glory*. They have avoided the gate and taken a shortcut by climbing over the wall as, they say, people have been doing for a thousand years. "And beside," they add, "if we get into the way, what [does it] matter which way we get in? If we are in, we are in" (3:103). They laugh at the objections of Christian, who goes on ahead of them.

Formalist and Hypocrisy appear when they do—almost immediately after Christian received his new clothes, the mark on his forehead, and the "roll with a seal upon it"—to point out the danger of two great errors. Formalist observes the law for its own sake. For him morality is an end in itself. Hypocrisy observes the law for appearance's sake. In neither case is keeping the law an authentic and grateful response to God's calling, as it is for the true Christian.

In due time Christian, with Formalist and Hypocrisy, comes to **Hill Difficulty**, where one false pilgrim takes the side road called *Danger*, and the other, *Destruction*, which leads him into a "wide field full of dark mountains" where he stumbles and falls, and does not get up again. Christian drinks from the spring at the bottom of the hill and begins to walk right up, along the narrow way. Soon he finds that he must climb the steep cliff on his hands and knees. About halfway up he comes to a pleasant *Arbour* made by the Lord of the Hill "for the refreshing of weary travellers" (3:105). He reads from the roll given to him at the cross and then sleeps until almost night. He is awakened suddenly by one who rebukes him, and as he makes haste to continue his journey he leaves behind the roll, which has fallen out of his hand while he was asleep.

When the pilgrim reaches the top of the hill he is met by two men, **Timorous** and **Mistrust,** who are running the other way. They call to him that the farther they have gone toward the City of Zion, the more dangers they have met, including a lion in the way; so they are going back. For a moment Christian wavers, then he remonstrates with them. "I must venture," he says. "To go back is nothing but death; to go forward is fear of death, and life everlasting beyond it. I will yet go forward" (3:105). So Mistrust and Timorous run down the hill, and Christian walks on his way.

> Civil and religious threats and persecution terrified many young Christians in Bunyan's time, and they, like Timorous and Mistrust, turned back. Alexander Whyte comments that "civil despotism and ecclesiastical tyranny do not stand in our way as they stood in Bunyan's way—at least not in the same shape: but every age has its own lions. . . ."[30]

Then Christian discovers that he has lost his roll that has brought him such comfort in difficult places. Regretfully, he turns back to search for it, finding it in the arbor in which he had fallen asleep. He retraces his steps, with joy that he has found his roll but sorrow that he has wasted so much time that night has fallen.

He goes on, fearful of the lions that had alarmed Timorous and Mistrust but encouraged by the view that he has of a palace called **House Beautiful**. "The Palace Beautiful is the church as Bunyan conceives it: a sort of *home* where one draws refreshment in communion with God and brotherly fellowship."[31] Hurrying toward that palace he sees the two lions (but not the chains that hold them). When he hesitates and ponders whether or not he, like Mistrust and Timorous, should go back, the porter *Watchful* calls out to him that the lions are chained (they are there, he says, for "the trial of faith"). Christian will be safe, he is told, if he keeps in the middle of the path. When Christian approaches the lions, he finds that they are chained.

> Alexander Whyte comments, "Whatever our past life may have been, whatever our past sins, past errors of judgment, past mistakes and mishaps, whatever of punishment or chastisement or correction or instruction or sanctification and growth in grace . . . all we have got to do at present is to leave the lions to Him who set them there, and to go on, up to them and past them, keeping always to the midst of the path."[32]

Interpreter's House, which Christian has already visited, represents the inner, spiritual life of the Christian; whereas the House Beautiful is an image of the church visible. It stands by the road, welcoming and genial. The house was built by "the Lord of the Hill," Christian is told, "for the relief and security of pilgrims." *Watchful* calls for "a grave and beautiful damsel" named *Discretion* to examine Christian "according to the law of the house" and, if she approves his answers, to bring him to "the rest of the family" (3:106-7). Discretion is impressed by Christian's clear, forthright testimony. She introduces him to *Prudence*, *Piety*, and *Charity*, who bring him into the family, and he is warmly welcomed. There is much more to be said, but Christian has proved himself a genuine pilgrim, and that is enough for his admission into the House Beautiful.

While they wait for supper, Piety, Prudence, and Charity talk with Christian, asking about his experiences along the way. To Piety's question "What moved you at first to betake yourself to a pilgrim's life?" Christian answers that it was both his fear of destruction and "it was as God would have it." Prudence asks, "And what is it that makes you so desirous to go to Mount Zion?" Christian answers, "Why, there I hope to see him alive that did hang dead on the cross. . . . For, to tell you truth, I love him, because I was by him eased of my burden; and I am weary of my inward sickness. I would fain be where I shall die no more, and with the company that shall continually cry, 'Holy, holy, holy'" (3:108). Charity asks Christian why he has not brought his wife and four children along. Christian recites with anguish his efforts to convince them to come but explains that his wife "was afraid of losing this world" and his children "were given to the foolish delights of youth" (3:107-9).

> AlexanderWhyte sees the supper in House Beautiful as the Lord's Supper in the church:"Let a man examine himself, says the apostle to the Corinthians, and so let him eat of that bread and drink of that cup. And thus it was, that before the pilgrim was invited to sit down at the supper table . . . quite a number of most pointed and penetrating questions were put to him by those who had charge of that house and its supper table."[33]

Finally supper is ready, the table "furnished with fat things" and "wine . . . well refined." As they eat they talk until late in the night about the Lord of the Hill and what he has done for pilgrims. Then Christian is shown a large bedroom named *Peace*, whose window opens to the sunrise, where he sleeps until daybreak. When he wakes refreshed he sings of the wonder of being forgiven and already, as it were, dwelling "next door to heaven" (3:109-10).

Christian remains several days at House Beautiful. He is shown the "rarities" of the house—the "pedigree" (or genealogy) of the Lord of the Hill, "that he was the son of the Ancient of Days, and came by that eternal generation"), the worthy acts of his servants, the armory, and ancient things such as the rod of Moses and the trumpets of Gideon's men. Finally, from the top of the house he spies the Delectable Mountains in the distance. That is only possible, he is told, "if the day be clear" (3:110). Such distant views are not always available to God's children. Sometimes the circumstances of life and the feebleness of our faith prevent us from enjoying the prospects of heaven.

Before leaving the House Beautiful, Christian is given weapons for his journey: "sword, shield, helmet, breastplate, *all-prayer*, and shoes that would not wear out" (3:110). His friends walk with him for a distance—not as symbolic virtues but as human friends who are part of the church. Christian hears from the porter that another pilgrim, **Faithful**, has passed by. Christian knows Faithful; he was his near neighbor in the City of Destruction. Discretion, Piety, Charity, and Prudence accompany Christian down the hill into the **Valley of Humiliation**. They give him farewell gifts—a loaf of bread, a bottle of wine, and a cluster of raisins—and send him on.

There are special delights and rest in the House Beautiful, but often the pilgrim's way lies through danger and difficulty. Just a little way into the Valley of Humiliation Christian encounters **Apollyon**.[34] The pilgrim is tempted to turn and run from this frightful, fiery creature with scales and wings, until he remembers that he has no armor for his back.

A war of words breaks out between Christian and his enemy. Apollyon claims that Christian is a deserter from his own country. Christian answers that although he was born in the City of Destruction, he left it when he found that he could not live on Apollyon's pay, because "the wages of sin is death." He refuses to return to the service of Apollyon because, as he puts it, "I have let myself to another, even to the King of princes." With flattery, sympathy, and threats, Apollyon tries to convince Christian to forsake his new Prince and serve him again. Christian answers well and stands resolute, but the next statement of Apollyon's strikes home: "Thou hast already been unfaithful in thy service to him; and how dost thou think to receive wages of him?" Apollyon recites Christian's failures and accuses him of inwardly desiring "vainglory." Christian replies that "all this is true, and much more, which thou hast left out," but "the Prince whom I serve and honour is merciful and ready to forgive."[35]

In great anger the roaring, yelling Apollyon announces that he is "an enemy to this Prince" and begins to throw flaming darts at Christian. Christian is wounded "in his head, his hand, and [his]

foot," that is, in his *thoughts*, his *deeds*, and his *conduct*, but he fights
on courageously "above half a day," when he falls and loses his sword.
It appears that he will be killed, but he recovers his sword and,
quoting Scripture as did Christ when tempted by the devil in the
wilderness, he gives Apollyon a "deadly thrust.""With that, Apollyon
spread forth his dragon's wings, and sped him away" (3:113).[36] A
Hand applies leaves from the tree of life to Christian's wounds
and they are healed. He eats some of his bread and drinks from the
bottle that was given him and is refreshed. Giving thanks to God
for his deliverance, Christian goes forward with drawn sword, now
watchful.

> The first African translation of **The Pilgrim's Progress** was made in
> Madagascar during a time of intense persecution of Christians by the
> royal court. Six or so handwritten copies circulated among the Malagasy
> Christians, who read and often memorized the text and found it a source
> of comfort in their persecution. One convert likened his experience to
> Christian's fight with Apollyon:"We read in **the Pilgrim's Progress**
> that when Christian saw Apollyon coming to meet him he began to be
> afraid and to hesitate whether to return or to stand his ground, but
> when he considered that he had no armour for his back he thought that
> to turn his back to him might give him greater advantage to pierce him
> with his darts, therefore he resolved to stand his ground, for, said he,
> 'had I no more in my eye than the saving of my life it would be the best
> way to stand.'When Christian entered theValley of the Shadow of Death,
> he said, 'though it be a gloomy valley, yet it is the way to the Celestial
> City.' These words of Christian and the passage quoted above express in
> few words our own feelings and views."Another convert wrote:"O God,
> do thou enable us to make the progress that Pilgrim made, and if thy
> kingdom in Madagascar is to be advanced by these means [persecution]
> be it so."[37]

At the end of the Valley of Humiliation, Christian comes to
another low place called **The Valley of the Shadow of Death**.
"And Christian must needs go through it, because the way to the
Celestial City lay through the midst of it" (3:114). This valley is not
death itself but the shadow of death, falling dark and deadly across

some part of life. Here Christian meets two men making haste to go back from this ominous place. When Christian asks them why they are in such a hurry, they tell him about the frightful things they have seen and heard. But the point—the only point—is, as Christian reminds them, Which is the way to "the desired haven?"[38]

Christian marches on. On one side of the valley is a deep ditch and on the other a dangerous mire, and the path is dark and "exceeding narrow." In the middle of the valley Christian passes the mouth of hell with its terrible noises and frightful sights; he puts up his sword and clutches another weapon called "All Prayer" (3:115). Christian's greatest trial comes when one of the wicked ones from the burning pit creeps up behind him and whispers "many grievous blasphemies to him, which he . . . thought had proceeded from his own mind." This experience was Bunyan's own, as related in *Grace Abounding*, and, like Christian, he at first "had not the discretion either to stop his ears or to know from whence these blasphemies came" (3:115).

As the traveler struggles through the valley, he thinks he hears "the voice of a man, as going before him, saying, Though I walk through the valley of the shadow of death, I will fear no evil, for thou art with me" (3:115). These are the words of Faithful, whom Christian overtakes early the next morning.[39] Christian is encouraged that another pilgrim who trusts in the Lord is going through this same awful valley, even though ahead is a dangerous route full of snares, traps, and pits. At the end of the valley he comes upon a gruesome scene, the "blood, bones, ashes, and mangled bodies" of pilgrims that have gone this way in times past. He sees a cave in which dwell *Pope* and *Pagan*, by whose power and tyranny many have been put to death. Christian passes through safely because "Pagan has been dead many a day" and Pope, although still alive, has "grown so crazy and stiff in his joints" that he can do little to threaten pilgrims.[40] As he leaves the valley, Christian bursts into one of his frequent (and better) songs, which ends with the words "But since I live, let Jesus wear the crown" (3:116).

As yet Christian has made no friends among other pilgrims, but from this point on we never see him alone again. As he climbs up a little hill he joins **Faithful**. Faithful is a stalwart figure—"strong of nerve, notable for momentum, braced in will." His characteristic phrase is "I firmly believe it."[41] As they go "very lovingly on together," they influence and shape each other. Faithful develops a richer human sympathy, and Christian gains robustness.

> *Alexander Whyte notes how completely unalike are these two pilgrims, Christian and Faithful, and comments:"John Bunyan is as fresh as nature herself in the variety, in the individuality, and even in the idiosyncrasy of his spiritual portrait gallery."[42]*

Faithful tells Christian about things that have taken place in the City of Destruction (from which both have come) after Christian's departure and reviews for him his own journey so far. He had escaped the Slough of Despond and come safely to the wicket gate, where he had been assaulted by *Wanton*, who had promised him "all carnal and fleshly content." Faithful had shut his eyes so that he would not "be bewitched by her looks" and gone his way (although he tells Christian that he is not sure that he "did wholly escape her"). At the foot of the Hill Difficulty, Faithful had met *Adam the First* from the town of *Deceit*, where he lived with his three daughters, *The Lust of the Flesh*, *The Lust of the Eyes*, and *The Pride of Life*. Old Adam had tried to convince Faithful to go to work for him. Though tempted, Faithful had resisted, not without feeling that Adam the First had pulled part of him after himself. Someone had come upon Faithful (at just about the place where Christian had lost his roll) and struck him because of his "secret inclining to Adam the First." This person (identified as Moses with the law) would have killed him but for the intervention of One whom Faithful did not know, "but as he went by, I perceived the holes in his hands and in his side; then I concluded that he was our Lord" (3:119).

Faithful had safely passed the lions, who were asleep, he thought. He had not stopped at Interpreter's House, much to Christian's regret. As he walked into the Valley of Humiliation, *Discontent* had tried to persuade him to go back by telling him that his friends *Pride*, *Arrogancy*, *Self-Conceit*, and *Worldly-Glory* would be much offended if he made such a fool of himself "as to wade through this valley." He also had met *Shame*, who had ridiculed religion and pilgrims for their "ignorance and want of understanding in all natural science."

Faithful had been hard put to answer him until he remembered that "that which is highly esteemed among men is had in abomination with God." Faithful had then "had sunshine all the rest of the way" through the Valley of Humiliation and through the Valley of the Shadow of Death (3:120).

Christian and Faithful meet **Talkative**, who enters into lengthy conversation with them, saying many good things.[43] At first Faithful is impressed, but not Christian, who knew Talkative in the City of Destruction. Speaking so that Talkative can't hear, Christian tells Faithful that Talkative is "best abroad; near home he is ugly enough" and "religion hath no place in his heart" but only in his "tongue" (3:121-2). Faithful accepts Christian's description of Talkative and sees, he says, that "saying and doing are two things." Then Faithful goes back to the impatient Talkative and asks him, "How doth the saving grace of God discover itself when it is in the heart of man" (3:123)? After Talkative's feeble attempts to answer, Faithful explains how God's grace manifests itself, both to a person and through that person to others who see and know him. When Faithful asks Talkative to apply this to his own life, he is much offended and departs. Christian is glad to be rid of him, and Faithful is thankful that he has been able to deal plainly with him. The length of this episode indicates Bunyan's concern for the problem of mere verbal profession of Christianity without real heart religion.[44]

Now the two pilgrims make their way through "a wilderness," where Evangelist overtakes them (3:125). He warns them about trouble they will face in a town ahead (one will be killed there) and encourages them to steadfastness. In the later editions of *The Pilgrim's Progress*, Bunyan gives Evangelist a wider sphere of work. Not only does he guide pilgrims to the wicket gate, but he comes to them from time to time as a pastor, to instruct and encourage.

Christian and Faithful arrive in the town of *Vanity* where the **Vanity Fair** is held all year long. The fair, founded five thousand years ago by *Beelzebub*, *Apollyon*, and *Legion*, is a place of merchandise, games, delights and pleasures of all kinds, and also "thefts, murders, adulteries, false-swearers." Different nationalities have their own special wares or forms of vanity, with the merchandise of Rome especially promoted in the fair. "Only our English nation," Bunyan adds, "with some others, [has] taken a dislike thereat" (3:127).

> Vanity Fair is a picture of life in the days of Charles II and the Restoration. Kelman comments that "in the figures of these two pilgrims austerely walking through the noisy streets of Vanity, we can see the forms of such men as Owen, Baxter, Goodwin, and Howe, walking apart amidst the dance of contemporary English life."[45]

Beelzebub is "the chief lord of the fair" through which pilgrims must pass because it is on the way to the Celestial City. Even "the Prince of princes" had had to come this way. Beelzebub had invited the Prince to buy of his vanities and even promised to make him lord of the fair if he would buy. "But he had no mind to the merchandise, and therefore left the town without laying out so much as one farthing" (3:128).[46]

The pilgrims attract the notice of the people of the town. A hubbub follows because their clothes and their speech are different and because they are not interested in the goods for sale.[47] When asked what they would buy, the two pilgrims reply, "We buy the truth." The "great one of the fair" orders that Christian and Faithful be questioned. Their examiners believe that they are mad or that they have come to "put all things into a confusion in the fair," so they beat them, and besmeared them with dirt, and put them in a cage so "that they might be made a spectacle to all" (3:128). When the pilgrims do not return evil for evil, some of the people begin to defend them, which leads to even greater disturbance. Christian and Faithful are blamed for this disorder and further mistreated. Their patient endurance continues and influences several of the bystanders at the fair. This more infuriates their enemies, who now resolve to kill them. The pilgrims comfort each other with Evangelist's words that the one to die will have the best of it because he will arrive first at the Celestial City and escape many trials along the way.

Christian and Faithful are brought before the judge, *Lord Hate-good*, and charged with disturbing business and creating a riot and division in the town.[48] Faithful begins his defense, but three witnesses—*Envy*, *Superstition* and *Pickthank*—are called to testify against him. After Faithful answers their accusations, he is turned over to the jury, whose names are *Mr. Blind-man*, *Mr. No-good*, *Mr. Malice*, *Mr. Love-lust*, *Mr. Live-loose*, *Mr. Heady*, *Mr. High-mind*, *Mr. Enmity, Mr. Liar*, *Mr. Cruelty*, *Mr. Hate-light*, and *Mr. Implacable*. The jury brings in a unanimous guilty verdict. Sad to read, the officials scourge and stone Faithful and burn him to ashes at the stake. But a chariot and horses were waiting, and he "was taken up into it, and straightway was carried up through the clouds, with sound of trumpet, the nearest way to the Celestial Gate" (3:132). Christian remained in prison for a while, "but he that overrules all things, having the power of their rage in his own hand, so wrought it about that Christian for that time escaped them and went his way." But he must have thought that Faithful had the better part, for "while he had mounted up with wings as eagles, Christian must yet, for a long while, walk and not faint."[49]

As lonely Christian left the town, **Hopeful**, who had been persuaded by the words and conduct of the two pilgrims at the fair, joined him. As one died to bear testimony to the truth, another rose "out of his ashes" to be a companion for Christian in his pilgrimage (3:132).

Christian and Hopeful overtake **By-ends**, who is from the town of *Fair-speech*. By-ends does not tell them his name, but he does tell them about some of his kindred, including *Mr. Facing-both-ways* and "the parson of our parish," *Mr. Two-tongues*, whose wife is "*my Lady Feigning's daughter.*" By-ends says that the people of Fair-speech differ somewhat in religion "from those of the stricter sort" in two small points: "First, we never strive against wind and tide; secondly, we are always most zealous when religion goes in his silver slippers; we love much to walk with him in the street, if the sun shines, and the people applaud him" (3:132). By-ends (he denies that that is really his name but a name given to him by some who "could not abide him") wants to go with Christian and Hopeful but cannot forsake his old principles, he says, "since they are harmless and profitable" (3:133).

A little later Christian and Hopeful look back and see that three others have joined By-ends: *Mr. Hold-the-world*, *Mr. Money-love*, and *Mr. Save-all*. By-ends tells his new companions that the two pilgrims ahead are so rigid and so in love with their own ideas that they will not accept others like himself. They discuss the question proposed by By-ends, of whether or not a minister or a merchant who has the opportunity of getting "the good blessings of this life" by becoming zealous, at least in appearance, in some point of religion may use this means to attain his end "and yet be a right honest man." They agree that such a use is quite proper. They call out to Christian and Hopeful to wait, and old Mr. Hold-the-world asks them the same question. Christian answers sharply, "Even a babe in religion may answer ten thousand such questions. For, if it be unlawful to follow Christ for loaves, as it is in John 6, how much more abominable is it to make of him and religion a stalking-horse to get and enjoy the world?" Christian illustrates his point with the Pharisees and Judas, concluding that a "man [who] takes up religion for the world will throw away religion for the world." Staggered by such an answer, Mr. By-ends and his friends are silent and wait for Christian and Hopeful to go on without them (3:136).

> By-ends "lives near enough to Vanity Fair to pass with its inhabitants for one of themselves, yet sufficiently clear of it to disclaim his citizenship when in the company of pilgrims. Everyone knows but too well that heartbreaking borderland in church membership wherein those live who (one cannot but suspect) would think little enough of the church or of religion if it were not for what these are supposed to be worth in other coin."[50]

Christian and Hopeful pass through a pleasant but narrow plain called *Ease*; on the far side of Ease is a little hill called *Lucre* in which there is a *silver mine*. Men have been injured and even killed in that area. As the pilgrims approach, one named *Demas* calls out to them to come over to the mine, where he will show them something.[51] Hopeful is tempted to go and see, but Christian recognizes the danger and stops him. By-ends and his companions do stop, however, and are never seen again in the way.

Near the highwayside the pilgrims find an old "monument" in the shape of a woman transformed into a pillar, with an inscription that reads "Remember Lot's wife."[52] Christian and Hopeful discuss how this should be to them a warning and example. The danger of the temptation and sin of covetousness is evidenced by the triple warning of By-ends, Demas, and Lot's wife.

Arriving at a pleasant river, the pilgrims wander happily along its banks, drinking, now and then, its refreshing water. There are groves of green trees bearing delicious fruit and leaves that are good for medicine. On either side of the river are fragrant meadows, very green and filled with lilies. Christian and Hopeful lie down safely and go to sleep. They stay in this delightful place for several days and nights. But, as Bunyan adds in a parenthesis, they are not yet at their journey's end.

> *"Another idyllic landscape unfolds itself before them, rich in associations from the Psalms and Isaiah, and in the deep spiritual [meaning] which Bunyan can always impart to fresh green meadows and clear water."*[53]

After the refreshment of their time at the river, Christian and Hopeful move on but soon feel discouraged because the road becomes rough and hard. They see a meadow on the left-hand side of the road (called **By-path Meadow**), with a path on the far side of the fence that runs along the way they are going. Discouraged, with sore feet, the pilgrims complain about the road and feel sorry for themselves. Christian wants to cross the stile and walk on the easier path, but Hopeful fears that it could eventually lead them out of the way.[54] However, Christian prevails (Bunyan's marginal note reads: "Strong Christians may lead weak ones out of the way" [3:139]). On the new path the pilgrims meet *Vain Confidence*, on his way, as he tells them, to the Celestial City. When night comes on, they lose sight of him but hear him fall into a deep pit.

As a ferocious storm, with thunder and lightning, pelts the frightened pilgrims, Christian asks Hopeful's forgiveness for having led him astray.[55] Christian and Hopeful try to go back, each man wanting to go first to warn the other of danger. They are nearly drowned several times by the rapidly rising rain water. Finally they stumble upon a little shelter, where they lie down and fall into exhausted sleep.

Alexander Whyte notes "how sudden and almost instantaneous is the fall of Christian and Hopeful, from the very gate of heaven to the very gate of hell. All the Sabbath and . . . Monday and . . . Tuesday before that fatal Wednesday, the two pilgrims had walked with great delight on the banks of a very pleasant river; that river, in fact, which David the King called the river of God, and John, the river of the water of life. . . . Now, could you have believed it that two such men as our pilgrims . . . could be in the enjoyment of all that the first half of the week, and then by their own doing should be in Giant Despair's deepest dungeon before the end of the same week? And yet so it was."[56]

Alarms are not over. **Giant Despair** discovers the pilgrims sleeping in his grounds and hauls them away to **Doubting Castle**, where he locks them in a dungeon.

*"In composing these terrible pages, Bunyan writes straight and bold out of his own heart and conscience," says Alexander Whyte. "Last week I went over **Grace Abounding** again and marked the passages in which its author describes his own experiences of doubt, diffidence, and despair, till I gave over counting the passages, they are so many."*[57]

"The main features of Doubting Castle are imprisonment and helplessness. This wretchedness comes late in the pilgrimage, as such moods often do come, amid the depressions of advancing age."[58]

Christian and Hopeful languish in the dungeon from Wednesday morning until Saturday night without light, food, or water. On Thursday, Giant Despair, at the counsel of his wife, *Diffidence,*[59] beats the pilgrims unmercifully. On Friday, again on the advice of his wife, the giant mocks them: Since they will never come out of the dungeon, they should kill themselves. Christian is tempted by the giant's counsel, but Hopeful reminds his companion that murder, of oneself as well as of others, is forbidden by the "Lord of the country" to which they are going. He urges ten reasons against suicide! Furthermore, he says, others have indeed escaped from Despair's dungeon. Reminding Christian of his own exploits in the past, Hopeful pleads with him to be patient. Although Christian has been a pilgrim longer, it is Hopeful who helps his companion endure. On Saturday, once again at his wife's suggestion, the giant takes the two pilgrims into the castle yard and shows them the skulls and bones of all those he has killed. Beating them again, he returns them to the dungeon.

> "The question might be asked, why Giant Despair did not do what he threatened? The answer is that he, like the rest of the universe, works within limits, and often seems much more powerful than he is. Also, his aim is not to work directly, but through the spirit of his prisoners. He will break their spirit if he can, or drive them into sin and madness."[60]

On Saturday night about midnight Christian and Hopeful begin to pray, and continue in prayer "till almost break of day."[61] It comes to Christian's mind that he has had all along a key called *Promise*, which he suspects will open the doors of the castle. Indeed this proves true and the two pilgrims escape from the clutches of Giant Despair. Brilliantly, Bunyan made the escape so difficult and yet so easy; Christian had only to be reminded that Scripture had provided him with the key, which he remembered when they earnestly prayed.

> "God's covenant with his elect has not been forgotten; Christian can only neglect it for a time, till his own regenerate heart recalls him to the promise of faith. No allegorical intermediary brings him the key; it is with him all the time."[62]

The two pilgrims recross the stile, where they build a signpost to warn future travelers. Then they walk on their way singing.

> "In the pillar which the pilgrims set up, with its warning to those that followed, we see Christian's incurable, undiscourageable need and impulse to evangelise. Neither the shame of his own late fall nor the joy of regaining the highway can hinder him from preaching to others and warning them. For deep in the man's heart there is a great compassion. It is a dangerous world, and he remembers other travellers in it, and sets up his pillar."[63]

It is a joyous day when Christian and Hopeful arrive in the

Delectable Mountains. Leaning upon their staffs, as is common with weary pilgrims, they converse with the shepherds they meet there. The shepherds tell Christian and Hopeful that "these mountains are Immanuel's Land, and they are within sight of his city; and the sheep also are his, and he laid down his life for them" (3:143). After questioning them and finding that they are true pilgrims, the shepherds look "very lovingly upon them" and welcome them to the Delectable Mountains. The next morning the shepherds, whose names are *Knowledge*, *Experience*, *Watchful*, and *Sincere*, show the pilgrims the wonders of the place.

> *AlexanderWhyte sees the four shepherds as representing four qualities of a faithful pastor. The names of the four shepherds sum up the life and work of the pastor. He is to labor in season and out of season to be a minister of the greatest possible knowledge and widest possible experience, the most alert and sleepless watchfulness, and the most earnest sincerity.*

Christian and Hopeful find themselves near three hills, two of which indicate danger, and the third, the brilliant spectacle of heaven. The hill called *Error* had brought about the deaths of those listening to *Hymeneus* and *Philetus*, who denied the resurrection.[64] That hill slopes upward innocently enough, but its farther side is a precipice.

> *"Men climb that hill to get a wide view of earth and heaven, and the fate of the climbers is a terrible commentary upon a certain kind of wide view," comments Kelman.*[65]

When, from the top of *Mount Caution*, Christian and Hopeful see men, blinded by Giant Despair, wandering among tombs, the pilgrims look at each other "with tears gushing out," but say nothing to the shepherds. The shepherds show them a door in the side of the hill, from which they hear tormented cries and smell brimstone. "This is a by-way to hell, a way that hypocrites go in," the shepherds explain (3:145). The door to hell, located among the mountains of lofty spiritual experience, does not mean that Bunyan believed that a person might lose his or her salvation; those for whom this door stands open are those who from the first were not true pilgrims.

As Christian and Hopeful come near the far foothills of the Delectable Mountains, which up to this point can hardly be said to live up to their name, the shepherds point them to the distant gates of the Celestial City. From the top of a high ridge called *Clear*, the travelers peer through the "perspective glass" of the shepherds and think they see "something like the gate and also some of the glory of the place" (3:145).

> *"This, then, is the Pilgrims' first definite glimpse of heaven. As years advance and the pilgrimage draws nearer to its close, it is fitting that [such glimpses] should come; and such optic glasses as the fourteenth chapter of [the Gospel of] St. John or the twenty-first of Revelation become the daily helpers of the aged saint."*[66]

With advice and encouragement—for a dangerous stretch of road is still ahead—the shepherds send the two pilgrims on their way.

"So I awoke from my dream. . . . And I slept, and dreamed again," wrote John Bunyan (3:145-6). Some believe that this break in the narrative marks the point at which Bunyan was released from jail, either to finish his book in freedom or to leave off writing until he found himself in prison again some years later.

As Christian and Hopeful trudge down from the mountains, they discover "a little crooked lane" winding from the country of *Conceit* and meet "a very brisk lad" named **Ignorance**, who is bound, he says, for the Celestial City. At first, Ignorance seems to be an honest enough citizen: calm, reserved, and "very English," with a reasonable faith.[67] No burden weighs him down and his path is "a fine pleasant green lane." However, his entrance to the way has not been by the wicket gate and the cross—the invariable test of genuineness for Bunyan—but down one of those many lanes that people wrongly decide will lead to heaven. Ignorance observes that he hopes to enter the city because of his good works "as other good people do." When Christian contradicts him, remarking that good works are not sufficient, he replies, "Gentlemen . . . be content to follow the religion of your country, and I will follow the religion of mine" (3:146).[68] Christian and Hopeful decide that Ignorance will not hear them at present, but they hope to have more to say to him later.

So the pilgrims go on and come to a very dark path, where they meet a man whom seven devils have bound with seven strong cords and are carrying back to a door in the side of the hill. At first Christian wonders if the man might be one *Turn-away* from the town of *Apostasy*, but then he recalls a story he has heard of a man named *Little-faith* from the town of *Sincere*. Little-faith was attacked and robbed by three brothers, *Faint-heart*, *Mistrust*, and *Guilt*. (We met Mistrust earlier, fleeing with Timorous from the imagined danger of the lions at the Palace Beautiful.)

> Kelman comments, "It may be permissible, without pressing the allegory too far, to see in the detailed account of the attack a very definite sequence of spiritual experiences. Faint-heart speaks, Mistrust robs, Guilt strikes down."[69]

Fearing that the King's champion, *Great-grace*, might be about, the three rogues fled. They had taken most of Little-faith's "spending money" but had missed his "jewels" and his "certificate," by which he was to receive his admittance at the Celestial Gate. Little-faith, however, was forced to beg, and often he went hungry as he continued his journey "with nothing but doleful and bitter complaints." When Hopeful wonders why Little-faith did not sell some of his jewels, Christian answers vehemently. Hopeful responds, "Why art thou so tart, my brother? Esau sold his birthright, and that for a mess of pottage, and that birthright was his greatest jewel; and if he, why might not Little-faith do so too?" Christian explains the difference between the two: Esau had not so much as a little faith, whereas Little-faith's mind was "on things divine." Though "faithless ones" can sell what they have and "themselves outright to boot; yet they that have faith, saving faith, though but a little of it, cannot do so" (3:148). Hopeful admits his mistake but adds that Christian's "severe reflection" has almost made him angry. Christian ends the unpleasant episode without apology, and Hopeful is big enough to let it pass, not demanding the last word (3:148-9). Bunyan, as a

Calvinist, was, of course, a firm believer in the perseverance of the saints; so he could not have had Little-faith lose his jewels. Hopeful was not the first or the last to be "almost angry" in an argument about the doctrine of perseverance!

> A Scottish woman "*underwent a dangerous operation that might have robbed her of her speech. After the operation, [her] pastor visited her in the hospital. Turning to him, she whispered, 'The jewels are all safe!' Her phrase refers to a scene in which the character Little Faith is robbed. The assailants make off with his spending money but fail to find his jewels—his belief in Christ. The woman in hospital uses the image to signal that both her voice and her faith have survived the operation.*"[70]

Hopeful fails to understand why Little-faith gave way so completely to the three men who were obviously cowards, running away as soon as they thought someone was coming. Christian is more sympathetic, and what follows has been called "a monologue on Christian tenderness." Christian says that "no man can tell what in that combat attends us, but he that hath been in the battle himself. . . . But for such footmen as thee and I are, let us never desire to meet with an enemy, nor vaunt as if we could do better, when we hear of others that . . . have been foiled" (3:149-50). Christian reminds Hopeful that allowance must be made for the limitations of a weak brother. Little-faith was not a great man or a hero of any kind. "Fortunately," Kelman points out, "this does not debar him from being one of God's true pilgrims."[71]

Christian and Hopeful turn their discussion to Great-grace. He is "the King's champion," but even Great-grace, Christian deplores, could face a terrible struggle if Faint-heart or Mistrust "[got] within him." The scars and cuts on his face show the battles Great-grace has fought. Christian warns Hopeful against overconfidence ("witness Peter, of whom I made mention before") and says that they must be sure to always have on their armor and carry a shield with them. It is also good, he adds, to "desire of the King a convoy, yea that he will go with us himself" (3:149-50).

"So they went on, and Ignorance followed." The pilgrims come to a place where they are perplexed as to which way to take. A man, "black of flesh, but covered with a very light robe," walks by and calls that they can follow him because he is going to the Celestial City.[72] Christian and Hopeful do so, but after a while they realize that the road is leading them away from the city. Before they can change their course, however, they find themselves entangled in a net. Too late they remember that the shepherds warned them to watch out for *the Flatterers*. Then a *Shining One* comes toward them with "a whip of small cord in his hand." He cuts the net, freeing the pilgrims, and leads them back to the way. But he also chastises them with the whip, saying as he does so, "As many as I love, I rebuke and chasten; be zealous, therefore, and repent" (Revelation 3:19) (3:151).

Christian and Hopeful see a man whose name is *Atheist* coming toward them "with his back toward Zion." When the pilgrims call to him that they are going to the Celestial City, he laughs, declaring that they are ignorant to take upon themselves "so tedious a journey" when they are likely to have nothing but their "travel for [their] pains." Atheist reports that he has been seeking this city in vain for twenty years, and now he is going back to refresh himself "with the things that I then cast away, for hopes of that, which I now see, is not" (3:152). Christian and Hopeful turn away from this man, and, laughing at them, he goes his way.

Bunyan, in his dream, watches the pilgrims as they walk into the **Enchanted Ground**. The air in that place makes people drowsy, and Hopeful wants to stop and take a nap.[73] Christian reminds him that one of the shepherds warned them to beware of this place; he suggests that to keep themselves awake, they "fall into good discourse."[74] Christian asks Hopeful how he first came to seek the good of his soul. Hopeful describes how he was taken up with the treasures and riches of the world until he heard the truth from "beloved Faithful" and Christian at Vanity Fair. For some time he struggled under conviction of sin before he decided to mend his life by forsaking sin and his sinful friends and give himself to good works. But he came to realize that all his good works were "as filthy rags." He did not know what to do until he spoke to Faithful, who told him that unless he could "obtain the righteousness of a man that never had sinned," neither his own righteousness nor "all the righteousness of the world" could save him. Faithful further explained the Gospel to Hopeful and taught him a prayer that he prayed again and again until the Father showed him his Son. Hopeful explained:

> *I did not see him with my bodily eyes, but with the eyes of my understanding, and thus it was: One day I was very sad, I think sadder than any one time in my life, and this sadness was through a fresh sight of the greatness and vileness of my sins. And as I was then looking for nothing but hell, and the everlasting damnation of my soul, suddenly, as I thought, I saw the Lord Jesus look down from heaven upon me, and saying, "Believe on the Lord Jesus Christ, and thou shalt be saved."*
>
> *But I replied, "Lord, I am a great, a very great sinner." And he answered, "My grace is sufficient for thee." Then I said, "But, Lord, what is believing?" And then I saw from that saying "He that cometh to me shall never hunger, and he that believeth on me shall never thirst" that believing and coming were all one; and that he that came, that is, ran out in his heart and affections after salvation by Christ, he indeed believed in Christ (3:155-6).*

In Hopeful's testimony we recognize Bunyan's own conversion experience and the most complete statement of God's way of salvation that we find in *The Pilgrim's Progress*.

Christian and Hopeful see Ignorance still following and decide to wait for him. In the conversation that follows, Christian questions Ignorance, rejecting or correcting his answers. Tired of Ignorance's constant reference to the thoughts of his own heart, Christian insists, in good Puritan fashion, on bringing everything to the test of the Scriptures. In the end, Ignorance falls into subversive Roman Catholic theology. His doctrine of justification, he tells them, is that "Christ makes my duties that are religious acceptable to his Father by virtue of his merits, and so I shall be justified" (3:158). Ignorance seizes on the obvious danger of the Protestant doctrine of free grace: if we are to trust simply in what Christ has done, he argues, we shall grow careless as to what we ourselves are to do. Christian's almost furious answer is understandable but has little effect on Ignorance, who waves them on because, he says, "You go so fast, I cannot keep pace with you" (3:159).

Christian continues to expound on the spiritual state of people like Ignorance but, when Hopeful appears to grow weary of the conversation, brings up the case of one *Temporary*, from the town of *Graceless*. Temporary desired to go on pilgrimage, but he met *Save-self* and gave up the idea. This talk introduces the subject of "sudden backsliding," which the two pilgrims explore until they are safely out of the Enchanted Ground.

Finally the travelers find themselves in the country of **Beulah**, where birds always sing, flowers always bloom, and the sun shines night and day. They are beyond the Valley of the Shadow of Death, out of the reach of Giant Despair, and within sight of the Celestial City. They meet some of the city's inhabitants, "the Shining Ones," who commonly walk in Beulah because it is "upon the borders of heaven" (3:161). Christian and Hopeful can clearly see the city, that it is built with pearls and precious stones and the streets are paved with gold; and they long to be there, but they have a little way yet to go. The King's *gardener* gives them fresh fruit to eat and a place to sleep in the King's leafy arbors.

At last Christian and Hopeful "address themselves" to go up to the **Celestial City**. Several men "in raiment that [shines] like gold" meet them and tell them that they have but two more difficulties "and then you are in the city" (3:162-3). Before them is the river of death, with the heights of heaven beyond. So the pilgrims go on together until they come within sight of the gate and reality overwhelms them. Between them and the gate is the very deep river and there is no bridge over it. The stunned travelers are told that they must go through. Only two pilgrims—Enoch and Elijah—have entered the city another way. With trepidation they step into the water. Christian becomes very troubled and seems to lose his senses and forget God's goodness. He begins to sink, and Hopeful calls out, "Be of good cheer, my brother, I feel the bottom, and it is good" (3:163). Hopeful has all he can do to encourage Christian. He is so busy attending to Christian's need that he quite forgets his own. Christian cheers up at the sight of Christ, who reminds him, "When thou passest through the waters, I will be with thee; and through the rivers, they shall not overflow thee." Both Christian and Hopeful cross safely and come to the bank on the other side. They meet the two shining men, who had waited for them, and go with them up the mighty hill, higher than the clouds. Christian and Hopeful climb with "much agility and speed" because they have "left their mortal garments behind them in the river" (3:164). As the Shining Ones prepare the pilgrims for the glory ahead, "a company of the heavenly host" comes out to welcome them with "shouting and the sound of trumpet" (3:165).

"Now I saw in my dream, that these two men went in at the gate; and lo, as they entered they were transfigured; and they had raiment put on that shone like gold. . . . Then I heard in my dream that all the bells in the city rang . . . for joy, and that it was said unto them, Enter ye into the joy of your Lord. . . . And after that, they shut up the gates; which, when I had seen, I wished myself among them" (3:166). Of these last words, Kelman comments, "There is no need of any note to that. It is the most perfect touch of all."[75]

> *The Pilgrim's Progress was recommended as "a book to live and die upon." One nineteenth-century commentator observed: "the descriptions of the pilgrims' crossing the river are full of instructions and comfort for dying believers, and have been helpful to many in looking forward to a dying day."*[76]

But there is a final, tragic scene. Ignorance arrives at the river and crosses it with little difficulty in the boat of a ferryman named *Vain-hope*. But when he comes to the gate he has no certificate, and so the king commands the two shining men to bind Ignorance and put him in the door in the side of the hill. "Then I saw that there was a way to hell," Bunyan writes, "even from the gates of heaven, as well as from the City of Destruction" (3:166). Ignorance is lost because he is willfully ignorant. Despite hearing the truth of the Gospel from Christian, he rejects it, saying that Christian's beliefs seem to him "the fruit of distracted brains" (3:158). His final fumbling for a certificate that he does not have represents Ignorance searching his heart for a faith that he never possessed. Ignorance stands for the cool, skeptical modern person who wants to ground his or her faith in conscience and conduct, not in the grace of God to an unworthy sinner.

Some people have wondered if it would have been better if Bunyan had ended with the beautiful words that close the story of the pilgrims' journey. *Kelman explains that Bunyan's ending is "bad art," but that Bunyan was "the Puritan preacher first, the artist and all else only afterwards."* [77] Because there is a hell, the last word of any faithful Christian must be a solemn word of warning.

> *C. S. Lewis writes: "In my opinion the book would be immeasurably weakened as a work of art if the flames of Hell were not always flickering on the horizon." On a deeper level, Lewis adds, "Many do not believe that either the trumpets 'with melodious noise' or the infernal den await us where the road ends. But most, I fancy, have discovered that to be born is to be exposed to delights and miseries greater than imagination could have anticipated; that the choice of ways at any crossroad may be more important than we think; and that short cuts may lead to very nasty places."* [78]

"So I awoke, and behold it was a dream," wrote John Bunyan (3:166). And "that dream of his," writes Kelman, "was and still remains truer than most men's waking thoughts." [79]

In his poetic conclusion to Part I, Bunyan warns against both misinterpreting his allegory and "playing with the outside" of his dream, that is, reading it for the story only. He urges his readers to look for "the substance" and when they find "dross," to throw it away but keep the "gold" (3:167).

Footnotes

[1] Samuel Taylor Coleridge, *Coleridge on the Seventeenth Century*, ed. Roberta Florence Brinkley (Durham, North Carolina: Duke University Press, 1955), 475-6.

[2] John Buchan, "Mr. Standfast," in *Adventures of Richard Hannay* (Boston: Houghton Mifflin Company, 1919), 18-19, 34. Buchan (Lord Tweedsmuir)— novelist, poet, fisherman, explorer, Member of Parliament, and Governor General of Canada—writes in his autobiography that as a child he and his siblings did not suffer from the rule in his strict Scottish Presbyterian family that barred secular books on Sundays. "We discovered a fruity line in missionary adventure, we wallowed in martyrologies, we had *The Bible in Spain*, and above all we had Bunyan. From *The Holy War* I acquired my first interest in military operations, which cannot have been the intention of the author, while *The Pilgrim's Progress* became my constant companion. Even today

I think that if the text were lost, I could restore most of it from memory. My delight in it came partly from the rhythms of its prose, which, save in King James's Bible, have not been equalled in our literature; there are passages, such as the death of Mr. Valiant-for-Truth, which all my life have made music in my ear. But its spell was largely due to its plain narrative, its picture of life as a pilgrimage over hill and dale, where surprising adventures lurked by the wayside, a hard road with now and then long views to cheer the traveller and a great brightness at the end of it." John Buchan, *Pilgrim's Way: An Essay in Recollection* (Cambridge, Massachusetts: Riverside Press, 1940), 7.

[3] In the third edition, which appeared in 1679, Bunyan placed the words "The Jail" in the margin to explain the sentence, "As I walked through the wilderness of this world, I lighted on a certain place, where was a Den, and I laid me down in that place to sleep" (3:89).

[4] Greaves, *Glimpses of Glory*, 218.

[5] U. Milo Kaufman, "*The Pilgrim's Progress and The Pilgrim's Regress*: John Bunyan and C. S. Lewis on the Shape of the Christian Quest" in *Bunyan in Our Time*, ed. Robert G. Collmer (Kent, Ohio: Kent State University Press, 1989), 189.

[6] Kaufman, "The Pilgrim's Progress," 191.

[7] Kaufman, "The Pilgrim's Progress," 191.

[8] Kaufman, "The Pilgrim's Progress," 189.

[9] C. S. Lewis, "The Vision of John Bunyan," *Selected Literary Essays by C. S. Lewis*, ed. Walter Hooper (Cambridge: The University Press, 1969), 147-8.

[10] Isabel Hofmeyr, *The Portable Bunyan: A Transnational History of The Pilgrim's Progress* (Princeton: Princeton University Press, 2004), 61. Blatchford was editor of the *Clarion*, an early and important Labour newspaper.

[11] Hugh Martin, *Great Christian Books* (London: S. C. M. :Press, 1945), 67.

[12] Robert Lewis Stevenson, "Introduction," *The Pilgrim's Progress* (London: Samuel Bagster and Sons, n. d.), v, viii.

[13] Lewis, "The Vision of John Bunyan," 150.

[14] Lewis, "The Vision of John Bunyan," 149.

[15] Lewis, "The Vision of John Bunyan," 148.

[16] Sharrock, *John Bunyan*, 54.

[17] "It came." C. S. Lewis wrote, "I doubt if we shall ever know more of the process called 'inspiration' than those two monosyllables tell us." Lewis, "The Vision of John Bunyan," 147.

[18] Sharrock, *John Bunyan*, 54.

[19] "One of the greatest dangers to life, and especially to travel, in the England of old days arose from those deep and treacherous morasses which it has taken centuries to drain. In every county of England there were many 'sloughs' in those days, and tradition has fixed upon one near Bedford for the suggestion of this picture." John Kelman, *The Road, A Study of John Bunyan's "Pilgrim's Progress"* (Port Washington, New York, 1970), 1:20.

[20] Alexander Whyte, *Bunyan Characters in The Pilgrim's Progress*, first series (Edinburgh: Oliphant, Anderson & Ferrier, n.d.), 51-2.

[21] C. H. Spurgeon, *Metropolitan Tabernacle Pulpit* (Pasadena, Texas: Pilgrim Publications, 1969-80), 13:592.

[22] Repeated knocking, as here and elsewhere in the two parts of *The Pilgrim's Progress*, does not symbolize God's reluctance to answer, but Bunyan's insistence on true and heartfelt faith and repentance.

[23] Whyte, *Bunyan Characters in The Pilgrim's Progress*, first series, 68.

[24] C. H. Spurgeon, *Metropolitan Tabernacle Pulpit* 46:211-2.

[25] Greaves, "Introduction" to Bunyan's *The Doctrine of the Law and Grace Unfolded* and *I will pray with the Spirit*, xxxiv-xxxv.

[26] Greaves, "Introduction," to Bunyan's *The Doctrine of the Law and Grace Unfolded* and *I will pray with the Spirit*, xxxv.

[27] As Alexander Whyte says, "Every minister of the Gospel is an interpreter, and every evangelical church is an interpreter's house." Whyte, *Bunyan Characters in The Pilgrim's Progress*, first series, 76.

[28] Whyte, *Bunyan Characters in The Pilgrim's Progress*, first series, 125-6.

[29] Whyte, *Bunyan Characters in The Pilgrim's Progress*, first series, 112.

[30] Whyte, *Bunyan Characters in The Pilgrim's Progress*, first series, 143.

[31] Talon, *Pilgrim's Progress*, 149.

[32] Whyte, *Bunyan Characters in The Pilgrim's Progress*, first series, 149.

[33] Whyte, *Bunyan Characters in The Pilgrim's Progress*, first series, 151.

[34] Revelation 9:11 states that the locusts that covered the earth when the fifth angel sounded his trumpet "had as king over them the angel of the Abyss, whose name in Hebrew is Abaddon, and in Greek, Apollyon."

[35] Christian's answer, says Kelman, is "one of the finest passages in the book. . . . With its repudiation of young folly, its trust in Christ's forgiveness, and its frank avowal of his heart's choice of his Saviour, it is worthy of a place in all books of devotion." Kelman, *The Road*, 1:134.

[36] The tempter seldom flies far away. In Part II we find that he went from Christian only into the next valley.

[37] Hofmeyr, *The Portable Bunyan*, 67.

[38] Kelman comments, "To go in that way is indeed the only safe course: but even if it were not, it is the only right course, and therefore the only course." Kelman, *The Road*, 1:145.

[39] Most commentators think that this was not only the voice of Faithful, but the voice of Martin Luther, who had served as Bunyan's guide during a most difficult time in his own pilgrimage.

[40] How was it that Bunyan was, seemingly, able to dismiss the dread of Catholicism that gripped so many others? Some have argued that when Bunyan wrote these words in the late 1660s, the papacy was preoccupied with the Jansenist challenge (an Augustinian movement in the Catholic Church) and

Louis XIV's aggressive policies and so represented no serious threat to English Protestantism; hence Giant Pope is chained. (This atmosphere would change soon, with allegations of a Catholic plot to assassinate King Charles II and set up a Catholic regime). Or it could be that Bunyan's portrayal of the weakness of the papacy depended more on eschatological (the Bible's teaching of last things) expectations than on observation of current events.

[41] Kelman, *The Road*, 1:162.

[42] Whyte, *Bunyan Characters in The Pilgrim's Progress*, 203.

[43] But, according to Sharrock, reducing them to "formulas and jargon." Sharrock, *John Bunyan*, 92.

[44] Talkative is one of three characters Bunyan creates to represent hypocrisy, the other two being By-ends and Ignorance.

[45] Kelman, *The Road*, 1:205.

[46] This is a reference to Christ's being tempted by the devil as recorded in Matthew 4:1-11.

[47] Kelman comments: "It is surely an insecure condition of affairs in which men raise a hubbub because somebody that they have met is unlike themselves." Kelman, *The Road*, 1:211.

[48] The account contains unmistakable references to Bunyan's experience with Bedfordshire justice. The portrait of Lord Hate-good, the trial judge in Vanity Fair, is drawn from the historical Sir John Kelynge and possibly Thomas Twisden, with whom Bunyan's wife had dealt. The name "Hate-good" comes from Micah 3:1-2—"Hear, O heads of Jacob, and ye princes of the house of Israel . . .who hate the good, and love the evil."

[49] Kelman, *The Road*, 1:229.

[50] Kelman, *The Road*, 2:5.

[51] In 2 Timothy 4:10 Paul writes, "Demas hath forsaken me, having loved this present world."

[52] Luke 17:32-3 records the words of Jesus: "Remember Lot's wife! Whoever tries to keep his life will lose it, and whoever loses his life will preserve it." The Old Testament story of Lot's wife is found in Genesis 19.

[53] Sharrock, *John Bunyan*, 85.

[54] As Kelman says, "No man who is quarreling with the road will travel long before he finds himself at a stile of this sort." Kelman, *The Road*, 2:42.

[55] "The gentleness of [Hopeful's] attitude to Christian is a notable piece of work, even for Bunyan's pen." Kelman, *The Road*, 2:47.

[56] Whyte, *Bunyan Characters in The Pilgrim's Progress*, first series, 226.

[57] Whyte, *Bunyan Characters in The Pilgrim's Progress*, first series, 225.

[58] Kelman, *The Road*, 2:55.

[59] The word "diffidence" had the stronger meaning in Bunyan's time of suspicion or mistrust.

[60] Kelman, *The Road*, 2:56.

[61] Kelman comments that "despair is powerless against a Sunday morning heart." Kelman, *The Road*, 2:62.

[62] Sharrock, *John Bunyan*, 86.

[63] Kelman, *The Road*, 2:64-5.

[64] The reference is to 2 Timothy 2:17,18—"Their teaching will spread like gangrene. Among them are Hymenaeus and Philetus, who have wandered away from the truth. They say that the resurrection has already taken place, and they destroy the faith of some."

[65] Kelman, *The Road*, 2:70.

[66] Kelman, *The Road*, 2:77.

[67] Talon, *John Bunyan*, 211.

[68] Ignorance's speech is "irritatingly complacent," but it has appealed to some people. An eighteenth-century preacher remarked that in his opinion, none of the characters of *The Pilgrim's Progress* spoke sense except Ignorance. Sharrock, *John Bunyan*, 92-3.

[69] Kelman, *The Road*, 2:90.

[70] Hofmeyr, *The Portable Bunyan*, 100.

[71] Kelman, *The Road*, 2:104.

[72] Luther warned against a white devil as much as against a black one, for Satan transforms himself into an angel of light, and his ministers as ministers of righteousness (2 Corinthians 11:14,15). It is Bunyan's point that the devil and his ministers deceive incautious souls by flattery.

[73] "The sweet danger—the fascinating and deadly danger—of rest before the time of rest has come, is well known to every pilgrim's heart." Kelman, *The Road*, 2:127.

[74] "Hopeful and his biographer have evidently experiences in common, and we may look in the conversation that follows for much autobiography," writes Kelman. Kelman, *The Road*, 2:134.

[75] Kelman, *The Road*, 2:196.

[76] Hofmeyr, *The Portable Bunyan*, 98-9.

[77] Kelman, *The Road*, 2:196.

[78] Lewis, "The Vision of John Bunyan," 152-3.

[79] Kelman, *The Road*, 2:199.

*John Bunyan's **The Pilgrim's Progress**, Thomas a Kempis, and a translation of the Bible; I don't want anything more.*

Vincent van Gogh[1]

*A mother had been reading her children **Pilgrim's Progress**. She asked them which one of the characters they liked best. One of the girls said, "Christiana, of course!" Christian is usually thought of as the hero of **Pilgrim's Progress**, and this mother said with some surprise, "You mean that you like Christiana better than Christian?" The girl said, "I certainly do . . . because she took the children with her."*

Robert A. Lapsley, Jr.[2]

3

The Pilgrim's Progress
Part Two

How right that we have the journey of Christian's wife, Christiana, as a story of her own apart from her husband's. Her conversion, faith, and perseverance are her own. Her disappointments, lessons learned, and encouragements are her own. Christian and Christiana travel the same route, but their stories are different. Whereas Part I of **The Pilgrim's Progress** *can be considered the account of an individual fighting alone, Part II has to do with an individual fighting in company—a family, a community, a congregation—on the way to the heavenly city. Bunyan's pilgrim Christian is already in Heaven when Christiana begins her trip with her four sons and her wonderful young friend Mercy. Our writer, perhaps made wiser by his two marriages and pastoral involvement in the Bedford church, did not stereotype conversion experiences. With the droll humor, sympathy, and insight into both grace and human nature that we enjoyed in Part I, Bunyan continued his pilgrim tale. We empathize with Christiana as she stands with and comforts the children through frightening times and illness, helps her daughters-in-law, cares for her friends in need, draws new friends into her life, intercedes for and feeds her group, makes decisions, and strengthens her faith, discovering delightful provisions along the way. In a divine riverside daycare center in the Delectable Mountains, the pilgrims' King houses, protects, carries, and nurtures the "babes of those women who [are] on pilgrimage" (3:228). That same King adjusts, to fit each pilgrim's strength of mind and body, the depth of the last great river the pilgrims have to cross (3:214, 240).*

Dr. Johnson remarked to his friend Boswell that *Don Quixote*, *Robinson Crusoe*, and *The Pilgrim's Progress* were the only three books that a reader might wish longer.[3] Bunyan's early readers, too, wanted more; and Part II of *The Pilgrim's Progress* was published in 1684, six years after the first volume appeared. Between the two parts of *The Pilgrim's Progress*, Bunyan wrote *The Life and Death of Mr. Badman*. He planned that book as a contrast to follow his *Pilgrim's Progress*, so as to give a dramatic account of a man who chooses hell instead of heaven. But the readers of *The Pilgrim's Progress*, understandably, were not satisfied. And apparently neither was Bunyan, because a continuation of the story of the pilgrims soon appeared.

Part II is the account of Christian's wife, appropriately named Christiana, who decides to take her children and a neighbor called Mercy and follow her husband. Christiana's love for Christian, her sorrow at the way she treated him when he became a pilgrim, and his determined example all play a role in her decision to follow him. Bunyan implies that had Christian not abandoned his family in what appeared to be a selfish desire to gain his own salvation, Christiana would never have set out on her pilgrimage. She tells her friend Mercy what her "good Christian" did for her when he left her: "he mourned . . . that I would not heed nor regard him; but his Lord and ours did gather up his tears and put them into his bottle; and now both I and thou, and these my sweet babes, are reaping the fruit and benefit of them" (3:178).

In Part II we are frequently reminded of Christian's pilgrimage. It is not that Bunyan's inspiration was flagging so that he had to repeat so much of Christian's story, but that Christian's prayers and example were to be seen as a constant encouragement and help to his wife, family, and others who joined them. Christian, therefore, helped "to define the road to be walked" and prepared the way for his wife and family by markers and victories.[4]

It is a common belief that Part II is inferior to Part I in artistic expression and theological significance. Michael Mullett, however, disagrees. He writes, "Often relegated to the status of a mere epilogue to Part I, the second part of *The Pilgrim's Progress* may be considered, in literary terms, . . . Bunyan's masterpiece."[5]

Women played a positive part in John Bunyan's life. His first wife, by her faith and love, awakened his thirst for higher joys. The women of the Bedford church pointed him to the Bible's way of salvation. His second wife, Elizabeth, stood by him and fought ably to save him from prison. Yet women hardly are given a favorable role in Part I of *The Pilgrim's Progress*. In Part II, however, Christiana and Mercy appear as major characters. In fact, the second part has been called "a female Pilgrim's Progress."[6] Still, it is difficult to argue with N. H. Keeble's evaluation that Bunyan "welcomes women on pilgrimage . . . as persons in need of especially solicitous ministerial care and guidance."[7] Of course Bunyan had the conventional seventeenth-century notion of women as "the weaker vessel," but many of the male characters in *The Pilgrim's Progress* (especially in Part II) also require "solicitous ministerial care and guidance." Elsewhere Bunyan asserts women's subordinate status, tracing it to the moment of their creation and not to Eve's sin. In *A Case of Conscience Resolved* (1683), Bunyan explains his conviction that women should not hold separate meetings for worship and prayer. In Part II of *The Pilgrim's Progress*, however, Bunyan sets forth, through the mouth of Gaius, an eloquent statement praising women and exhorting them to continue the exemplary work for the Gospel undertaken by women in the Bible. To Bunyan, it seems, deeply believed that women are "highly favoured" and "sharers with us in the grace of life" (3:219).

Although not without images of the church and pictures of Christian fellowship, Part I is primarily the account of a solitary pilgrim or, for the last part of the book, two pilgrims together. In Part II, however, Bunyan develops the biblical, Protestant, and Puritan emphasis on family religion and highlights the role of the church as an agency of saving grace for all its true members, both feeble and robust. As Kaufman puts it, "Christiana and the others, like Feeble-mind and Ready-to-halt, who constitute the entourage of Great-heart, are, in their diverse weaknesses, a clear figuration of the church as redemptive community, healing and strengthening the less advantaged of the world."[8] Part II of *The Pilgrim's Progress* is a complement rather than a correction to Part I. There is both an individual and communal aspect to salvation, and Bunyan creates two allegories to present both. As N. H. Keeble explains it, "A writer cannot, with equal force, say everything at once: the stress does fall differently in Part II, but there is neither contradiction, rejection, nor retraction; there is completion of the portrait of the saint."[9] Before John Bunyan wrote Part II, he had been for some years pastor to the Bedford congregation. His pastoral experiences doubtless enriched the second part of his greatest book.

Although there are marked similarities between the two parts of *The Pilgrim's Progress*, there are, as we have noted, some differences in emphasis. With pardonable exaggeration, Neil Keeble, alluding to 1 Corinthians 13:13, wrote, "If Part I had handled faith and hope, Part II turns to charity."[10] The second journey is more leisurely. Christiana and her companions spend a month at the Palace Beautiful, more than a month at Gaius's inn, a "great while" at the town of Vanity. Marriages take place; children are born.

> "In the second part [of **The Pilgrim's Progress**], in place of the lonely figures of Christian and his companion, battling with demons or disputing with heretics, there is a bustling, and on the whole a cheerful, picture of the life of a separatist church."[11]

Part II begins with a long poem, entitled **"The Author's Way of Sending Forth his Second Part of the Pilgrim."** The clever opening lines read:

> Go now, my little book, to every place,
> Where my first Pilgrim has but shewn his face,
> Call at their door. If any say, Who's there?
> Then answer thou, Christiana is here (3:168).

Bunyan employs the poem to deal with four objections to his work. First, some people will not believe that Part II is really from John Bunyan since so many had plagiarized Part I. (Answer: send for Bunyan and he will testify that the work is his.) Second, some people very much dislike *The Pilgrim's Progress*. (Answer: plenty of people do like it, however, not only in England but France, Holland, Scotland, Ireland, and even in faraway New England.) Third, some say that Bunyan's "words and stories are so dark." (Answer: there is a purpose in the book's style; furthermore Part II will make clear some obscurities of the first part.) Fourth, some despise the book as a "romance." (Answer: you can't please everyone!) A brief description of some of the characters of Part II and a prayer that the story of his "second pilgrim" might "persuade some that go astray to turn their feet and heart to the right way" conclude the poetic apology (3:168-70).

Bunyan begins Part II with a statement that when Christian left the City of Destruction to go on his pilgrimage, he left behind his wife and children, who were unwilling to go with him. "Now, it hath so happened, through the multiplicity of business, that I have been much hindered and kept back from my wonted travels into those parts whence [Christian] went, and so could not, till now, obtain an opportunity to make further enquiry after whom he left behind, that I might give you an account of them. But having had some concerns that way of late, I went down again thitherward. Now having taken up my lodgings in a wood about a mile off the place, as I slept I dreamed again" (3:171).

In his dream Bunyan meets an old man called **Mr. Sagacity**, who talks to him about Christian and his journey. Bunyan learns that Christian is now admired by people in the City of Destruction, though some are afraid that his King might come and punish them for their earlier mistreatment of him. Bunyan asks Mr. Sagacity if he has heard any news of Christian's wife and children. He learns from the old man that a great change has come over them and "so they have packed up, and have also gone after [Christian]" (3:172).

After her husband has "gone over the river" and **Christiana** can receive news about him no longer, she begins to be sorry for her behavior toward him and her stubbornness in refusing to accompany him on his journey. She had thought him mad but now she realizes that "the Light of Life" had been given him, so that he had escaped "the snares of death" (3:173). When Christiana sees, in a dream, a parchment containing "the sum of her ways," she cries aloud, "Lord have mercy upon me, a sinner." In a second dream she sees Christian in a place of great bliss. The next morning a visitor arrives at her door and announces himself as *Secret*. He has come from *the Merciful One*, he says, with an invitation to Christiana "to come into his Presence" (a fine statement of the doctrine of effectual calling—God's special working in the elect so that they respond in faith). He tells her to go to the wicket gate, as Christian did, and gives her a letter from the King, which he advises her to learn by heart and to keep to present at "the further gate" (3:174).

As Christiana and her children load their backpacks and prepare for their journey, two neighbours, **Timorous** and **Mercy,** visit. Timorous tries to talk Christiana out of her plans by recalling the great troubles that came upon Christian during his pilgrimage and urges her not to take her "four sweet babes" on such a dangerous journey. Mercy, who loves Christiana and is concerned also for her own soul, wants to know more about the reason for Christiana's dramatic change of heart. Mercy decides to "walk this sun-shine morning, a little way with her, to help her on the way" (3:176). Timorous goes back home and calls her neighbors—Mrs. Bats-eyes, Mrs. Inconsiderate, Mrs. Light-mind, and Mrs. Know-nothing—to gossip about Christiana.

Meanwhile Christiana urges Mercy to go with her, telling her that "the King who hath sent for me and my children is one that delighteth in mercy." Mercy is persuaded and they set out, with Mercy weeping for her lost relatives and then, with Christiana's guidance, praying for them—"Lord, make them pray they may be thine, with all their heart and mind" (3:177-8).

The two women and four boys right away arrive at the **Slough of Despond**, which has gotten worse since Christian's misfortunes there. But, with Mercy's encouragement, the little company proceeds safely across by carefully searching out the steps. As soon as they have gotten over, they hear the words "Blessed is she that believed, for there shall be a performance of those things which were told her of the Lord" (Luke 1:45). The slough presents scarcely any dangers for the women and children, who are aware of Christ's promises (3:178).

So far, Christiana's story has been related in John Bunyan's dream by Mr. Sagacity, and the reader may well be daunted at the prospect of a secondhand account of her entire pilgrimage. Bunyan apparently was of the same opinion, because when Christiana reached the wicket gate, he wrote, "Mr. Sagacity left me to dream out my dream by myself" (3:179). Thus Bunyan cleverly got rid of the old man who was becoming tiresome.

Christiana, Mercy, and the boys approach **the wicket gate,** where Christiana's knocking is answered only by the barking of a huge dog. After a long time the keeper of the gate answers and welcomes her and the children as a trumpeter plays, but Mercy stands waiting outside since she has not received an invitation from the King. While Chistiana is interceding for her friend, Mercy begins to knock loudly ("for each minute [is] as long to her as an hour") and then faints because she is so afraid that the gate will not be opened to her. When the door *is* opened, she cries, "If there is any grace or forgiveness of sins to spare, I beseech that I, thy poor handmaid, may be partaker thereof." The keeper of the gate lifts her up, takes her hand, and leads her gently in. **The Lord of the Way** receives them all and grants them pardon "by word and deed; by word, in the promise of forgiveness; by deed, in the way I obtained it," he tells them. The gatekeeper leads them to the top of the gate, where he shows them "by what deed they were saved" (3:180). Here Bunyan attempts to clear up any doubt left by his former story concerning the relationship between the wicket gate and the cross. (A marginal note earlier in Part II indicates that "the gate . . . is Christ" [3:177]).

The Lord leaves them for a while in "a summer parlour below," where Christiana and Mercy discuss what they have just experienced. The two women are puzzled as to why the Lord keeps such a ferocious dog, but they take comfort in the fact that they are safely in. When the Lord returns, Mercy asks him about the dog. She is told simply that he has another owner. The dog belongs to a nearby castle and can only come up to the walls of this place, where pilgrims can hear his fierce barking. The Lord goes on to say that sometimes the dog has broken out and "worried some that I [love]; but I take all at present patiently. I also give my pilgrims timely help, so they are not delivered up to his power" (1:181). This disturbance speaks of Satan's antagonism toward the Lord and his pilgrims, the Lord's permitting the devil's wicked activity, but its future termination.

With glad hearts, the pilgrims travel on in "very comfortable weather." Christiana sings, perhaps better than Christian, although the lyrics of her song leave much to be desired. The boys pick and eat some fruit that hangs over the wall from trees in the garden of the one who owns the dog. Two *Ill-favored ones* try to rape the women, who cry out and struggle, until a *Reliever* appears and chases the men over the wall into the garden where the dog is. The Reliever is a bright figure, undefined, but one who brings help and hope. The Reliever explains to the women that since they knew that they were "but weak women," they should have asked the Lord for a *Conductor* (3:183).[12]

Christiana admits their mistake in not asking for a conductor but wonders why the Lord, knowing their need, did not send one with them. Reliever replies that help is not always appreciated until the want of it is felt and that gifts not asked for are not always granted. He tells them, however, that he will present to the Lord their confession and their request.

The pilgrims come to **Interpreter's House**, where they are joyously welcomed by *Innocent*, who answers Christiana's knock, and by the whole house. "One smiled, and another smiled, and they all smiled for joy that Christiana was become a pilgrim" (3:184).

Before supper, Interpreter shows them his *Significant Rooms* that Christian had seen and also seven other scenes. They see "the man with the muck-rake" who can only look down at the dirty floor, even though there stands above him one holding "a celestial crown in his hand." "Heaven is but a fable to some," explains Interpreter, whereas the straws, the small sticks, and dust of the floor . . . "are counted the only things substantial." When Christiana prays "O! deliver me from this muck-rake," Interpreter replies sadly, "That prayer has lain by 'till it is almost rusty" (3:184-5). They go next to the very best room in the house, where they see "an ugly spider" on the wall. The spider, Interpreter explains, despite the venom that remains in her, dwells in the best room in the King's house. The little group understood the point and "seemed all to be glad; but the water stood in their eyes" (3:185). (Sin and evil exist in the very best places and persons in this world.) Next the pilgrims are shown a hen and chickens. They watch a little chick drink, "and every time she drank, she lifted up her head, and her eyes towards heaven." The message is plain. They see a butcher killing a sheep "and behold the sheep was quiet, and took her death patiently." As the Lord's sheep, "you must learn to suffer," they are told, "and to put up [with] wrongs without murmurings and complaints." Other scenes follow—the flowers in the field that stand where "the gardener has set them . . . and quarrel not one with another" (the love of Christians for each other); the field sowed with wheat and corn (the danger of not reaping the crop); and the robin and the spider (a good-looking person that loves sin) (3:186-7).

At Christiana's request, while she and her family and friend wait for supper, Interpreter discloses a number of proverbs with lessons attached, including one about women's dress (women like pretty clothes, so they should desire to be adorned with righteousness) and another about a ship's captain in a storm (one throws overboard first that which is of least value, but the person who does not fear God throws out first that which is of greatest value). Two of Interpreter's sayings are particularly memorable:

- *"He that forgets his friend is ungrateful unto him; but he that forgets his Saviour is unmerciful to himself" (3:187).*

- *"If a man would live well, let him fetch his last day to him, and make it always his company keeper" (3:187).*

Supper is still not ready so Interpreter and his new friends walk out into the garden, where they see a rotten tree that nonetheless grows and has leaves. It is a picture of people in "the garden of God" whose "leaves are fair" but whose heart is corrupt (that is, hypocrites in the church) (3:187).

"And then with a sly stroke at us old ministers," comments Alexander Whyte, Bunyan "points out to us how much better furnished the Interpreter's House was by the time Christiana and the boys visited it compared with that early time when Christian was entertained in it. . . . Let every long-settled, middle-aged, and even grey-headed minister read the life of the Interpreter at this point and take courage and have hope. Let it teach us all to break some new ground in the field of divine truth with every new year."[13]

At last supper was ready! "And they sat down and did eat, when one had given thanks" (3:188). There is music during the meal and good conversation. Christiana explains how she became a pilgrim, and so does Mercy. Interpreter compares Mercy to Ruth, "who did, for the love she [bore] to Naomi, and to the Lord her God, leave father and mother, and the land of her nativity, to come out, and go with a people that she knew not heretofore" (3:189). The evening closes with a song that translates in sweet, simple verses the beginning of Psalm 23. That night Mercy cannot sleep for joy because her doubts are "removed further from her than ever they were before" (3:189).

The next morning, before their departure from Interpreter's House, the pilgrims bathe in the garden to be cleansed "from the soil, which they [have] gathered by travelling" (3:189). We can picture our friends in a lovely garden with evergreens, flowering trees, and roses, a pool with fountains, and birds singing. They come out of "the bath of sanctification" (Bunyan's marginal note) "not only sweet and clean, but also much enlivened and strengthened in their joints." Interpreter pronounces them "fair as the moon" and places a mark between their eyes so "they might be known in the places whither they were yet to go." The mark "greatly added to their beauty, for it was an ornament to their faces. It also added to their gravity, and made their countenances more like [that] of angels" (3:189). "Fine linen white and clean" was brought, and the women dressed themselves in it. When they were "thus adorned, they seemed to be a terror one to the other; for . . . they could not see that glory each one on herself, which they could see in each other" (3:190).

The Interpreter then calls for a man-servant of his, **Great-heart**, and bids him take sword, helmet, and shield, and take "these my daughters . . . and conduct them to the house called Beautiful" (3:190). Mr. Great-heart appears only in Part II. His characterization emphasizes the value Bunyan had come to put upon spiritual leaders and pastors. Mutual help and encouragement, especially for the weaker members of the congregation, is, as we have seen, especially stressed in Part II.

As the travelers set out, they sing a sort of ballad about what they have seen and felt in Interpreter's House (3:190). They come to the place where Christian's burden fell off, and Great-heart discourses appropriately on justification by Christ. He tells his companions that their pardon was obtained by the perfect life and sacrificial death of the One who had let them in at the gate. This One, explains Great-heart, had two natures in one person, "plain to be distinguished, impossible to be divided" (3:190) The orthodox doctrine of the two natures of Christ—that he is both God and man in one person—is briefly and accurately stated. As the God-Man, the righteous Christ perfectly kept the law and so earned a righteousness that he did not need. The doctrine of the substitutionary atonement of Christ—his dying in the place of the sinner—is set forth in these words. He hath indeed "two coats, one for himself, and one to spare; wherefore he freely bestows one upon those that have none." The Protestant doctrine of justification by faith alone is here stated. Further, said Great-heart, this One who earned righteousness for sinners also provided pardon for them by the shedding of his blood. He "came and stood in your place and stead," explains Great-heart, "and died your death for your transgressions" (Galatians 3:13) (3:191). Christiana asks if it was this pardon that made Christian's burden fall off. Great-heart answers that it was "the belief of this that cut those strings that could not be cut by other means; and . . . to give him a proof of the virtue of this, that he was suffered to carry his burden to the cross" (3:192). Again Bunyan, maybe unsuccessfully, tries to explain why Christian was allowed to carry his burden so long. He suggests, undoubtedly from his own experience, that the delay strengthened Christian's conviction of the power and efficacy of Christ's cross.

As Christiana and her sons and Mercy walk on, they discover a place where *Simple*, *Sloth*, and *Presumption* were hanged for their crimes of turning out of the way would-be pilgrims—including *Slow-pace*, *Short-wind*, *No-heart*, *Linger-after-lust*, *Sleepy-head*, and a young woman named *Dull*.

At the **Hill Difficulty** they find the going hard. The pilgrims become overheated and out of breath. The smallest child starts crying. Great-heart leads them to *the Prince's Arbor*, where they are allowed to rest in the shade for a short time. Christiana makes a little picnic with the pomegranates and honeycomb that Mr. Interpreter had given her. When they leave, Christiana forgets her bottle of spirits (just as Christian here lost his roll) and sends her little boy "back to fetch it." When Mercy remarks that this is "a losing place," Great-heart explains that pilgrims need to be watchful of forgetfulness when they have been resting (3:195). They see where Mistrust and Timorous tried to turn Christian back from his pilgrimage (and were "burnt through the tongue with a hot iron" for their evil deed) (3:195).

The pilgrims arrive at the place of the lions. The boys, who have been running ahead, now fall back behind Great-heart, who smiles at their timidity. Great-heart draws his sword; he does not meet the lions but the lions' "backer," a giant named *Grim*. (Kelman remarks, "John Bunyan always brightens up at the sight of a giant."[14]) Great-heart slays the giant (who may here personify civil persecution) and leads the pilgrims past the lions, who are chained, and delivers them safely into the care of the porter, *Mr.Watchful*. Great-heart announces that he will return that very night to his Lord, much to the dismay of Christiana, Mercy, and the boys. Great-heart explains that he is at his Lord's command and tells his friends that they should have asked the Lord for his company to their journey's end. Bunyan's marginal note reads: "Help lost for want of asking for (it)" (3:197).

Christiana and the others receive a cordial welcome at **the Porter's Lodge** and, after a supper, retire to rest. At Christiana's request, they are all put to bed in the same room in which Christian slept. As the two women talk quietly, they hear music. Mercy exclaims, "Wonderful! Music in the house, music in the heart, and music also in heaven for joy that we are here" (3:198). Bunyan's works vibrate with music, and we are never allowed to forget how much he loved it. While he was in prison, he carved a flute from one of the legs of a stool. In existence also are a metal violin and a cabinet decorated with musical instruments that are believed to have belonged to him. That night Mercy, who still struggles with doubts concerning her invitation to the Celestial City, dreams that she is taken to the city by a being with wings. She is brought before the One who sits on the throne and he says to her, "Welcome, daughter." When Mercy wakes and tells Christiana her dream, Christiana encourages her by saying that God can speak to us when we sleep as well as when we are awake.

The pilgrims spend "about a month or above" in this delightful house. One of the maids of the house, *Prudence*, catechizes the children, beginning with the young *James*. James answers splendidly, as do all the boys. Prudence commends Christiana for "thus bringing up your children" (3:199). When Prudence asks the oldest, *Matthew*, what he does when he reads things in the Bible that he does not understand, he replies, "I think God is wiser than I. I pray also that he will please to let me know all therein that he knows will be for my good" (3:200). Prudence sums up the proper sources of the education of children—first the mother, then other people, then nature, then the Bible, and finally the church.

Mr. Brisk, "a man of some breeding, and that pretended to religion, but a man that stuck very close to the world," comes to court Mercy. His courtship is in vain because Mercy is determined "never to have a clog to [her] soul" (3:200). Mr. Brisk gives up his plan to make Mercy his wife when he discovers that her industriousness, which he had so much admired, is for the purpose of making things for the poor.

Matthew becomes very sick, and the physician *Mr. Skill* is sent for. He learns that Matthew ate some of the fruit that hung over the wall when the pilgrims came in at the gate—the fruit of *Beelzebub's orchard*. The doctor prepares a purge with the blood of a goat and the ashes of a heifer (Old Testament ceremonies) but it is too weak; so he makes another, *ex carne & sanguine Christi* (of the body and blood of Christ). Bunyan notes in the margin, "The Latin I borrow." Bunyan confesses that he got all his Latin from the prescription papers of his doctors. Like children of all times the world over, Matthew is reluctant to take the medicine until his mother tastes it with the tip of her tongue and tells him that it is "sweeter than honey."[15] Mr. Skill refuses to accept any payment, saying, "You must pay the Master of the College of Physicians, according to rules made in that case and provided" (3:202). When Mr. Skill tells Christiana that the pills he has given Matthew are "good against all the diseases that pilgrims are incident to," she orders twelve boxes of them! (3:202) Matthew spends his time asking Prudence questions about medicine and nature, to which she replies with spiritual lessons and applications.

It is time to depart, but first Joseph reminds his mother that she should not forget to send to the house of Mr. Interpreter, "to pray him to grant that Mr. Great-heart should be sent unto us, that he may be our conductor the rest of our way." The marginal note reads: "The weak may sometimes call the strong to prayers" (3:203). Before they leave the house, the pilgrims are shown many things on which they can meditate as they travel: one of the apples that Eve ate; Jacob's ladder with angels ascending it; a golden anchor, which is given to them to enable them to "stand steadfast" in case they meet "turbulent weather"; and the altar, wood, fire, and knife used in Abraham's "sacrifice" of his son, Isaac. This is a strange scene for a Puritan writer to create. Protestant rejection of relics would seem to preclude Bunyan's introduction of them. Of course they do not function as meritorious, as in Catholic theology, but as instructional.

As the travelers walk down the path from the house, the birds in the grove sing to them from Sternhold's and Hopkins's version of Psalm 23![16]

> *Through all my life thy favour is*
> *So frankly show'd to me,*
> *That in thy house for evermore*
> *My dwelling-place shall be.*
>
> *For why? The Lord our God is good,*
> *His mercy is for ever sure;*
> *His truth at all times firmly stood,*
> *And shall from age to age endure (3:205).*

By this time Mr. Great-heart has arrived with gifts of wine and food from his Lord for them. They take their farewell of the porter, who gives them good words of blessing and instruction. Prudence and Piety go with them, and they soon come into the **Valley of Humiliation**. It was here that Christian had his great fight with Apollyon, but now the valley is a quiet place, a place of meditation, a place where there are no travelers except "those that love a pilgrim's life" (3:206). Mercy is delighted. No spot has so suited her spirit, she says, because "I love to be in such places where there is no rattling with coaches, nor rumbling with wheels" (3:207).

The group comes upon a boy singing as he cares for his father's sheep. "Hark," calls Mr. Great-heart, "to what the shepherd's boy saith."

> He that is down needs fear no fall;
> He that is low, no pride;
> He that is humble, ever shall
> Have God to be his guide.
> I am content with what I have,
> Little be it, or much;
> And, Lord, contentment still I crave,
> Because thou savest such.
> Fulness to such a burden is,
> That go on pilgrimage;
> Here little, and hereafter bliss,
> Is best from age to age (3:206).

They learn that the Lord, in the days of his flesh, had his "country house" in this valley and loved to be there and walk in the meadows. He has endowed the grounds for the refreshment and encouragement of pilgrims. It is true, Great-heart affirms, that Christian fought Apollyon in this valley (in a narrow canyon called Forgetful Green), but others "have met with angels here, have found pearls here, and have in this place found the words of life" (3:207). They come to the place where Christian encountered Apollyon and see some of his blood still on the stones and a monument telling about the battle and Christian's victory.

The little party leaves the Valley of Humiliation and begins to walk into the **Valley of the Shadow of Death**. Despite the daylight and the presence of Mr. Great-heart, the women and children are very much afraid. They hear groans and hissing and feel the earth shake under them. James gets sick from fear, but Interpreter's glass of spirits and Mr. Skill's pills that Christiana has with her soon make him right. Mr. Great-heart protects them against a fiend and against a lion who would have done them harm. Christiana pities her husband, who had to go through the valley alone and at night. Many have spoken of this valley, she says, but "none can tell what the Valley of the Shadow of Death should mean until they come in it themselves." Mr. Great-heart reminds them to pray "for light to him that can lighten our darkness." God sends them "light and deliverance" (3:209), for they have to walk through snares in a gloomy place where many have been slain, including *Heedless*, whose body still lies in a ditch.

At the end of the valley their way is barred by another giant, named *Maul*, who attempts "to spoil young pilgrims with sophistry." He challenges Great-heart and accuses him of kidnapping "women and children" and carrying them "into a strange country" to the weakening of the kingdom of the giant's master (3:210). A battle ensues in which Great-heart, after receiving many blows himself, kills the giant. This giant may stand for the reviving power of the Roman Catholic Church in England (earlier, Christian had found Giant Pope in his cave, impotently sitting and biting his nails) or, as Talon suggests, Maul might stand for a rationalism that was threatening the church.[17]

The travelers come to an oak tree, under which an old pilgrim lies fast asleep. He is alarmed when they wake him, because he is afraid that they are those who, sometime before, robbed *Little-faith* of his money. The man explains that he is from the town of *Stupidity*, not far from the City of Destruction. Great-heart guesses that the man is "old Honesty." The man replies, "Not *Honesty* in the abstract, but *Honest* is my name, and I wish that my nature shall agree to what I am called" (3:212). Honest is a plain man who goes straight to the point, and most of what he says is memorable. His hometown of Stupidity is even further off "from the sun" than the City of Destruction, but, as Honest testifies, "the frozen heart" of "a man in a mountain of ice" will feel a thaw "if the Sun of Righteousness will arise upon him." "The old gentleman [is] taken" when he meets Christiana, skipping, smiling, and "blessing them with a thousand good wishes," because he has heard much of her husband and "his faith, . . . courage, . . . enduring, and . . . sincerity" (3:212).

As the friends walk along together they talk about *Mr. Fearing*, who was from the area from which Mr. Honest came. Honest says, "He was a man that had the root of the matter in him; but he was one of the most troublesome pilgrims that ever I met with in all my days" (3:212).

Great-heart had served as Mr. Fearing's guide from his "Master's house to the gate of the Celestial City." He "was dejected at every difficulty," Great-heart remembers, "and stumbled at every straw that anybody cast in his way." He could hardly get through the Slough of Despond, and when he did he could not believe it. "He had, I think, a Slough of Despond in his mind," observes Great-heart, "a slough that he carried everywhere with him" (3:213). Surprisingly, Mr. Fearing did not hesitate when he came to the Hill Difficulty, neither did he much fear the lions. His trouble "was not about such things as those," says Great-heart; "his fear was about his acceptance at last" (3:214). He did very well in the Valley of Humiliation; "I think there was a kind of sympathy between that valley and him," says Great-heart. But at the entrance to the Valley of the Shadow of Death, Great-heart recalls, "I thought that I should have lost my man" for he was "ready to die for fear." Yet that valley, says Great-heart, "was as quiet while he went through it, as ever I knew it before or since." And when Mr. Fearing at last came trembling to the river across which there is no bridge, "the water of that river was lower at this time than ever I saw it in all my life, so he went over at last not much above wet-shod." "He was a man of choice spirit," continues Great-heart, and despite his fear and despondency, he would not turn back. But his low spirits "made his life . . . burdensome to himself, and . . . troublesome to others" (3:214).

To Honest's question as to why "such a good man should be all his days so much in the dark," Great-heart answers that there are two "sorts of reasons." One is that "the wise God will have it so." The other is that Mr. Fearing played upon the "bass" string. True, it is an important and necessary note, and "God also plays upon this string first, when he sets the soul in tune for himself" (3:215). But the problem was that Mr. Fearing could play no other string until his end. Christiana recognizes something of herself in the account of Mr. Fearing. Her personality expresses itself differently, though, because whereas Mr. Fearing could hardly bring himself to knock at the gate and the houses along the way, her trouble made her "knock the louder" (3:215).

> "For humour, for pathos, for tenderness, for acute and sympathetic insight at once into nature and grace, for absolutely artless literary skill, and for the sweetest, most musical, and most exquisite English, show me another passage in our whole literature to compare with John Bunyan's portrait of Mr. Fearing."[18]

Conversation then turns to another, *Mr. Self-will*. He pretended to be a pilgrim, says Honest, "but I persuade myself, he never came in at the gate that stands at the head of the way" (3:216). Self-will argued that Scripture allowed him to "follow the vices as well as the virtues" of a pilgrim. As Honest speaks of other strange sights that he has observed in his long journey on the road, the travelers are met by a man who warns them that there are robbers ahead. Imagine how these words strike fear to the hearts of the boys! But the robbers do not appear, perhaps because they hear that Mr. Great-heart is conducting this group of pilgrims.

The tired Christiana and her children and friends arrive happily at the inn of **Gaius**, who welcomes them warmly for he is "a lover of pilgrims."[19] Gaius instructs his cook, whose name is *Taste-that-which-is-good*, to prepare supper, and, as the host and guests wait, they entertain each other with "some good discourse" (3:218). Gaius had known Christian, as well as Christian's father and grandfather. "Many have been good of this stock," he says; "their ancestors dwelt first at Antioch" (3:218).[20] He tells them about some of Christian's relatives—Stephen who was killed with stones; James who was slain by the sword; also Paul and Peter; Ignatius who was cast to the lions; Romanus whose flesh was cut from his bones; and Polycarp "who played the man in the fire."[21] It would be impossible, he declares, "to count up all of that family that have suffered injuries and death for the love of a pilgrim's life" (3:218). Gaius then talks about Christian's and Christiana's sons and suggests that the oldest marry Mercy! He goes on to "speak on behalf of women": "For as death and the curse came into the world by a woman, so also did life and health: God sent forth his Son, made of a woman." And when the Savior came, Gaius continues, "women rejoiced in him, before either man or angel." Furthermore, he adds, "I read not that ever

The Pilgrim's Progress – Part Two

any man did give unto Christ so much as one groat, but the women followed him, and ministered to him of their substance." "Women therefore are highly favored," he concludes, "and show by these things that they are sharers with us in the grace of life" (3:219). We catch here, perhaps, a glimpse of the real Bunyan, who, despite sometimes bending to the seventeenth-century ideas of women in his words, seems to appreciate the spiritual and human qualities of women.

When the party sits down to a bountiful supper there is course after course, with some symbolic meaning or spiritual application for each, all accompanied by wine from the true vine, good talk, and joy. Mercy put the boys to bed, "but the rest sat up all night, for Gaius and they were such suitable company that they could not . . . part" (3:220). Old Honest puts forth a riddle: "A man there was, though some did count him mad, the more he cast away, the more he had." Gaius knows the answer: "He that bestows his goods upon the poor, shall have as much again, and ten times more" (3:220). More talk, riddles, and stories follow until daybreak, when Gaius proposes that he and Great-heart and the others "walk into the fields, to see if we can do any good." He has in mind the killing of a giant, one *Slay-good*, who very much annoys "the King's highway in these parts" (3:221).

They find the giant; he has captured *Feeble-mind* and is preparing to kill him. Great-heart slays the giant, rescues Feeble-mind, and brings him to the inn, where the consoled man tells his story. He had come from the town of *Uncertain*, and had been determined to be a pilgrim despite his weakness of body and mind. Many had been kind to him and helped him along the way, but he was captured by the giant and taken to his den. He expected to be rescued since he "went not with him willingly" (3:222). Bunyan's marginal note reads: "Mark this." Now indeed he has been saved from the giant, "for the which I thank my King as author," exults Feeble-mind, "and you as the means." Even though he was not strong, he had courage and resolved "to run when I can, to go when I cannot run, and to creep when I cannot go." "I am fixed," continues Feeble-mind, "my way is before me, my mind is beyond the river that has no bridge" (3:222).

103

The little group stays in the house of Gaius for more than a month. There are two weddings—Matthew and Mercy are married, as are Phebe, the daughter of Gaius, and James.[22] After happy festivities and banqueting, the pilgrims prepare to leave. Gaius refuses to accept any payment, saying that he will be paid by the "good Samaritan" when he comes again. Gaius says goodbye to them all and they depart, but Feeble-mind delays, saying that he is afraid that he shall be both a burden to himself and to them. Great-heart encourages him to come with them, promising that they will wait for him and help him. About this time *Ready-to-halt* appears, and he and Feeble-mind gladly welcome each other's company. "Thus therefore they went on; Mr. Great-heart and Mr. Honest went before, Christiana and her children went next, and Mr. Feeble-mind and Mr. Ready-to-halt came behind with his crutches" (3:224).

> "*The collection of weaklings is growing now, and before long we shall have a company like that in the parable—'the poor, and the maimed, and the halt, and the blind' (Luke 14:21). It may, indeed, have been this passage that was in the mind of Bunyan. Certainly the insistence upon the care and compassion of Christianity for weaklings is intentional and emphatic.*"[23]

As the party returns to the trail, Great-heart recounts the adventures of Christian and Faithful along that same road. When Christiana and her friends arrive at the town of **Vanity**, where **Vanity Fair** is held, they lodge at the house of "*Mr. Mnason, a Cyprusian by nation, an old disciple.*"[24] From him they learn that there are a few good people in the town ("just as there have often been saints in the wicked courts of Rome, France, and England," comments Kelman).[25] Mr. Mnason sends his daughter *Grace* to bring *Mr. Contrite, Mr. Holy-man, Mr. Love-saint, Mr. Dare-not-lie,* and *Mr. Penitent* to meet his guests. The people of the town, the visitors are told, are much more "moderate" than they were when Christian and Faithful were persecuted there. (Faithful was the last to be burned in the town.) Indeed, in some parts of the town "religion is counted honourable" (3:225). The point Bunyan apparently is making is that wicked cultures and people can outwardly reform and that genuinely good and righteous people can live in such environments. Great-heart tells the good people of Vanity about their adventures on the journey.

Christiana and the others remain in Vanity "a great while, at the house of Mr. Mnason, who, in process of time, gave his daughter Grace unto Samuel, Christian's son, to wife, and his daughter Martha to Joseph" (3:226). While the party of pilgrims are at Vanity, a *Monster* (with a body like a dragon, seven heads, and seven horns) comes out of the woods and murders people in the town. Those who "[love] their lives more than their souls" accept the monster's conditions, but Great-heart and some of his friends determine to go out and engage the monster in battle (3:227). They wound him so seriously that it is believed he will die. Bunyan's point here may be that preaching and Christian action may decrease many evils that they cannot destroy.

The pilgrims reach the place where Faithful was put to death. They stand there and thank "Him that had enabled him to bear his cross so well" (3:227). Approaching the river that is "on this side of the Delectable Mountains," they see a meadow beside the river and a place for "the nourishing and bringing up of lambs, the babes of those women [who] go on pilgrimage." Christiana exhorts her four daughters to commit their children into the care of the One who "[can] have compassion, and that [can] gather these lambs with his arm, and carry them in his bosom, and that [can] gently lead those that [are] with young" (3:228).

At **By-path Meadow** they decide to try to kill *Giant Despair* and destroy **Doubting Castle**. Great-heart, Mr. Honest, and Christiana's four sons set out on this dangerous mission. After a fearsome battle they kill both the giant and his wife and spend the next seven days destroying the castle. They find dead bodies here and there and bones everywhere, but they also discover *Mr. Despondency* and his daughter, *Much-afraid*, still alive. When the others learn that the giant is dead, they celebrate with music and dancing. The poetic lines that follow this passage, however, issue a warning that "sin can rebuild the castle" and "make Despair the Giant live again" (3:229).

While Great-heart's party heroically battles their foes, Feeble-mind and Ready-to-halt are left to guard the women, prompting one writer to observe that "the least male is to be preferred to the best female" by "the misogynist Bunyan." Bunyan, however, affixed the text Isaiah 11:6 to his narrative and stated that even though Giant Despair dealt nearby, "they keeping in the road, a little child might lead them" (3:228). "Isaiah 11 is not about gender or age," Richard Greaves explains, "but the promised salvation of the remnant of God's people. . . . As they travel on God's Highway, they are beyond danger. . . . No guard is necessary, which is why the least qualified male pilgrims can serve in what is a merely symbolic role."[26]

The party walk on to **the Delectable Mountains**, where the **Shepherds** welcome both "the strong" and "the feeble," for, they assure the pilgrims, "Our Prince has an eye to what is done to the least of these." The weak are invited in by name, because "they are most subject to draw back" (3:230). Mr. Great-heart responds to the shepherds' gracious words and actions by stating that he sees that grace shines in their faces and that they are the "Lord's shepherds indeed" (3:230). The next day the shepherds show the pilgrims "some rarities," including *Mount Marvel* where the son of Great-grace teaches pilgrims to overcome difficulties by faith.

> Great-grace is "a man who neither makes nor feels difficulties, and to whom nothing is impossible. . . who, taking Christ literally, believes that faith can remove mountains," says Kelman.[27]

Next they can see *Mount Innocent*, where two rascals, *Prejudice* and *Ill-will*, are trying in vain to cast dirt upon the white garments of *Godly-man*.

> "It is interesting to remember that we have already met innocence in the person of the damsel at the House of the Interpreter. There the lesson was that of the lowliness of innocence; here we are to learn its loftiness."[28]

At *Mount Charity* they observe a man making clothes for the poor out of a bundle of cloth that always remains the same size.

At a certain *place* they watch *Fool* and *Want-wit* washing an Ethiopian to make him white but succeeding only in making him blacker.[29] To Bunyan this represents the folly of trying to reform a person's conduct without a real conversion of his heart.

Mercy wants to see the hole in the hill that is called the *by-way to hell*. The earth groans and quakes under her feet as she hears someone saying, "Cursed be my father for holding . . . my feet back from the way of peace and life"; and another, "O that I had been torn in pieces, before I had, to save my life, lost my soul"; and still another, "If I were to live again, how would I deny myself, rather than come to this place" (3:231).

Back at the house of the shepherds, Mercy, who is expecting a child, covets a rare looking glass that hangs in the dining room. Turned one way it would show one's own face; turned another way it showed the face of "the Prince of Pilgrims himself." The shepherds give her the wonderful looking glass. "It was the Word of God," reads the marginal note (3:231).

> "It is extremely interesting to notice how, as Bunyan comes near the end of his work, he closes in upon the thought of the Word. . . . It is the sword in the hand of Valiant, and the crutches of Mr. Ready-to-halt, a map, a light struck suddenly. Here it is a magic mirror, which, if held one way, will show a pilgrim the uttermost truth about himself, but held another way will reveal Christ to him."[30]

When the company of pilgrims arrives at the place where Little-faith was robbed, they see "a man with his sword drawn and his face all bloody." The man is *Valiant-for-truth*, one of Bunyan's noblest characters. He has just engaged in a three-hour battle with three men. When Great-heart remarks about the odds of three against one, Valiant replies, "It is true; but little and more are nothing to him [who] has the truth on his side" (3:233). Great-heart inspects Valiant's sword and judges, "It is a right Jerusalem blade" (Isaiah 2:3). When Great-heart wonders why his new friend has not become weary in such a long fight, Valiant-for-truth replies, "I fought till my sword did cleave to my hand; and when they were joined together, as if a sword grew out of my arm, and when the blood ran through my fingers, then I fought with most courage" (3:233).

> "In these few words we have an epitome of the requisites for successful spiritual warfare. First, there is the Word, that sword of the Spirit, the 'true Jerusalem blade.' Then there is the grip of faith, which identifies the man with the Word he uses. And lastly, there is a dash of his own blood upon the fighting—that element of experience, and even of pain, which brings all such warfare to its highest perfection and its surest victory."[31]

Valiant-for-truth now joins the expedition, telling, as they travel on, the story of how Christian's adventures and his happy end at last had moved him greatly and caused him too to go on pilgrimage. Great-heart sums it all up with the words "Then this was your victory, even your faith" (3:235). And Valiant replies, "It was so. I believed, and therefore came out, got into the way, fought all that set themselves against me, and, by believing, am come to this place" (3:235). He ends his testimony with a powerful song:

> Who would true valour see,
> Let him come hither;
> One here will constant be,
> Come wind, come weather.
> There's no discouragement
> Shall make him once relent,
> His first avow'd intent
> To be a pilgrim (3:235).

The travelers make their way through the **Enchanted Ground**. As we saw in Part I, this place near the journey's end is a special danger to weary pilgrims. A dark mist falls, the path is boggy, and bushes "grab" them. They have to call to each other to know where each one is because they walk "not by sight" (3:236). They resist stopping at an inviting arbor called *The Slothful's Friend*. They would have become lost and sunk in the mud except for a map (the margin reads "God's book") that shows them all the ways leading to and from the Celestial City. In another arbor they see *Heedless* and *Too-bold* fast asleep. They try to wake them up but only cause them to talk in their sleep, words governed neither "by faith or reason" (3:237).

> *This experience is "a time of bitterness and disheartening depression, such as but too often comes upon the elderly. Everything seems to go wrong, and everybody to be disagreeable. The whole business of life looks vulgar, commonplace, and difficult; and there is no longer that resilient spring of youthful energy which made such things of little account in former days."[32]*

Almost at the end of the Enchanted Ground the group comes upon "a man upon his knees, with hands and eyes lift up, and speaking, as they [think], earnestly to one who [is] above" (3:238). His name is *Stand-fast*, and he tells them how "one in very pleasant attire, but old" presented herself to him and offered him "three things, to wit, her body, her purse, and her bed." To escape from this person, *Madame Bubble* she was called, Stand-fast "prayed to him that had said he would help" (3:238). The verse at the end of the passage contains two memorable lines that seem to hint at surprise that such temptations should come back in later life: "How many ways there are to sin no living mortal knows" (3:239).

At last the companions arrive in the land of **Beulah**, "where the sun shineth night and day." There they are refreshed without sleeping, "for the bells . . . so ring and the trumpets continually sound so melodiously" (3:240). More pilgrims come and wait to cross the river, which is reported to have been almost dry for some and overflowing for others. The pilgrims taste the water of the River of Death and find it bitter to the taste, but afterwards sweet and comforting.

A letter "of great importance" arrives for Christiana, stating that "the Master calleth for thee, and expecteth that thou shouldest stand in his presence, in clothes of immortality, within these ten days" (3:240). Imagine the feelings of her family and friends as Christiana offers blessings to her children and says goodbye to her fellow pilgrims. Crowds of people have come to see her end her journey. The banks beyond the river are full of horses and chariots that have arrived to accompany her to the city gate. She steps into the river with a wave of farewell, and the last words that she is heard to say are, "I come, Lord, to be with thee, and bless thee." Then she "went and called, and entered in at the gate with all the ceremonies of joy that her husband, Christian, had [had] before her" (3:241).

Mr. Ready-to-halt is summoned to come to the Master's table "the next day after Easter." When he reaches the river he declares, "Now I shall have no more need of these crutches, since yonder are chariots and horses for me to ride on." With the words "Welcome, life," he slides into the water (3:242). Then Mr. Feeble-mind is called, and Mr. Despondency and his daughter, Much-afraid. The last words of Mr. Despondency are "Farewell night, welcome day." His daughter walks through the current singing, but "none could understand what she said" (3:242).

Mr. Honest comes next. The river is overflowing its banks in some places, but *Good-conscience* meets him and helps him over. It is not because of his good deeds that Mr. Honest crosses the waters safely. His last words are "Grace reigns" (3:243). Next Mr. Valiant-for-truth is summoned. He says, "My sword I give to him that shall succeed me in my pilgrimage, and my courage and skill to him that can get it. My marks and scars I carry with me, to be a witness for me, that I have fought his battles, who now will be my rewarder" (3:243). Then Mr. Stand-fast is called, "for his Master was not willing that he should be so far from him any longer." Stand-fast commissions Great-heart to let his wife and five children know what has happened to him and sends them his prayers and tears. As he crosses the river he speaks memorable words:

> *I see myself now at the end of my journey, my toilsome days are ended. I am going now to see that head that was crowned with thorns, and that face that was spit upon for me. I have formerly lived by hearsay and faith; but now I go where I shall live by sight, and shall be with him in whose company I delight myself. I have loved to hear my Lord spoken of; and wherever I have seen the print of his shoe in the earth, there I have coveted to set my foot too. His name has been to me as a civet-box; yea, sweeter than all perfumes. His voice to me has been most sweet; and his countenance I have more desired than they that have most desired the light of the sun (3:243).* [33]

> "It was this passage that made Helen Waddell, that remarkable Christian scholar, take back everything she had said in criticism of Bunyan. Waddell's eminent mentor, Professor George Saintsbury, had told her that **Pilgrim's Progress** was 'one of the cheerfullest books in the world.' As a child Waddell had been haunted by the wicket-gate, and wished that Bunyan had made clear to her not only 'strait is the gate' but also 'I am the door.'"[34]

"But glorious it was to see how the open region was filled with horses and chariots, with trumpeters and pipers, with singers and players on stringed instruments, to welcome the pilgrims as they went up, and followed one another in at the beautiful gate of the city" (3:244). What a scene—to erase the fear of death from pilgrims' hearts!

"As for Christian's children, the four boys that Christiana brought with her, with their wives [including Mercy] and children, I did not stay where I was till they were gone over. Also, since I came away, I heard one say that they were yet alive, and so would be for the increase of the church in that place where they were, for a time." Part I ended with a brief mention of hell, to which Ignorance was taken from the very gates of the Celestial City; Part II closes with a reference to those who are left behind for a while to build the church in this world.

Footnotes

[1] *The Complete Letters of Vincent van Gogh* (Boston, 1958) 1:170. The letter is dated May 1875. For Bunyan's influence on Vincent van Gogh, see Kathleen Powers Erickson, "Pilgrims and Strangers: The Role of *The Pilgrim's Progress* and *The Imitation of Christ* in Shaping the Piety of Vincent van Gogh," *Bunyan Studies: John Bunyan and His Times* 4 (Spring 1991): 7-36.

[2] Robert A. Lapsley, Jr., *Like As We Are* (Richmond: John Knox Press, 1939), 42.

[3] Martin, *Great Christian Books*, 65, quoting James Boswell, *Life of Johnson*, ed. G. B. Hill (Oxford, 1934) 2:239 (footnote).

[4] U. Milo Kaufman, *"The Pilgrim's Progress" and Traditions in Puritan Meditation* (New Haven: Yale University Press, 1966), 115.

[5] Mullett, *John Bunyan*, 259.

[6] Mullett, *John Bunyan*, 244.

[7] Johnson, Galen, "'Be Not Extream': The Limits of Theory in Reading John Bunyan," in *Christianity and Literature* 49 (Summer 2000): 453.

[8] Kaufman, "*The Pilgrim's Progress*," 198-9.

[9] N. H. Keeble, "Christiana's Key: The Unity of *The Pilgrim's Progress*," in *The Pilgrim's Progress: Critical and Historical Views*, ed. Vincent Newey (Totowa, New Jersey: Barnes & Noble Books), 12, 14. Keeble writes, "The fellowship of Part II is made possible only because Christian in Part I had not overvalued the creature. Had he done so, he and his family would be squabbling yet in the City of Destruction" (13).

[10] Keeble, "Christiana's Key," 14.

[11] Sharrock, *John Bunyan*, 138.

[12] Surely it would have been better to say that all pilgrims, both strong and weak, both female and male, need a "conductor."

[13] Alexander Whyte, *Bunyan Characters in The Pilgrim's Progress*, second series, 84.

[14] Kelman, *The Road*, 2:221.

[15] A well-known remedy of the Restoration period was called "Matthew's powders."

[16] Hill, *John Bunyan*, 264. The earliest metrical Psalter with tunes issued for use in England was dated 1560 and reprints the Anglo-Genevan Psalter of 1558. Another edition in 1561 had eighteen more Psalms, mainly by Sternhold and Hopkins.

[17] Talon, *John Bunyan*, 163.

[18] Alexander Whyte, *Bunyan Characters in The Pilgrim's Progress*, second series (Edinburgh: Oliphant, Anderson and Ferrier), 149.

[19] Gaius is mentioned by Paul in Romans 15:23—"Gaius, whose hospitality I and the whole church here enjoy, sends you his greetings."

[20] This is a reference to Acts 11:26, which states that "the disciples were first called Christians at Antioch."

[21] The list includes biblical figures from the book of Acts, as well as persons from early church history.

[22] The time scheme of the story is greatly altered, notes Sharrock, who comments, "Mercy is now married to Matthew, who only a short time before was a naughty boy robbing orchards; and Christiana is described as 'an aged matron,' which seems totally at variance with the impression made by her words and carriage elsewhere" (Sharrock, *John Bunyan*, 151).

[23] Kelman, *The Road*, 2:258.

[24] Another host of Paul's, mentioned in Acts 21:16.

[25] Kelman, *The Road*, 2:258.

[26] Greaves, *Glimpses of Glory*, 506-7.

[27] Kelman, *The Road*, 2:267.

[28] Kelman, *The Road*, 2:268.

[29] This is a reference to Jeremiah 13:23. Like other seventeenth-century English writers, John Bunyan, unfortunately, identifies blackness with sin and evil.

[30] Kelman, *The Road*, 2:271.

[31] Kelman, *The Road*, 2:274.

[32] Kelman, *The Road*, 2:280.

[33] The last sentence refers to a perfume obtained from the civet cat, a small animal of North Africa. The perfume was regarded as especially precious and is often referred to by Shakespeare.

[34] Davies, *Genius and Grace*, 76-7.

Mr. John Bunyan, who was of the meanest occupation, a notorious Sabbath-breaker, drunkard, swearer, blasphemer . . . by habitual practice: . . . yet, through rich, free, sovereign, distinguishing Grace, chosen, called, and afterwards formed, by the all-powerful operations of the Holy Ghost, [was] a scribe ready instructed to the kingdom of God.

George Whitefield[1]

The Pilgrim's Progress *is accepted among the dozen greatest books in the English language; and neither* **Grace Abounding** *nor* **Mr. Badman** *will be neglected by anyone who cares to understand English Puritanism at its greatest.*

G. B. Harrison[2]

4

The Life and Death of Mr. Badman

> This short piece contains horror stories, somber theological warning, a treatise on the doctrine of original sin and human choice, social satire, curious incidents, good business guidelines, and excellent child-rearing advice. The tale is told in the conversation of two neighbors who meet and visit under a tree. Knowledgeable neighbor Wiseman discusses the life of their profane, fraudulent, immoral, and recently deceased townsman, Badman. Wiseman, who speaks for Bunyan himself, amusingly draws out the story's suspense, as his friend Attentive becomes more and more anxious to get to the end and know the details of what he guesses must have been, for such a wicked man, a terrible death.

The Life and Death of Mr. Badman was published in 1680, between the two parts of *The Pilgrim's Progress*. After Bunyan's story of the journey of Christian "from this world to glory," he wrote "of the life and death of the ungodly, and of their travel from this world to hell" (3:590). Bunyan wrote *The Life and Death of Mr. Badman*, he tells his readers, because of the "wickedness" that "like a flood, [was] like to drown our English world" (3:586). He hoped by the book "to stop a hellish course of life, and 'to save a soul from death'" (3:592).[3]

Mr. Badman's story is a faithful, detailed account of the life of a middle-class scoundrel during the reign of Charles II and is Bunyan's nearest approach to a novel. In fact, as G. B. Harrison writes, "it is scarcely an exaggeration to call it the first modern English novel."[4]

The story is concerned with the moral state of England during the time of the Restoration. With its preoccupation with status, fashion, and pleasure and its hostility to godly values, the nation was desperately in need of hearing and heeding a prophetic message of repentance and reform. "Wickedness, like a flood, is like to drown our English world," Bunyan wrote. "It begins already to be above the tops of the mountains; it has almost swallowed up all: our youth, middle age, old age, and all, are almost carried away of this flood" (3:592). Though appalled by what he saw around him, Bunyan had by no means abandoned concern for English society or become exclusively concerned with the internal affairs of the church. Rather, he retained a sense of moral concern for the state of the nation. Bunyan's book offers a revealing critique of some of the sins of Restoration England—including sexual offenses, swearing, drunkenness, and dishonesty in business.

With convincing local color and abundance of detail, Bunyan tells the story of **Mr. Badman** in spirited, vernacular, and idiomatic English. "As a picture of the trader in a small country town it is invaluable."[5] The book, however, does not really present an engaging story, because Bunyan does not succeed in bringing Mr. Badman and the other characters to life. The method of narration sets the real action at a distance from the reader and is interrupted by long digressions. The unrelieved recital of the "badness" of Mr. Badman is horrifying but predictable and almost mechanical. According to Talon, "We do not watch a man live so much as learn a good deal about the customs of the time; we are offered a series of little pictures, but they are juxtaposed rather than interwoven."[6]

Badman's story unfolds in the conversation of two of his neighbors, **Wiseman** and **Attentive**, who meet while walking early one morning. Wiseman can be seen as Bunyan himself, recounting incidents from his pastoral experience and dealing with issues of church discipline he regularly confronted—mixed marriages, drunkenness, avarice, uncleanness, Sabbath breaking, dress and fashion. Wiseman (Bunyan) states that he has personally observed "all the things that here I discourse of" (3:590).

As the neighbors meet, Wiseman remarks that he has been saddened by "the death of that man for whom the bell tolled at our town yesterday" (3:595). Attentive asks who the man is, and they sit down in the shade under a tree to talk about Mr. Badman. Attentive is anxious to know how Badman died. Wiseman sighs but does not tell him. Instead he gives him a detailed account of Badman's life from childhood on. The conversation is laced with anecdotes about other people as well.

Wiseman tells Attentive that Badman was bad from the beginning—an example of the doctrine of original sin (corruption and guilt with which all descendants of Adam are marked). Later in the story he explains more fully, "For they be not bad deeds that make a bad man, but he is already a bad man that doth bad deeds. A man must be wicked before he can do wickedness. . . . It is an evil tree that bears evil fruit. Men gather no grapes of thorns; the heart therefore must be evil before the man can do evil, and good before the man doth good" (Matthew 7:16-18) (3:627). Wiseman does assert that Badman "chose death rather than life" (3:608). But at the same time he insists that his choosing evil arose from his evil nature, which predisposed him to that choice.

Badman was the child of honest parents, carefully brought up and taught to know and do good; and yet he sinned from his earliest childhood, sins that "manifested him to be notoriously infected with original corruption" (3:596). Much to the grief of his godly parents, he was given to lying. He could not "endure the Lord's day" (3:600). Even as a boy he engaged in "grievous swearing and cursing" (3:601) (like young John Bunyan himself).

Badman was apprenticed to an honorable master, lived in a good family, had many spiritual helps, but nothing took "hold of his heart." After about a year and a half he met "three young villains": one given to "uncleanness," another to drunkenness, and the third to stealing. Because he could not endure the godliness of his master's house, he ran away and joined another ungodly man in his own trade. Wiseman judges that "for a wicked man to be by the providence of God turned out of a good man's doors, into a wicked man's house to dwell, is a sign of the anger of God" (3:614).

When Badman completed his apprenticeship, he asked his father for money to set himself up in business. His "loving and tender-hearted" father gave him the money. Attentive is of the opinion that the father should not have helped his son, because if the son had suffered some he might have come to his senses like "the prodigal."Wiseman agrees but generously states that "we are better at giving good counsel to others than we are at taking good counsel ourselves" (3:617). He goes on to say:

> I tell you that if parents carry it lovingly towards their children, mixing their mercies with loving rebukes, and their loving rebukes with fatherly and motherly compassions, they are more likely to save their children than by being churlish and severe towards them: but if they do not save them, if their mercy do them no good, yet it will greatly ease them at the day of death to consider: I have done by love as much as I could, to save and deliver my child from hell (3:617).

After he had wasted the money given to him by his father, Badman very much wanted to marry a rich wife. Since the woman he chose was a religious person, he knew that he would have to pretend to be religious too in order to win her. And this is what he did. Owing to his acquaintance with religion in his father's house and in the house of his first master, he knew how to put on a good appearance. He would often speak well of godly ministers, "especially of those that he perceived she liked and loved most." The young woman was an orphan and, without good advice from others, she was swept off her feet by the tall, handsome Badman and agreed to marry him. Wiseman points out that "it is too much the custom of young people now to think themselves wise enough to make their own choice; and that they need not ask counsel of those that are older, and also wiser, than they" (3:619).

Badman got the money he wanted, but of course the marriage was a disaster for his wife, because he "brought her not only almost to beggary but robbed her of the Word of God" (3:621). They had seven children. One loved its mother dearly, and "she had the opportunity to instruct" that child in "the principles of Christian religion." It "became a very gracious child," but Badman could not abide it and so made life miserable for it. Three of the children "did directly follow [Badman's] steps," whereas the others were not "so bad as their father, nor so good as their mother" (3:623). Wiseman mourns these poor children, and Attentive agrees that such children have all kinds of disadvantages but adds that "we must say nothing, because this also is the sovereign will of God" (3:623). Badman forbade his wife to attend church services and threatened to "make both her and her damnable brotherhood" sorry for their meetings. He would, in other words, "turn informer"—a practice well known to Bunyan and the Puritans. Wiseman tells several stories of other informers he has heard about and the sorry end to which they all have come (3:624).

In the eyes of Bunyan and the Puritans, informers were particularly obnoxious characters. Fanatically devoted to the Church of England, they spied on unauthorized gatherings and reported them to the authorities. In *Mr. Badman* Bunyan described the spying activities of one W. S., who diligently searched for dissenting meetings day and night, in the woods and fields, even climbing trees to discover offenders.

Wiseman relates that Badman used the money he got from his wife to pay his debts and set up again in business. But soon he was once more heavily in debt. A long discussion follows between Attentive and Wiseman concerning economic morality. Mr. Badman was a treacherous bankrupt, "breaking" two or three times to his own financial advantage. In "breaking," the systematic exploitation of bankruptcy, he got his creditors to accept repayment at terms of 25 per cent – profit to himself. He also was guilty of fraud, using deceitful weights and measures and many other tricks. He took advantage of his neighbors' distress and needs by hoarding until prices rose. Long passages of the book deal with "economic advice to shopkeepers and small traders, whose traditional standards have been upset by the perplexing advance of the capitalist economy" (3:624-42).[7]

In the midst of this lengthy discourse on economics, Attentive asks Wiseman to continue his story but "with as much brevity" as possible. Wiseman, a little offended, asks, "Why, are you weary of my relating of things?" "No," answers Attentive, "but it pleases me to hear a great deal in few words" (3:633). Wiseman asks what Badman gets by dishonest means? He answers his own question: "Why he getteth sin and wrath, hell and damnation, and now tell me how much he doth get" (3:636).

Economic concerns continue to dominate the conversation as Bunyan (speaking through Wiseman) attempts to set forth a Christian philosophy of buying, selling, and profit. He states that no man should under all circumstances buy as cheaply as he can and sell as dearly as he can. The rule here, as in every area of life, is supplied by the words of Jesus, who said, "Do unto all men even as ye would that they should do unto you" (Matthew 7:12). Attentive asks, "You know that there is no settled price set by God upon any commodity that is bought or sold under the sun, but all things that we buy and sell do ebb and flow, as to price, like the tide; how then shall a man of a tender conscience do, neither to wrong the seller, buyer, nor himself, in buying and selling . . . commodities?" (3:640). After more discussion, Wiseman sums up: "This is to buy and sell with good conscience: thy buyer thou wrongest not, thy conscience thou wrongest not, thyself thou wrongest not, for God will surely recompense thee (Isaiah 58:6-8). I have spoken concerning corn, but thy duty is to 'let your moderation' in all things 'be known unto all men. The Lord *is* at hand' (Philippians 4:5)" (3:641-2).

Bunyan had no interest in defending traditional practices for their own sake or opposing commercial development as such. He based his critique of England's economic practices primarily on New Testament principles. To take advantage of people's ignorance or need was unconscionable, Bunyan argued, but this did not prohibit fair profits or a capitalist economy. According to Bunyan, unbridled profit was evil, but reasonable gain was not. At the same time, his treatment of prices, weights, measures, and quality protected the consumer.

Attentive entreats, "Well, sir, . . . I have heard enough of Mr. Badman's naughtiness, pray now proceed to his death" (3:642).

Wiseman replies that there are yet three hours until night; and he continues with the story of Badman's life!

He discusses Badman's pride. Badman loved to be proud but could not bear to be called a proud man, Wiseman explains. A discourse on pride follows. Then Wiseman states that Badman refused to reverence the Word of God; instead he questioned its truthfulness and authority. He ridiculed Christians. He was "an angry, wrathful, envious man" (3:647). He argued against the Christianity of his wife much as the Ranters of Bunyan's day ridiculed the Bible as "a nose of wax" that anyone can twist to say anything. He believed in "fortune, ill luck, chance" rather than in providence and held that Scripture was the source of all the "dissensions and discords that [were] in the land" (3:646).

One day Mr. Badman broke his leg after becoming drunk in an alehouse. When his leg healed he was dangerously ill, and during his long recovery he had thoughts that he would go to hell, so he asked his wife to pray for him. He promised God that if He would spare him a little longer, he would be "a penitent man" toward God and "a loving husband" to his wife. "Now she was his good wife, his godly wife, his honest wife, his duck and dear and all" (3:650). "But, alas, alas!" says Wiseman, "in little time things all proved otherwise." When he recovered "he never minded religion more, but betook him again to the world, his lusts and wicked companions: and there was an end of Mr. Badman's conversion" (3:651). This broke his wife's heart and she died, "with a soul full of grace, a heart full of comfort, and by her death ended a life full of trouble" (3:653). As she lay dying she instructed her bad children to turn to God, and her good child to love the Bible, Christ, his ministers and a good conscience, and to be kind and dutiful to his father and love his brothers and sisters, because he had "grace but they [had] none." In Bunyan's story Badman's wife is an undeveloped character, with few traits beyond her piety and goodness. If she had a fault, says Wiseman, it was her "unadvisedness" in relying on "her own poor, raw, womanish judgment" (3:622). This surely is one of Bunyan's most unfortunate statements about women!

Badman married again quickly, this time a woman as wicked as himself. As Wiseman puts it, Mr. Badman "met . . . his match." The two of them wasted what they had with their evil companions, "he with his whores, and she with her rogues" (3:655).

Wiseman comes at last to Mr. Badman's death! In his final illness, Badman talked about "trades, houses, lands, great men, great titles, great places, outward prosperity or outward adversity." The one thing that he avoided was "a sense and sight of his sin, that he might repent and be saved" (3:658). Attentive asks, "How was he in his death? Was death strong upon him? Or did he die with ease, quietly?" "As quietly as a lamb," Wiseman answers, and adds, "He that dies quietly, suddenly, or under consternation of spirit, may go to heaven, or may go to hell; no man can tell whither a man goes, by any such manner of death." Here Bunyan counters the "frivolous and vain" opinion "among the ignorant" that a quiet death is a good, hopeful sign (3:659). Bunyan was not suggesting that all wicked people perish so calmly. Earlier in the book he had told the story of an adulteress who died in great emotional distress.

Attentive concludes, "This is a dreadful story. And I would to God that it might be a warning to others" (3:661). Perhaps it is, but, understandably, the story is not read and loved as is *The Pilgrim's Progress*.

Footnotes

[1] Whitefield, "Recommendatory Preface," *The Works of John Bunyan*, iii.

[2] G. B. Harrison, "Introduction," to John Bunyan, *Grace Abounding & The Life and Death of Mr. Badman* (London: Dent, 1969), xii.

[3] Mullett believes that "Bunyan achieves considerable success in combining a horror story with an essay in Reformed soteriology." Mullett, *John Bunyan*, 229.

[4] Harrison, "Introduction," to Bunyan, *Grace Abounding & The Life and Death of Mr. Badman*, xii. James Forrest and Richard Greaves assert that "whereas some scholars were once willing to regard Bunyan's book as the first novel, there is now general concurrence that at most it was a precursor." James F. Forrest and Richard Lee Greaves, *John Bunyan: A Reference Guide* (Boston: G. K. Hall & Co., 1982), xvi.

[5] Harrison, "Introduction," to Bunyan, Grace Abounding & The Life and Death of Mr. Badman, xii.

[6] Talon, *John Bunyan*, 228.

[7] Hill, *John Bunyan*, 234.

[8] Whyte, *Bunyan Characters in The Holy War*, 301.

The Pilgrim's Progress sets forth the spiritual life under the scriptural figure of a long . . . uphill journey. *The Holy War*, on the other hand, is a military history; it is full of soldiers and battles, defeats and victories. . . . Its devout author had much more scriptural suggestion and support in the composition of the *Holy War* than he had even in the composition of the *Pilgrim's Progress*. For Holy Scripture is full of wars and rumours of wars: the wars of the Lord, the wars of Joshua and the Judges, the wars of David, with . . . magnificent battle-songs. . . . The best-known name of the God of Israel in the Old Testament is the Lord of Hosts, and . . . in the New Testament we have Jesus Christ described as the captain of our salvation. Paul's powerful use of armour and armed men is familiar to every student of his epistles; and . . . the whole Bible is crowned with a book . . . sounding with the battle cries, shouts, and songs of soldiers, till it ends with that City of peace where they hang the trumpet in the hall and study war no more.

Alexander Whyte[1]

5

The Holy War

Though perhaps not as durable as his pilgrim allegory, **The Holy War** is John Bunyan's second greatest work, an amazingly clever metaphor and chilling war story. One scholar has observed that **The Holy War** by itself would have entitled Bunyan to a place among the masters of English literature.[2] The sparkling allegory is alive with drums, swords, and bloodshed; castles, tower gates, and banners; spies, strategic planning, and military action. The plot of the story, made clear by its subtitle, unveils the intrigue of a Great War—made by Shaddai, through his Son, Emmanuel, upon Diabolus, to regain the town of Mansoul. Shaddai's creation of Mansoul was "good and perfect," but Diabolus had taken it from him. Against the fury of hell, Emmanuel declares "Mansoul is mine!" The picture of God's grace as He fights for Mansoul makes, to use Bunyan's phrase, "the water stand in our eyes." The fifty-four-year-old Bedford tinsmith, clearly writing from experience of his own soul's battles, has produced a book that "reveals a wide knowledge of war and a deep understanding of human nature and the Holy Scriptures."[3]

Having already displayed the Christian life under the image of a journey, John Bunyan, in 1682, published *The Holy War*. In this book he made use of the other great metaphor of the Christian life: war. This biblical image abounded in Puritan sermons and lectures, but Bunyan cast it in a sustained story. Scholars have pointed out that Richard Bernard's *Isle of Man Or the Legal Proceedings in Manshire Against Sin* undoubtedly was in Bunyan's mind as he wrote his *Holy War*. Bernard's popular allegory was published in 1627 and had reached its sixteenth edition in 1681 when Bunyan's work was in progress.

The Holy War may reflect something of the political battle in Restoration England, during the 1660s, for the control of the nation's cities and towns; however, the central point of the book is not politics but war. Bunyan characterizes those who conformed at the Restoration as Mr. Tradition, Mr. Human-wisdom, and Mr. Man's-invention. These had served King Shaddai, but after the victory of Diabolus they decided that "they did not so much live by religion as by the fates of fortune," and so they changed sides (3:277).

For *The Holy War*, John Bunyan could draw from memories of the Civil War of the 1640s in which he had played a small part, serving in the Parliamentary Army for several years. Bunyan makes direct allusions to the events of the English Revolution. Diabolus warned Mansoul that Shaddai was "raising . . . an army to come against you, to destroy you root and branch" (3:268). Puritans in the early 1640s had insisted on destroying episcopacy, "root and branch." Yet *The Holy War* contains splendid passages describing the excitement of battle, such as, "O how the trumpets sounded, their armour glittered, and how the colours waved in the wind! The Prince's armour was all of gold" (3:285). This is not a picture of actual seventeenth-century warfare; it derives more from Bunyan's youthful reading and imagination. Primarily, however, it draws on Scriptural language: the breastplate of righteousness, the shield of faith, the sword of the Spirit, and many other biblical images.

The book's full title is *The Holy War, Made by Shaddai upon Diabolus, for the Regaining of the Metropolis of the World; Or, the Losing and Taking Again of the Town of Mansoul*. *The Holy War* combines several stories. First, it is the history of salvation: the failure of the covenant of works in the fall of Adam and Eve, Christ's redemption of the elect (those whom God has eternally chosen to inherit salvation) through the covenant of grace, Christian commitment tested by sin and Satan, the perseverance of the saints, and the second coming of Christ. Second, the book also records the story (like Bunyan's own story) of the awakening of an individual soul by the hearing of the Word of God, conviction of sin, the vain attempt to live a moral life, fresh despair, an understanding of Christ's justification of sinners by his death on the cross, and the work of sanctification by which the believer grows in holiness. *The Holy War* is Bunyan's story, the account of the fearful combat waged within his soul and the victory he experienced through the grace of God and the power of the Holy Spirit. Bunyan begins *The Holy War* with a poetic introduction in which he claims:

> *For my part, I (myself) was in the town,*
> *Both when 'twas set up, and when pulling down,*
> *I saw Diabolus in his possession,*
> *And Mansoul also under his oppression.*
> *Yea, I was there when she own'd him for lord,*
> *And to him did submit with one accord (3:253).*

Bunyan describes Emmanuel's advance for Mansoul's relief in words that come from his own experience:

> *. . .What is here in view,*
> *Of mine own knowledge, I dare say is true.*
> *I saw the Prince's armed men come down,*
> *By troops, by thousands, to besiege the town.*
> *I saw the captains, heard the trumpets sound,*
> *And how his forces cover'd all the ground.*
> *Yea, how they set themselves in battle-ray,*
> *I shall remember to my dying day (3:253).*

Some interpreters have suggested readings of *The Holy War* as setting forth English history from the tyranny of Charles I and Archbishop Laud, through the all-too-brief rule of the saints during the Commonwealth, to the return of the Stuart Monarchy in 1660, and its ultimate overthrow. Sensitive to the possibilities, contemporary readers probably saw numerous allusions to historical events in England.

The Holy War was an ambitious undertaking but is generally held to be less successful than *The Pilgrim's Progress*. Sharrock calls it "a magnificent failure."[4] Talon calls it "a heavy work."[5] Edward Dowden describes it as "an allegory rather manufactured than inspired."[6] This is only true in part. *The Holy War* is a more complex allegory than *The*

Pilgrim's Progress, but it has its own power and appeal. The number of books published on military history indicates the continuing interest this topic has for many people. Moreover, the threat of war in our time concerns us all; it gives Bunyan's allegory a modern relevance. To read *The Holy War*, as Alexander Whyte puts it, "kindles our cold civilian blood like the waving of a banner and like the sound of a trumpet."[7]

Chapter 1[8]

Like *The Pilgrim's Progress*, *The Holy War* begins with a memorable sentence: "In my travels, as I walked through many regions and countries, it was my chance to happen into that famous continent of Universe." There the author found "a fair and delicate town called *Mansoul*" (the human soul or mankind). The people were not "all of one complexion, nor yet of one language, mode, or way of religion," but differed (3:255). The "first founder and builder" of the town was *Shaddai* (the Hebrew word for "almighty" that often refers to God the Father in the Old Testament). "And he built it for his own delight." In the middle of the town was "a most famous and stately palace" (the human heart). The town, interestingly, had five gates: Ear-gate, Eye-gate, Mouth-gate, Nose-gate, and Feel-gate (the five senses) (3:255-6).

Diabolus (the devil, who at first was one of the servants of King Shaddai) and his followers had been cast out of the court of King Shaddai and his Son, *Emmanuel*. Diabolus resolved to seek revenge by seizing the newly created town of Mansoul, "one of the chief works and delights of King Shaddai" (3:257).

And so the war begins! To their pride and rebellion, Diabolus and his followers add malice and rage against Shaddai and his Son. Diabolus knows that he cannot take the town of Mansoul "without its own consent" (3:257), so a council is held to decide how best to do this. One of the devils, whose name is *Legion*,[9] argues that the way to win the town is to assault the townspeople in "pretended fairness, covering our intentions with all manner of lies, flatteries, delusive words." In this way, he says, we will cause the people of Mansoul of themselves to open their gates to us (3:258). And so Diabolus and the others make for Ear-gate to put their plan into operation.

Diabolus, "as if he had been a lamb", courted the citizens of the town who came to the walls to see what was happening (3:258). Through his spokesman, a man named *Illpause*, Diabolus tried to persuade the people to eat forbidden fruit. The allegory is awkward here, because Bunyan tries to combine the biblical account of the fall of Adam and Eve with the idea of a siege. During the long speech of Illpause, one of Diabolus's men shot and killed *Captain Resistance*, who was standing on the gate (3:259). Then "the townspeople saw that the tree was good for food, and that it was pleasant to the eye, and a tree to be desired to make one wise," and "they did as old Illpause advised; they took and did eat thereof" (3:260). At that moment, in some unexplained way, "My *Lord Innocency*" died. The people then "opened the gate, both Ear-gate and Eye-gate, and let in Diabolus with all his bands, quite forgetting their good Shaddai, his law, and the judgment that he had annexed with solemn threatening to the breach thereof." This disastrous event pictures the fall of mankind through the sin of Adam and Eve, with the implication in Bunyan's story that all who are now born in the town of Mansoul are born sinners and servants of Satan.

Chapter 2
Diabolus repudiates the laws of Shaddai and sets about to "remodel" the town. He expels from office the Lord Mayor, whose name is *Lord Understanding*, and the recorder, whose name is *Mr. Conscience*. These officials are replaced by a new mayor, *Lord Lustings*, and a new recorder, whose name is *Forget-good*. *Lord Will-be-will* (the human will), who has agreed that Diabolus should be let into the town, now expresses his willingness to serve Diabolus. *Mr. Mind*, Lord Will-be-will's clerk, and *Mr. Affection* join Will-be-will in his rebellion. Thus Bunyan describes the Calvinistic doctrine of "total depravity." This teaching holds that all people are totally or radically depraved; sin controls the mind, the will, and the emotions. The mind, the affections, and the will are all brought into bondage to Satan.

Diabolus vengefully defaces the image of hallowed King Shaddai that stands in the marketplace in Mansoul and also upon the gates of the castle. This act sets forth the marring (but not the destruction) of the image of God in fallen mankind. Diabolus carefully arms the town so as to prepare it for resistance if Shaddai should try to take Mansoul back.

Chapter 3

Shaddai hears the sad news of the surrender of his beloved Mansoul. He is not taken by surprise, however, because he and his Son have known this would happen "long before," and indeed they have "suffered" the town to be lost (3:266). As a Calvinist, Bunyan believed that God knows and plans all. God and his Son have "sufficiently provided for the relief" of the town. In fact, they have already planned to recover it "in such a way . . . that both the King and his Son will get themselves eternal fame and glory thereby." The Son, "a sweet and comely person, and one that had always great affection for those that were in affliction, but one that had mortal enmity in his heart against Diabolus," promises that he will be Shaddai's servant to recover Mansoul (3:266). They agree that at a certain time fixed by both, the King's Son will "take a journey into the country of Universe; and there, in a way of justice and equity, by making . . . amends for the follies of Mansoul," he will lay a foundation of her "perfect deliverance from Diabolus, and from his tyranny." He will put Mansoul, "through the power of his matchless love, into a far better and more happy condition than it was in before it was taken by Diabolus." Bunyan's story here aptly portrays "the covenant of redemption," as it was called by some Puritan theologians, in which God the Father and God the Son entered into a covenant for the recovery of fallen mankind. Then the *Lord Chief Secretary* is ordered to draw up and publish "a fair record" of what has been determined (3:266). The Lord Chief Secretary represents the Holy Spirit, and the record he draws up, "the holy Scriptures."

To resist the plans of Shaddai and his Son, Diabolus charges Lord Will-be-will to keep watch day and night at all the gates of the town and not to let any enter who are not "favorers of our excellent government." This means, according to Bunyan, that "all good thoughts and words" in the soul were to be suppressed (3:267). Diabolus arms the people for the expected battle with the breastplate of "a hard heart, a heart as hard as iron and as much past feeling as a stone." He gives them a sword, which is "a tongue that is set on fire of hell." He gives them a shield, which is "unbelief, or calling into question the truth of the Word" (3:269).

Chapter 4

Thankfully, all this time the sovereign Shaddai is preparing to send an army made up of more than forty thousand men to recover the town. The army is led by "four stout generals": *Boanerges* ("son of thunder," or powerful preaching),[10] *Conviction, Judgment,* and *Execution* (descriptions of the Mosaic law). The generals, who are also called captains, speak to the rebellious town. Like Cromwell's Ironsides, Shaddai's officers could preach as well as fight! Captain Conviction calls on Mansoul to repent, reminding the people of the "amazing grace" of their King, who has given opportunity for repentance when he might have simply destroyed the town. Mansoul refuses to hear the words of the captains; but a noise beats against Ear-gate, "though the force thereof could not break it open" (3:275). The words of the law can be heard by fallen people, but more is needed to bring about conviction and conversion.

The traitorous Lord Will-be-will takes special care that the gates are secured with double guards, double bolts, and double locks and bars—especially Ear-gate, for that was the gate that the King's forces sought most to enter. Will-be-will appoints old *Mr. Prejudice* captain of the ward at that gate and puts under his power sixty "deaf men." This precaution illustrates the concern of the devil to protect his followers from biblical preaching.

Chapter 5

King Shaddai's captains add more forces against Ear-gate, for they know that they have to take that gate or they cannot enter the town. Their repeated attacks cause some of the townspeople to become alarmed. After some "brisk skirmishes," Conscience, who had been the recorder before Diabolus took over the town, "began to talk aloud, and his words were now to the town of Mansoul as if they were great claps of thunder" (3:278). Conscience is still active in fallen people, convicting of sin and warning of judgment. Furthermore, "things began to grow scarce in Mansoul" and "upon all her pleasant things there was a blast, and burning instead of beauty" (3:278).

In addition to the voice of conscience, external circumstances may warn of God's wrath, as in Jesus' parable of the Prodigal Son: "After he had spent everything, there was a severe famine in that whole country, and he began to be in need."[11]

The townspeople propose a truce, but the King's captains reject their "weak and feeble offer" (3:279). The good Captain Boanerges demands unconditional surrender, but the Lord Mayor, old *Incredulity*, warns Mansoul against giving itself up "so that you are no more your own" (3:280). A party under the former lord mayor, Lord Understanding, and the former recorder, Mr. Conscience, is able to make some headway; and soon there is a mutiny in Mansoul. A debate between Understanding and Incredulity follows, in which Understanding reminds his opponent that Incredulity and his prince are both foreigners to Mansoul and not natives of the town. The devil and unbelief have no place in man as created by God. The debate turns into blows and there are "knocks on both sides" (3:282). The author especially enjoyed seeing "how old *Mr. Prejudice* was kicked and tumbled about in the dirt." Very active in the fight was a "brisk man," *Mr. Anything*, "but both sides were against him because he was true to none" (3:282). Meanwhile Mr. Will-be-will stood by, indifferent to the struggle. This account describes the human soul under conviction but still struggling against God.

Chapter 6

When the uproar dies down, Diabolus puts Lord Understanding and Mr. Conscience in prison for their part in the uprising. King Shaddai's captains send a trumpeter to renew their message to the town. The trumpeter's speech against Mansoul's pride is one of Bunyan's most stirring: Do the people think they are stronger than the King, to stop the sun, hinder the moonlight, count the stars, stay the rain, flood the earth with the sea, and abase the proud? Do they think the King entreats them because he is as afraid of them as if he were a grasshopper? (3:283). The trumpeter is answered by Diabolus, who persuades the people so that they "again harden their hearts yet more against the captains of Shaddai." Thoughts of Shaddai's "greatness . . . quite quash" the people, and "thoughts of his holiness [sink] them in despair." (This was Bunyan's own experience as recorded in *Grace Abounding* [1:29].) The captains continue their assault on the town while they send to Shaddai for reinforcements, "so that his Majesty [might] not lose the benefit of these his good beginnings but [might] complete his conquest upon the town of Mansoul." When the petition reaches the palace of the King, it is delivered to the King's Son, who, after he has made such "amendments and additions" as he thinks convenient, with his own hand carries it to the King (3:284). King Shaddai is glad for the petition and more so when he sees that it is seconded by his Son. The King calls to himself Emmanuel, his Son, who answers, "Here am I, my Father." The King makes Emmanuel the leader of his forces, over the five "noble captains": *Credence*,[12] *Goodhope*, *Charity*, *Innocent*, and *Patience*. The attack of Shaddai's army to bring guilt and conviction is now followed by the promise of the Gospel. Note that Captain Credence and the other captains are not residents of Mansoul, but Emmanuel's officers sent by him to the rebellious town. Likewise, faith, as well as hope, love, innocence, and patience, are not natural qualities but gifts of God.

The Prince begins his march to the town, with Captain Credence leading the way and Captain Patience bringing up the rear. What a picture! They bring with them fifty-four battering rams and twelve slings ("the holy Bible containing 66 books" [3:286, margin]). The infantry surrounds the town and raises two mounds—called *Mount Gracious* and *Mount Justice*. On them they place their slings and put five of their best battering rams on *Mount Hearken*—a mountain near Ear-gate. The Prince puts out a white flag (mercy) among the golden slings on Mount Gracious, to give notice to Mansoul that he can and will yet be gracious if they turn to him. When there is no response, he raises the red flag (warning of judgment) upon Mount Justice. Still there is no response, so the Prince sets out the waving black flag of defiance (execution of judgment). But Mansoul remains unconcerned (3:286).

When the Prince's messenger comes to further set forth Emmanuel's cause, the people respond by saying that they will have to consult their own prince. When "good Prince Emmanuel hears this answer, and sees the slavery and bondage of the people," his heart is grieved (3:287). Diabolus goes to the town's gates and makes a reply in his own language to Emmanuel. The people cannot understand his words, nor do they see how he crouches and cringes before Emmanuel. Emmanuel answers that he has come to avenge the wrong done to Mansoul, which he claims for his own because his Father has built it and he is his Father's heir. Furthermore, he himself has bought it, for, at the appointed time, he explains, "I gave body for body, soul for soul, life for life, blood for blood, and so redeemed my beloved Mansoul" (3:288). The atonement provided by Christ on the cross, the basis for the recovery of Mansoul, is displayed here. The cross of Christ is present in *The Holy War* but stands somewhat in the background.

Chapter 7

Mansoul and Diabolus propose a compromise, sent to Prince Emmanuel by *Mr. Loath-to-stoop*. Diabolus offers to give up "one half of the town of Mansoul." The marginal note here, and repeated six more times in this chapter, is "Mark this!"—a warning against compromise (3:290). Diabolus proposes that Emmanuel become the "nominal and titular Lord of all" if he, Diabolus, can "possess but a part." (How can Christ be Lord of all and Lord of only a part!) The wiley Diabolus then asks for some place in Mansoul where he can live privately. He asks for permission to enter the town occasionally, for a few days or a month or so. Other requests of this kind are made and all are rejected by Emmanuel, who sums up his position with the words "No. For if Mansoul [comes] to be mine, I shall not admit of, nor consent, that there should be the least scrap, shred, or dust of Diabolus left behind" (3:290). Christ claims full Lordship over the soul he has redeemed.

A fierce battle follows for several days, during which the posts of Ear-gate shake, Eye-gate is "well nigh broken quite open," Will-be-will is completely daunted, and many of the soldiers of the town are "maimed, and wounded and slain" (3:292). When the battle is over, the Prince commands that the white flag again be flown on Mount Gracious "to show that yet Emmanuel [has] grace for the wretched town of Mansoul." Diabolus, now desperate, slyly attempts to convince Emmanuel to lift the siege and depart, allowing Diabolus to persuade the town to reform and receive Emmanuel for its Lord and Diabolus as his deputy. Emmanuel rejects this proposal, stating that "the greatest proficiency that man can make in the law and the righteousness thereof will amount to no more, for the taking away of a curse from Mansoul, than just nothing at all" (3:293). Emmanuel tells the enraged Diabolus, "I will pull down this town and build it again, and it shall be as though it had not been, and it shall then be the glory of the whole universe" (3:293). Bunyan's Protestant and Puritan theology is emphasized by the fact that Mansoul cannot save itself by its own efforts but has to be taken by divine assault.

The Prince's soldiers make another foray against the town; Ear-gate is shattered and its bars and bolts broken in a thousand pieces! "Then . . . the Prince's trumpets sound, the captains shout, the town [shakes], and Diabolus retreats to his hold" (3:294). Emmanuel's captains make straight for the heart of the town, where the Recorder, Mr. Conscience, is locked up in his house. They occupy the strategically placed house and make it their headquarters. Mr. Conscience tells the people that death and destruction have been attending Mansoul. "I have transgressed greatly," says the old man sadly, "in keeping silence when I should have spoken, and in perverting . . . justice when I should have executed the same."This, notes Bunyan, is "the office of conscience when he is awakened" (3:295, margin).

The captains of the Prince execute many of the enemy, so that Diabolonians lie "dead in every corner"; but the chapter ends with the solemn words, "though too many yet were alive in Mansoul" (3:295).

Chapter 8

Emmanuel strips Diabolus, binds him with chains to chariot wheels, displays him as an object of derision, and drives him to "the parched places of a salt land," where he seeks rest but finds none (3:297). The Prince, who remains in a "royal pavilion in the camp, and in the midst of his Father's forces," orders Captain Boanerges to imprison Lord Understanding, Mr. Conscience, and Lord Will-be-will. The townspeople send Emmanuel a petition, pleading for him to spare these men "according to the greatness of [his] mercy" (3:298). Another petition is sent with the plea, "Oh that Mansoul might live before thee." A third petition to Emmanuel states that if he should condemn the town, "we cannot but say [he is] righteous." It adds, "But, oh! Let mercy reign, and let it be extended to us!" (3:299, 300). Yet Mansoul fears that no mercy will be given to such a wicked and rebellious town as it knows itself to be. All the inhabitants of the town, that is, all the natives who have lived there before the Diabolonians came in, join in ashamed confession of their sin. The merciful Prince, accompanied by music, gives the prisoners "a large and general pardon": "beauty for ashes, the oil of joy for mourning, and the garment of praise for the spirit of heaviness" (Isaiah 61:3). "The grace, the benefit, the pardon, [is] sudden, glorious, and so big that they [are] not able, without staggering, to stand up under it" (3:303). The town's noblemen are sent to tell Mansoul what the Prince has done. Captain Credence marches into the town and takes possession of the castle. Captain Judgment and Captain Execution leave the castle and withdraw from Mansoul.

Chapter 9

The people of Mansoul, waiting sadly to hear of the prisoners' deaths, are amazed to see these prisoners returning happily to town. In John Bunyan's words that absolutely sing, we read:

> [The prisoners] went down to the camp in black, but they came back to the town in white; they went down to the camp in ropes, they came back in chains of gold; they went down to the camp with their feet in fetters, but came back with their steps enlarged . . .; they went also to the camp looking for death, but they came back from thence with assurance of life (3:304).

The recorder reads the Prince's pardon to the people of the town and the Prince displays "his grace before Mansoul." The townspeople praise him "for his abundant favor" and beg him to come into Mansoul "with his men, and there to take up their quarters forever." "O, Lord," they plead, "come to our Mansoul; do what thou wilt, so thou keepest us from sinning and makest us serviceable to thy Majesty" (3:306-7). This prayer depicts our reliance on God's preserving and sanctifying grace after our salvation.

Emmanuel makes a feast for the town with "food that came from his Father's court, water that was made wine, honey from the rock," and musicians who were "masters of the songs that were sung at the court of Shaddai" (3:308). The best of everything!

And so all the citizens of Mansoul learn that sin and rebellion against God deserve punishment and death, and they learn that God's grace is greater than all their sin.

Chapter 10

A court is called and Diabolonians tried and condemned: *Mr. Incredulity*, *Mr. Lustings*, *Mr. Forget-good*, aldermen *Hardheart, Atheism*, and *Falsepeace*, and the burgesses *Notruth*, *Pitiless*, and *Haughty*. This process of the cleansing of the town of Mansoul is, in theological terms, the sanctification of the justified sinner. Bunyan's own prison experience had given him a good working knowledge of court procedure. Note the case of Falsepeace, who swears (falsely) at the bar that his name is not "Falsepeace" but "Peace" and therefore he cannot be indicted. In seventeenth-century criminal law, extreme precision was required in the wording of an indictment; an inaccurate naming of the prisoner could enable the defense to plead that the whole indictment was invalid. The trial of Atheism is a fascinating account, and would especially be so to a Christian student in a secular university. The Diabolonians are put in prison to be executed the next day; but one, *Incredulity*, escapes and reports to Diabolus "what sad alteration Emmanuel [has] made in Mansoul." Diabolus and Incredulity angrily plot to take Mansoul back again. Meanwhile, some Diabolonians in Mansoul, who had been a plague, a grief, and an offence to the town, are put to death in obedience to the teaching of Romans 8:13, "If by the Spirit you put to death the misdeeds of the body, you will live."

Chapter 11

Emmanuel renews the charter of the town and enlarges it, "mending several faults therein, that Mansoul's yoke might be yet more easy." The revised charter is "a better, a new one, more steady and firm by far" (3:318). Here is the covenant of grace, which cannot fail. Emmanuel sets up a ministry among the people so that he may instruct them in "the things that . . . concern their present and future state." His ministry comprises two persons: "one . . . of his Father's court, and one . . . a native of Mansoul." The minister from the court, Emmanuel tells the town, is "a person of no less quality and dignity than . . . my Father and I." This one, the Holy Spirit, is to be their "chief Teacher" (3:319). The other appointed minister, Mr. Conscience, who had been the recorder of the town, receives clearly defined duties. You must, said the Prince to Mr. Conscience, confine yourself to "the teaching of moral virtues, to civil and natural duties." But you must not attempt to presume to be "a revealer of those high and supernatural mysteries that are kept close in the bosom of Shaddai, my Father. For those things know no man, nor can any reveal them but my Father's Secretary only" (3:320). Conscience can urge righteousness and convict of sin; the Holy Spirit through the Scriptures reveals the will and purposes of God.

Emmanuel warns Mansoul that Diabolonians still lurk in the town and commands the people "to take, mortify, and put them to death." Emmanuel teaches his people with a "standing ministry" in the place: with "a weekly—yea, if need be, a daily—lecture" (3:322). Here is an example of the Puritan practice of frequent preaching for instruction and edification.

"And now was Mansoul . . . a town redeemed from the hand and from the power of Diabolus—a town that the King Shaddai loved, and that he sent Emmanuel to regain from the prince of the infernal cave . . . a town that Emmanuel loved to dwell in" (3:323).

When the Prince completes "the modeling of the town," he sets up his standard to wave upon the castle (3:323). He visits with the elders of the town often, and they walk together and talk about all the great things that he has done and yet promises to do for Mansoul. If Mansoul townspeople do not frequently call on him as he desires they should, he walks to their houses and knocks at their doors. If they hear and open to him, as commonly they do if they are at home, he renews his former love and confirms it too with some fresh tokens and signs of continued favor, such as banquets, gold tokens of marriage, honor, beauty, and pardon, and—best of all—his smile (3:323-4).

A new officer, *Mr. God's-peace*, is brought to the town as governor.

He is not a native of the town but came with Prince Emmanuel. This reminds us that true peace is never a human achievement; it always comes as a gift from God.

Chapter 12

Mr. Carnal-security, whose father was a Diabolonian, had served Diabolus against Emmanuel; now he pretends to serve the Prince. But he brings Mansoul "into great and grievous slavery and bondage" by turning the people away from loving and serving Emmanuel (3:324). The people reject a warning from the Lord Chief Secretary, who is grieved and goes away. When the Secretary reports to Prince Emmanuel, he too is grieved and makes "provision to return to his Father's court" (3:326). Mr. God's-peace resigns. The people of the town, however, are amazingly unmoved; the departing of their Prince does not touch them, nor is he remembered by them when gone (3:326). This startling development does not mean that Mansoul has "fallen from grace" and is lost again; the town has, however, fallen away temporarily from fellowship with God. The Holy Spirit and Christ are grieved and are no longer at home in Mansoul.

Mr. Carnal-security gives a feast for the town. *Mr. Godly-fear*, "one now but little set by, though formerly one of great request," is invited by Diabolus so that he can make fun of him (3:326). But the sad Godly-fear speaks out bravely for Emmanuel, and the "subordinate preacher," old Mr. Conscience, begins to support his words. The people listen, becoming perturbed and dejected at what they have done in forsaking their Prince, and they take Mr. Carnal-security and burn him and his house. Conscience acknowledges his fault in falling in with Carnal-security and calls for a day of fasting.

This change initiates a long winter of sending messages beseeching Emmanuel to return to Mansoul. Remaining in Mansoul are many of the old Diabolonians who either came with the tyrant when he invaded the town or were born there "by reason of unlawful mixtures." These include *Lord Adultery*, *Lord Murder*, *Lord Anger*, *Lord Lasciviousness*, *Lord Deceit*, *Lord Evil-eye*, *Lord Blasphemy*, and "the old and dangerous" *Lord Covetousness*. Mansoul neglects to destroy these Diabolonians and, by degrees, these old men take courage "to show themselves to the inhabitants of the town" (3:330).

Chapter 13

When Emmanuel leaves the backsliding town, the Diabolonians gather to plot how they can take over Mansoul again. They send a letter to Diabolus in hell to ask for his advice. *Mr. Profane* carries it to Hell-gate-Hill and brings back Diabolus's answer. The devilish ruler proposes either persuading the townspeople to "a vain and loose life," tempting them "to doubt and despair," or blowing up the town "by the gunpowder of pride and self-conceit" (3:332). He charges his "trusty Diabolonians" to spy out the weakness of Mansoul and determine the best method of assault. During further discussion among the Diabolonians in Mansoul, Mr. Deceit proposes driving Mansoul into desperation by causing its people to "question the truth of the love of the heart of their Prince towards them" (3:332). It is decided that three disguised Diabolonians should offer themselves as servants to Mansoul: namely, Lord Covetousness, Lord Lasciviousness, and Lord Anger, who now call themselves *Prudent-thrify*, *Harmless-mirth*, and *Good-zeal*. These three corrupt the town as much as they can and begin to plan as to when Diabolus should make his attack. They send a message to Diabolus by Mr. Profane, suggesting that "an army of doubters" would be the most likely to succeed against the town. They further suggest that a market day would be best for the attack, for then Mansoul would be most busy and have fewest thoughts of a surprise (3:333-4). Diabolus's counselor, the Lord Lucifer, says, "Let this therefore stand with us for a maxim, and be to Diabolonians for a general rule in all ages, for nothing can make this to fail but grace, in which I would hope that this town has no share" (3:335). Even (especially!) the devil knows that mankind's only hope is God's grace!

The town is indeed in desperate condition! She has offended her Prince and he is gone; she has "encouraged the powers of hell, by her foolishness, to come against her to seek her utter destruction" (3:339). Mansoul sends petition after petition to Emmanuel, but he answers all with silence (3:339). Why does God not answer them? As long as the people of Mansoul regard iniquity in their hearts their King will not hear their prayers (Psalm 66:18).

Sadly, there is now a confusing mix in Mansoul. Diabolonians and Mansoulians walk the streets together, and there is no great difference in their behavior. The backsliding Christian looks more and more like a person of the world.

Chapter 14

One man, *Mr. Prywell*, "a great lover of the people of Mansoul," learns of the Diabolonian plans to possess Mansoul again and warns the lord mayor, who tells the subordinate preacher, who raises the alarm in the town.

> *"Bunyan employs pry . . . in a more favorable sense than it now bears. As, for instance, it is said in another part of this same book that the men of Mansoul were allowed to* pry *into the words of the Holy Ghost and to expound them to their best advantage. Honest anxiety for the welfare of his fellow-townsmen was Mr. Prywell's chief characteristic. Pry is another form of* peer—*to look narrowly, to look closely. And God, says John Bunyan, would have it so."[13]*

The ashamed citizens of Mansoul realize their folly and double their petitions to Shaddai and his Son. They make the gates of the town fast with bars and locks, conduct a strict search for all kinds of Diabolonians, and proclaim a public fast and a day of humiliation.

Meanwhile, an army of terrible *doubters* approaches the town. The doubters do not represent intellectual questions about the truth of Christianity but different forms of doubt and despair concerning salvation. They are divided into nine companies under nine captains. These are *Captain Rage* over the Election-doubters, *Captain Fury* over the Vocation-doubters, *Captain Damnation* over the Grace-doubters, *Captain Insatiable* over the Faith-doubters, *Captain Brimstone* over the Perseverance-doubters, *Captain Torment* over the Resurrection-doubters, *Captain Noease* over the Salvation-doubters, *Captain Sepulcher* over the Glory-doubters, and *Captain Pasthope* over the Felicity-doubters! Over these companies are seven superior generals, *Beelzebub, Lucifer, Legion, Apollyon, Python, Cerberus,* and *Belial.* Incredulity is the lord-general; and Diabolus is the king (3:341-2).

The Mansoulians frantically seek help from the Lord Chief Secretary, but he sadly answers them that as yet he is "ill at ease" and therefore cannot do as he formerly did (3:344). After another petition, he answers that the people have offended their Emmanuel, and have also grieved himself, and that they must yet help themselves. His answer falls "like a millstone" upon the people. The Lord Mayor, "my Lord Understanding," points out that the Lord Secretary has said that "we must yet suffer for our sins." "The word 'yet,'" he continues, "sounds as if at last we [will] be saved from our enemies; and that after a few more sorrows, Emmanuel will come and be our help" (3:344).

The constant noise of Diabolus's drum troubles the people of the town, and the stones (Scripture truths) that are slung by the captains of the Prince (who delight in "warlike achievements" for their Prince) into the army of Diabolus terrify his soldiers. Diabolus decides to change his tactics and flatter the Mansoulians into his net. He says to them, "Consider, you never had so many hard, dark, troublesome and heart-afflicting hours while you were mine as you have had since you revolted from me; nor shall you ever have peace again until you and I become one as before." He offers the people an enlarged charter so that their "license and liberty" should be to take, hold, enjoy, and make their own all that is "pleasant from the east to the west" (3:345). The Lord Mayor responds to the speech of Diabolus, stating that it is "empty and void of all truth" and that the Mansoulians are ready to die rather than "fall in" with the "flattering and lying deceits" of Diabolus again (3:345). Furthermore, the transformed Lord Will-be-will takes two young Diabolonians and hangs them on a very high cross at Eye-gate! The marginal note explains that "mortification of sin is a sign of hope of life" (3:346).

Chapter 15

The Mansoulians make an attack on the camp of Diabolus at night. "And there was the folly of Mansoul, for the night is always the best for the enemy, but the worst for Mansoul to fight in" (3:348). They fail and have to make "as safe and good retreat" as they can (3:349). Encouraged by this success, Diabolus demands the surrender of the town, but the Lord Mayor replies that as long as Emmanuel their Prince is alive (though he at present is not with them as they wish), they shall "never consent to yield Mansoul up to another" (3:349).

One night Diabolus makes a surprise attack on Feel-gate and succeeds in entering the town. "For the truth is," we are told, "those gates [are] but weak, and so most easily made to yield" (3:350).[14] The Prince's men and their captains are forced to retreat to the castle. Diabolus quarters his soldiers in the houses of the inhabitants of the town of Mansoul and lays siege to the castle. But Mr. Godly-fear is keeper of the castle, a man of such "courage, conduct, and valor" that the siege is in vain. This standoff continues for "about two years and a half" (3:351). (Perhaps this is a piece of autobiography, for much of the struggle in Mansoul reflects Bunyan's own long struggle for assurance, as described in *Grace Abounding.*) During this time "the body of the town was the seat of war, the people of the town were driven into holes, and the glory of Mansoul was laid in the dust" (3:351).

This sad picture is unfortunately an accurate one. Christians are sometimes so under attack by the world, the flesh, and the devil that we hardly seem to possess faith, and our courage and hope almost fail. "Because there remains in every part" of Christians "some remnants of corruption," there is within us a "continual and irreconcilable war." Even though, as the Westminster Confession of Faith further states, "the remaining corruption, for a time, may much prevail, yet, through the continual supply of strength from the sanctifying Spirit of Christ," we will overcome. "And so, the saints grow in grace, perfecting holiness in the fear of God."[15]

At last the inhabitants of the town agree to send another petition for relief to Emmanuel. Mr. Godly-fear states that the Prince will not receive such a petition "unless the Lord Secretary's hand [is] to it" (3:351). He adds that the Lord Secretary will not set his hand to any petition that he himself has not had a part in composing and drawing up (3:352). The Lord Secretary agrees to draw up the petition for Mansoul but states that they "must be present at the doing of it; yea, [they] must put [their] desires to it. True, the hand and pen shall be mine," he says, "but the ink and paper must be yours" (3:352). Real prayer must be by and from the Holy Spirit but at the same time contain the honest supplications of the ones praying. The petition is drawn up and carried by "the brave and most stout Captain Credence" to Emmanuel.

Diabolus is enraged and renews his efforts against "the wretched town of Mansoul." He demands that the gates of the castle be opened to him but Godly-fear refuses, saying that "Mansoul, when she [has] suffered awhile, [shall] be made perfect, strengthened, settled" (3:353). Diabolus reminds Mansoul of its wickedness and states that "it is not only I but your Emmanuel [who] is against you" (3:353). The Lord Mayor replies in these wonderful words:

> We have sinned indeed, but that shall be no help to thee, for our Emmanuel hath said it, and that in great faithfulness: "And him that cometh to me I will in no wise cast out." He hath also told us, O our enemy, that "all manner of sin and blasphemy shall be forgiven" to the sons of men. Therefore we dare not despair, but will look for, wait for, and hope for deliverance still (3:353).

Again, these words came from Bunyan's experience and were written out of his heart.

The Prince takes notice of the many petitions from Mansoul. He states that he has placed the town in the hands of the Lord Secretary and under the conduct of Captain Credence. The people send word of their wishes to the Lord Secretary that "all that ever they were and had might be put under the government, care, custody, and conduct of Captain Credence" (3:355).

Chapter 16

Diabolus calls a council of war to plan revenge on Mansoul. *Apollyon*,[16] the president of the council, advises that the Diabolonians withdraw and allow Mansoul to think that its problems are over, which will "give them a bigger blow than we can possibly give them ourselves" (3:355). So the army of Diabolus withdraws to a plain outside the town, first instructing the Diabolonians still in the town to set to work to betray Mansoul to them. Diabolonians such as *Mr. Sweetworld* and *Mr. Present-good* are commissioned to encourage Mansoul to be taken up "in much business." "Remember ye not," says *Lucifer* to his colleagues, "that thus we prevailed upon Laodicea, and how many at present do we hold in this snare?"[17] (3:356) They know they can count on *Mr. Penny-wise-pound-foolish* and *Mr. Get-in-the-hundred-and-lose-in-the-shire*. "A hundred" in the old county geography of England was a political subdivision of a shire. The proverb means that one might gain part of the shire but lose the whole shire.

> *"And thus after tonight," said Alexander Whyte, "we shall always call this shrewd proverb to mind when we are tempted to take a part at the risk of the whole; to receive this world at the loss of the next world; or, as our Lord has it, to gain the whole world and to lose our own soul. Lot's choice of Sodom and Gomorrah, and Esau's purchase of the mess of pottage in the Old Testament; and then Judas's thirty pieces of silver, and Ananias and Sapphira's part of the price in the New Testament, are all so many well-known instances of getting in the hundred and losing in the shire."*[18]

Emmanuel sends a letter to Captain Credence, telling him to meet him in a field in the plains outside Mansoul on the third day. Captain Credence has the King's trumpeters "play the best music the heart can invent" from the castle battlements. Hearing this, the Diabolonians realize that Emmanuel is coming to the aid of his town and retire from Mansoul. Their army, however, is caught between the Prince's army and the soldiers of Captain Credence—including the ill Captain Experience on his crutches! Battle is joined, and "betwixt Christ and faith" the army of Diabolus is destroyed. Emmanuel, delighted with the valiant fight of his people, comes, and he comes "with colors flying, trumpets sounding," and the feet of his soldiers "scarcely touching the ground"! All the gates of the town are thrown open, and the gates of the castle, to receive the Prince and his army. The Mansoulians bury in the plains the army of doubters and their leaders and commit themselves anew to the destruction of all Diabolonians remaining hidden in the town (3:358-61).

Chapter 17

Far from giving up, Diabolus raises another army of ten thousand doubters, whose nature is "to put a question upon every one of the truths of Emmanuel" (3:361), and fifteen thousand *Bloodmen* under the command of eight captains, beginning with *Captain Cain* and ending with *Captain Pope*. Diabolus puts a great deal more trust in these Bloodmen than he did in his army of doubters. Having failed to gain his goal by creating internal doubt in Christians,

Satan now attempts to win using external persecution. Bunyan himself had experienced first spiritual doubts, then persecution and imprisonment.

The town prepares for the new onslaught. Captain Credence and Captain Patience are sent to the part of Mansoul in which the Bloodmen have gathered. *Captain Self-Denial* is stationed at Ear-gate and Eye-gate. The surviving doubters, however, are able to enter the town and find shelter in the house of an old Diabolonian named *Evil-questioning*. But their plans are overheard by one of Lord Will-be-will's faithful soldiers, *Mr. Diligence*. Diligence leads Will-be-will to Evil-questioning's house, where he breaks open the door and captures the doubters.

At the trial that follows, Evil-questioning denies that "Evil-questioning" is his name; rather, he announces, it is "Honest-inquiry." The doubters are called. Election-doubter admits that rejection of the doctrine of election is "the religion that he [has] been brought up in" and by which he will die. The judge tells him that "to question election is to overthrow a great doctrine of the Gospel; to wit, the omniscience, and power, and will of God; to take away the liberty of God with his creature; to stumble the faith of the town of Mansoul; and to make salvation to depend upon works and not upon grace" (3:368). Vocation-doubter is accused of denying "a great part of one of the most experimental truths of the Prince of the town of Mansoul; for he has called, and she has heard a most distinct and powerful call of her Emmanuel." Grace-doubter admits that he believes that Mansoul shall "never be saved freely by grace." They are all "sentenced to the death of the cross" (3:368-9). This severe sentence is a theological statement, of course. Because Paul in Galatians 5:24 speaks of Christians crucifying "the sinful nature with its passions and desires," the doubters are put to death.

Chapter 18

Lord Will-be-will and Diligence search out the remaining Diabolonians in the town. *Clip-promise* is apprehended—"he was a notorious villain, for by his doings much of the King's coin was abused." The name "Clip-promise" originated with thieves who, with shears, clipped slivers of silver or gold off the rough rims of coins, debasing the money and producing confusion about its value. Clip-promise is whipped and then hanged. John Bunyan observes that "some may wonder at the severity of this man's punishment; but those that are honest traders in Mansoul are sensible of the great abuse that one clipper of promises, in little time, may do to the town of Mansoul" (3:369).

Also arrested is *Selflove*, whose sentence is deferred because there are many who are "allied to him in Mansoul" (3:369). *Mr. Self-denial* threatens to lay down his commission if "such villains" are allowed to go unpunished. He takes Selflove from the crowd and has him put to death. Some mutter at this act, indicating that all is not right as yet in the town. But Mansoul does "arrive to some good degree of peace and quiet," and the Prince lives within her borders (3:370).

In *The Holy War* John Bunyan dramatically preaches his theology, expresses his love for his Savior and for the church, and ends his allegory with the mighty words of Prince Emmanuel.

The Prince tells his people that he has redeemed them "not only from the dread of [his] Father's law, but from the hand of Diabolus" (3:370). He tells them that during their rebellion, he has compassed them about and afflicted them on every side to make them weary of their ways. Furthermore, he has lodged within the town a company of his Father's host: "captains and rulers, soldiers and men of war, engines and excellent devices to subdue and bring down [their] foes." It is Emmanuel who has stirred up their consciences and understanding, their wills and affections, and who has put life in them to seek him and, in finding, find their "own health, happiness, and salvation" (3:371).

Emmanuel tells the people that, after a little while, he will "take down this famous town of Mansoul . . . and carry the stones thereof, and the timber thereof, and the walls thereof, and the dust thereof, and the inhabitants thereof, into mine own country, even into the kingdom of my Father; and will there set it up in such strength and glory, as it never did see in the kingdom where now it is placed" (3:371). Bunyan is describing the new heaven and the new earth that God will bring about in his own time and the happy life of the redeemed in heaven.

Prince Emmanuel arrives in state with his chariot and dignitaries to meet with his people in the marketplace. He describes his sacrifice for them:

> O my Mansoul, I have lived, I have died, I live, and will die no more for thee. I live that thou mayest not die. Because I live thou shalt live also. I reconciled thee to my Father by the blood of my cross, and being reconciled thou shalt live through me. I will pray for thee, I will fight for thee, I will yet do thee good. Nothing can hurt thee but sin; nothing can grieve me but sin (3:372).

What incredible words! But this is not yet heaven, and the Prince explains to his people that he will allow Diabolonians to continue to live in the walls of the town "to keep thee wakening, to try thy love, to make thee watchful, and to cause thee yet to prize my noble captains, their soldiers, and my mercy." He ends his loving address:

> Remember, therefore, O my Mansoul, that thou art beloved of me; as I have therefore taught thee to watch, to fight, to pray, and to make war against my foes, so now I command thee to believe that my love is constant to thee. O my Mansoul, how have I set my heart, my love, upon thee, watch. Behold I lay none other burden upon thee than what thou hast already. Hold fast till I come (3:373).

AlexanderWhyte summed up "Emmanuel's Last Charge" to his people, the recipients of his grace throughout their lives, in these words: "You are to be at that day the highest monument in heaven or earth to the redeeming, pardoning, and saving grace of God. Yes, this is the name that shall be written on you; this is the name that shall be read on you of all who shall see you in heaven; this name that Emmanuel pronounced over Mansoul that day from His ascending chariot-steps, a very Spectacle of wonder, and a very Monument of the mercy and the grace of God."

Footnotes

[1] Alexander Whyte, *Bunyan Characters in The Holy War* (Edinburgh: Oliphant, Anderson and Ferrier, 1895), 2.

[2] Wilbur M. Smith, "Introduction," *The Holy War: The Losing and Taking Again of*

the Town of Mansoul (Chicago: Moody Press, 1978), 48.

[3] Smith, "Introduction," *The Holy War*, 48.

[4] Sharrock, *John Bunyan*, 136.

[5] Talon, *John Bunyan*, 240.

[6] Quoted in Talon, *John Bunyan*, 256.

[7] Whyte, *Bunyan Characters in The Holy War*, 12.

[8] Chapter divisions were not used when Bunyan's book was first published, but they did appear in later editions.

[9] This is a reference to Jesus' healing of a demon-possessed man in Mark 5. When Jesus asked the evil spirit "What is your name?" the spirit replied, "My name is Legion, for we are many" (Mark 5:9).

[10] Boanerges is the name given to two of the disciples of Jesus, James and John, the sons of Zebedee. The name refers to their fiery temperaments, which can be seen in Luke 9:54 and Mark 9:38.

[11] Luke 15:14.

[12] "Credence" means "trust, confidence; hence, trustworthiness."

[13] Alexander Whyte, *Bunyan Characters in The Holy War*, 151.

[14] The feelings and emotions are favorite targets of attack by Satan because they appear most vulnerable.

[15] *Westminster Confession of Faith*, chapter 13, sections 2 and 3.

[16] Apollyon is the Greek translation of the Hebrew "Abaddon," which means "destroyer" (Revelation 9:11).

[17] Lucifer (shining one) is applied to the king of Babylon in Isaiah 14:12. It is often used as a term for Satan. Bunyan uses it for one of the devil's followers. Laodicea is a reference to the blackslidden, lukewarm church of the city of Laodicea in Revelation 3:17.

[18] Whyte, *Bunyan Characters in The Holy War*, 130-1.

Here's sixty pieces of his labours, and he was sixty years of age.

Charles Doe[1]

Bunyan's sermons were not made of novelty, but of accepted doctrine, and he could make it as powerful as though it were being heard for the first time.

Ola Elizabeth Winslow[2]

6

Other Writings

John Bunyan's reputation rests on four of his sixty books—his spiritual autobiography, **Grace Abounding to the Chief of Sinners**, and three notable others: **The Pilgrim's Progress**, **The Holy War**, and **The Life and Death of Mr. Badman**. His remaining books, largely forgotten today, are not without interest and flashes of the power and imagination that we find in his four major works. In this chapter we survey briefly some of Bunyan's other writings.

The variety in Bunyan's writing is remarkable: autobiography, allegory, fiction, polemics, poetry, and books for children. Most of Bunyan's books, however, are practical expositions of Scripture, growing out of his preaching. As a Puritan preacher, Bunyan wanted above all to be biblical; then he wanted to be simple and clear. In his sermons he uses proverbs, antitheses, repetition, and homely illustrations. He is a master in the use of everyday events and scenes in his sermons. Talon says, "The tact and lightness of touch are always there, indispensable in the blending of day-to-day things with eternal things, in interweaving earth's coarse brown linen with the gold and silk of heaven."[3]

During the 1550s Bunyan wrote his first manuscripts—works of polemics and theology.[4]

In **Some Gospel Truths Opened** (1656) Bunyan sharply, and at length, attacks the Quakers' doctrine of the inner light and their mystical treatment of Scripture. He sets forth the mainstream Protestant doctrine of salvation by grace alone through the "death of Christ upon the cross, without the gates of Jerusalem" against the Quaker notion that "salvation was not fully and completely wrought out for poor sinners by the man Christ Jesus" (2:133). Bunyan felt that the Quakers, by stressing a Christ "crucified within, dead within, and ascended within," were denying the importance of the historical Christ (2:134-5). Bunyan's primary purpose in this writing, however, was not to combat Quaker errors, but to preach the Gospel to the unconverted. Richard Greaves writes, "This incorporation of an evangelical invitation to the unregenerate would become a hallmark of nearly all [Bunyan's] writings."[5]

In *A Vindication of Gospel Truths Opened* (1657) Bunyan replies to Quaker objections to his first book and endeavors to prevent other Christians from accepting Quaker teaching. He again champions the historicity of the life and death of Jesus, insisting that salvation was obtained by Christ "when he did hang on the cross without Jerusalem's gate" (2:176). Bunyan insists on both the work of Christ "without" and the work of the Holy Spirit "within" the believer. He writes: "If thou hast laid Christ, God-man, for thy foundation, though thou hast the spirit of this man Christ within thee, yet thou dost not look that justification should be wrought out for thee, by that Spirit of Christ that dwelleth within thee, for thou knowest that salvation is already obtained for thee by the man Christ Jesus without thee, and is witnessed to thee by his Spirit that dwelleth within thee" (2:184).

Despite their antagonism, Bunyan and the Quakers shared some important convictions. Both stressed the internal work of the Holy Spirit, both opposed the Anglican establishment, and both rejected sacramental theology. Living with Quakers in prison and sharing hardships with them may have softened Bunyan's hostility toward them. Bunyan's release from prison in 1672 is said to have been because of the mediation of some Quakers.

A Few Sighs from Hell appeared in 1658 with a preface by Bunyan's friend and pastor, John Gifford. (A royalist inserted an advertisement for the book in a newspaper immediately after the announcement of Cromwell's death in 1658!) This small book is an expansion of a sermon that Bunyan preached on the parable of the rich man and Lazarus. In it he constantly urges his readers to accept

God's mercy through Christ and escape the fearful end of the rich man in the flames of hell.

John Bunyan's most important theological treatise, **The Doctrine of the Law and Grace Unfolded**, followed in 1659. Bunyan's principal exposition of covenant theology, this book sets forth "the freeness and fulness of the Gospel" (the covenant of grace) and "the terror, horror, and severity of the law" (the covenant of works) (1:493). Like his mentor Luther, Bunyan contrasts law and grace, so that people will "understand what grace is" and "how to come from under the law to meet God in and through that other most glorious covenant, through which, and only through which, God can communicate of himself grace, glory, yea, even all the good things of another world" (1:493). This early book by Bunyan provides a theological foundation for a fuller understanding of *The Pilgrim's Progress*, *The Holy War*, and all Bunyan's writings.

During the 1660s Bunyan published ten works of poetry and prose that made the prisoner in Bedford a famous author.

Profitable Meditations (1661) is Bunyan's first attempt at writing verse. Bunyan's poetry is not as successful as his prose usually is (indeed, he often achieves poetry in his prose). But his poetry has its own appeal in what C. S. Lewis calls its "harsh woodcut energy."[6] Marcus Loane writes: "It may be true that his muse was clad in russet and spoke with a country accent; but there was pith and point in his rudest rhyming, and a certain dash of beauty in his best lines."[7] Christopher Hill makes the point that "anyone attempting to write about Bunyan's poems must depend on Graham Midgley's introduction to the Oxford University Press edition of Bunyan's works. Midgley has established the case for regarding Bunyan not as a failed Herbert, Vaughan, Crashaw, or Herrick, but as the "inheritor and refiner of a folk-tradition of verse, drawing on ballads, broadsides, chap-books, and metrical psalms."[8] In his poetry Bunyan uses the pattern of the ballad, an art form that enjoyed enormous popularity in seventeenth-century England. With Bunyan, however, a clear, practical message is more important than the poetry itself. He follows *Profitable Meditations* with **Prison Meditations** (1663)—seventy short verses of four lines each. *Prison Meditations*, says Richard Greaves, is "spiritual autobiography in verse."[9] For example, Bunyan writes concerning his imprisonment:

> *For though men keep my outward man*
> *Within their locks and bars,*
> *Yet by the faith of Christ I can*
> *Mount higher than the stars (1:64).*

> *For, as the devil sets before*
> *Me heaviness and grief,*
> *So God sets Christ and grace much more,*
> *Whereby I take relief (1:64).*

In *I will Pray with the Spirit* (1663), Bunyan teaches that Christians are to pray with the Spirit and the understanding also, as Paul wrote in 1 Corinthians 14:15. In contrast to the set prayers of the Book of Common Prayer, Bunyan describes prayer as "a sincere, sensible affectionate pouring out of the heart or soul to God through Christ, in the strength and assistance of the Holy Spirit, for such things as God hath promised, or according to the Word, for the good of the church, with submission, in faith, to the will of God" (1:623). Bunyan was opposed to the use of the Book of Common Prayer (or any liturgy) and claimed that those who required its use "love and advance the form of their own or others' inventing before the Spirit of prayer, which is God's special and gracious appointment" (1:640).[10]

In the early months of 1663, Bunyan composed what he thought might be his final work, *Christian Behaviour; or the Fruits of True Christianity*, the title page of which identified him as "a prisoner of hope." From the jail in Bedford, Bunyan explained that he had written this book to encourage his readers to faith and holiness "before I die." He deals with proper conduct of husbands, wives, parents, children, masters, and servants. Bunyan's book is filled with biblical teaching and good advice on how to behave in these various relationships "so as to please God" (2:548). For example, Bunyan explains how parents are to instruct their children. "Do it in terms and words easy to be understood," he advises; "affect not high expressions, they will drown your children." But teach as

"God spake to his children" (2:558). Parents also must correct their children, but let it "be mixed with such love, pity, and compunction of spirit, that if possible they may be convinced you dislike not their persons, but their sins. This is God's way" (2:559).

A Map Showing the Order & Causes of Salvation & Damnation was produced by Bunyan sometime during 1663 and 1664. This chart, inspired by similar works by the early Puritan William Perkins, and Theodore Beza, Calvin's successor in Geneva, illustrated how God's glory is manifest in both the eternal happiness of the elect and the everlasting damnation of the reprobate. Hung on the wall of a home, Bunyan's *Map* served as a visual reminder that God is sovereign in all things, including human salvation. At the same time it set forth the urgency of a person's knowing where he or she stood before God. Bunyan's theology did not lead to fatalism, however. The *Map* reminded the faithful to make their "calling and election sure" (2 Peter 1:10) and the unconverted to "seek . . . the Lord while he may be found" (Isaiah 55:6). The wicked are damned, Bunyan explained in a book he wrote at this time (*The Resurrection of the Dead*), because they sinned, not because they were denied saving grace. They deliberately, knowingly, turned away from God, yielding to Satan; thus, the responsibility for their fate rests directly upon them.

One Thing is Needful (1665) is a long poem concerning the four "last things": death, judgment, heaven, and hell (3:725). It contains these lines about heaven:

> *There he will show us how he was*
> *Our prophet, priest, and king,*
> *And how he did maintain our cause,*
> *And us to glory bring (3:731).*

> *That head that once was crown'd with thorns,*
> *Shall now with glory shine,*
> *That heart that broken was with scorns*
> *Shall flow with life divine (3:732).*

Another poem, **Ebal and Gerizim; or the Blessing and the Curse**

(1665), is a kind of "aftcr-word" (3:737) to *One Thing is Needful.*
The title of the poem comes from Deuteronomy 27, in which the
mountains Ebal and Gerizim symbolize, respectively, a curse and
a blessing. Bunyan describes his poem as "a short exhortation to
sinners" concerning "the mercy and severity of God" (3:737).

The Holy City (1665) grew out of a sermon Bunyan preached
in prison. One Sunday when it was Bunyan's turn to preach, he was
not prepared. He turned through the pages of his Bible until, at the
very end, his eye fell upon the description of the New Jerusalem
in Revelation 21. "His soul was enlarged and enlightened with
the dazzling splendour of that sacred city," George Offor wrote.
Bunyan's heart, which had felt "empty, spiritless, and barren," was
so blessed that he preached with great power to his fellow prisoners.
"While distributing the truth," Offor continued, "it did so increase
in his hand, that of the fragments he gathered up a basket full, and
furnished this heavenly treatise"—*The Holy City (3:395).*

In this beautiful piece, an exposition of Revelation 21:10 through
22:4, Bunyan describes in detail "that great city, the holy Jerusalem,
descending out of heaven from God" (Revelation 21:10). He writes:

> *Never was fair weather after foul—nor warm weather after cold—nor
> a sweet and beautiful spring after a heavy, and nipping, and terrible
> winter, so comfortable, sweet, desirable, and welcome to the poor birds and
> beasts of the field, as this day will be to the Church of God (3:409).*

The Holy City, states Richard Greaves, is "a triumphal work, its
author certain of the elect's victory over persecution and secure in
the faith that Antichrist, the source of despair, doubt, and blasphemy,
will soon be bound with chains for a thousand years." Bunyan's "work
of exegesis," Greaves adds, "had not opened his prison door, but it
had uplifted his spirit."[11]

The Resurrection of the Dead (1665) is the sequel to *The
Holy City*, carrying the account of last things, from Christ's second
coming to the last judgment. The book came out of Bunyan's grief
and hope at the death of his beloved blind daughter, Mary. In the
spring of 1663, Mary fell sick and died soon after. With the news of
her death, Bunyan began the outline of *The Resurrection of the Dead.*

He completed the book in 1665 while the plague raged in England. Bunyan writes that "this doctrine of the resurrection of the dead hath that power, both to bear up and to awe; both to encourage and to keep within compass, the spirit and body of the people of God" (2:86). He explains:

> *Though God's saints have felt the power of much of his grace, and have had many a sweet word fulfilled on them; yet one word will be unfulfilled . . . so long as the grave can shut her mouth upon them: but, as I said before, when the gates of death do open before them, and the bars of the grave do fall asunder; then shall be brought to pass that saying that is written, "Death is swallowed up of victory"; and then will they hear that most pleasant voice, "Awake and sing, ye that dwell in dust: for thy dew is as the dew of herbs, and the earth shall cast out the dead" (2:97).*

The Heavenly Footman was written in 1667 and 1668, although it was not published until after Bunyan's death. Like its great successor *The Pilgrim's Progress*, *The Heavenly Footman* compares the Christian life to a journey and a race. "They that will have heaven," Bunyan writes, "must run for it" (3:381). He sets forth nine directions as to how to run, nine motives that cause us to run, and nine applications, such as "the danger they are in [who] grow weary before they come to their journey's end" (3:380). He writes:

> *Because the way is long . . . , and there is many a dirty step, many a high hill, much work to do, a wicked heart, world, and devil, to overcome; I say, there are many steps to be taken by those that intend to be saved, by running or walking, in the steps of that faith of our father Abraham. Out of Egypt thou must go through the Red Sea; thou must run a long and tedious journey, through the vast howling wilderness, before thou come to the land of promise (3:382).*

During the 1670s, Bunyan produced not only Part I of *The Pilgrim's Progress* (1678) but a number of other manuscripts.

In *A Defence of the Doctrine of Justification by Faith* (1672), Bunyan's final work during his twelve-year confinement, the Dissenter Bunyan defended the "wholesome" teaching of the Thirty-Nine Articles on the doctrine of justification, against Edward Fowler, a Presbyterian who had turned Anglican when the Act of Uniformity came into force in 1662. Fowler was appointed rector of Northill in Bedfordshire. In *The Principles and Practices of Certain Moderate Divines of the Church of England*, Fowler set forth "the reasonableness of the Gospel precepts" against what he considered extremists of all types. He denounced the doctrine of predestination and what he called "the antinomian opinion of imputed righteousness." He followed with another book, *The Design of Christianity*, in which he asserted that the purpose of Christ's coming into the world was simply to inspire people to a holy and moral life. Bunyan could not keep quiet. He attacked Fowler's "unstable weathercock spirit" as well as his theology. Fowler's views were no more than "heathenish" moralism, and Bunyan said so vehemently. Fowler, Bunyan charged, made Jesus a schoolmaster rather than a savior. The title of Bunyan's *Defence of the Doctrine of Justification by Faith* continues *Or, Mr. Fowler's Pretended Design of Christianity, Proved to be Nothing More than to Trample under Foot the Blood of the Son of God; and the Idolizing of Man's Own Righteousness.* The heart of Bunyan's assault on Fowler was his defense of the Lutheran (and Protestant) doctrine of the believer's justification solely by Christ's imputed righteousness. Bunyan patiently but sharply answered the twenty-seven chapters of Fowler's *Design of Christianity*. He ended by quoting articles ten, eleven, and thirteen of the Thirty-Nine Articles and stating:

> *These articles, because they respect the points in controversy betwixt Mr. Fowler, and myself; and because they be also fundamental truths of the Christian religion, as I do heartily believe, let all men know that I quarrel not with him about things wherein I dissent from the Church of England, but do contend for the truth contained, even in these very articles of theirs, from which he hath so deeply revolted, that he clasheth with every one of them, as may farther be shewn when he shall take heart to reply (2:332).*

Fowler (or more likely his curate) replied in a book called *Dirt Wip't Off*, accusing Bunyan of being "a ranting antinomian" and pointing out his lack of education. Bunyan ignored the book, but in early 1675 he wrote **Light for Them That Sit in Darkness**, to prevent

Christians from embracing the tenets of the Latitudinarians and others who rejected salvation by Christ's imputed righteousness.

Latitudinarians *like Edward Fowler regarded themselves as defenders of a "reasonable" version of Christianity. Emphasizing reason, tolerance, and suspicion of creeds and doctrine, they anticipated the new world of deism and rationalism brought in by the Enlightenment. During the seventeenth century, Latitudinarianism replaced Calvinism as the dominant strain in English Protestantism. Its basic message was of how piety and religion can contribute to success and happiness in this world.*

In 1672 Bunyan published ***A Confession of My Faith, and A Reason of My Practice in Worship.*** He set forth a detailed confession of his faith as a basis for his discussion of ecclesiastical separation. He asserts that there must be a strict separation from the "open profane," even though these say, "We have been christened, we go to church, we take . . . communion" (2:615). But "in the midst of your zeal for the Lord," Bunyan added, "remember that the visible saint is his . . . . Quarrel not with him about things that are circumstantial" (2:615).

Bunyan continues this thought in ***Differences in Judgment about Water Baptism, No Bar to Communion*** (1673). To Bunyan, baptism was not an essential prerequisite for church membership—a view that he derived from John Gifford (2:616). In ***Peaceable Principles and True*** *(1674),* Bunyan answers his Baptist critics who were pressing him to declare whether or not he was a Baptist. He replies:

> *And since you would know by what name I would be distinguished from others; I tell you, I would be, and hope I am, a Christian; and choose, if God should count me worthy, to be called a Christian, a Believer, or other such name which is approved by the Holy Ghost. And as for those factious titles of Anabaptists, Independents, Presbyterians, or the like, I conclude, that they came neither from Jerusalem, nor Antioch, but rather from hell and Babylon, for they naturally tend to divisions; "you may know them by their fruits" (2:648-9).*

The Barren Fig-tree (1673), an exposition of Luke 13:6-9, deals with a constant Puritan concern: the hypocrites, or "fruitless professors," those who claim to be Christians but who give little or no evidence of it in their lives (3:561). The preacher's task, asserted Bunyan, is to warn such people to repent and become fruitful Christians while they still have time. In **The Strait Gate** (1676), an exposition of Luke 13:24, Bunyan addressed professing Christians, distinguishing between genuine conversion, repentance, and faith, and their counterfeits.

In 1678 Bunyan brought out his **Come, and Welcome to Jesus Christ**, a beautiful book with music in its title. It grew from a sermon on words that had helped to heal his own spiritual wounds: "All that the Father giveth me shall come to me; and him that cometh to me I will in no wise cast out" (John 6:37). Probably his greatest sermon, *Come, and Welcome to Jesus Christ*, was already in its sixth edition when Bunyan died in 1688. Bunyan writes:

> *They that are coming to Jesus Christ are ofttimes heartily afraid that Jesus Christ will not receive them. . . . [But] this word "in no wise" cutteth the throat of all objections; and it was dropped by the Lord Jesus for that very end; and to help the faith that is mixed with unbelief. And it is, as it were, the sum of all promises; neither can any objection be made upon the unworthiness that thou findest in thee, that this promise will not assoil [assuage].*

> *But I am a great sinner, sayest thou.*
>   *"I will in no wise cast out," says Christ.*
> *But I am an old sinner, sayest thou.*
>   *"I will in no wise cast out," says Christ.*
> *But I am a hard-hearted sinner, sayest thou.*
>   *"I will in no wise cast out," says Christ.*
> *But I am a backsliding sinner, sayest thou.*
>   *"I will in no wise cast out," says Christ.*
> *But I have served Satan all my days, sayest thou.*
>   *"I will in no wise cast out," says Christ.*
> *But I have sinned against light, sayest thou.*
>   *"I will in no wise cast out," says Christ.*

> But I have sinned against mercy, sayest thou.
>
> "I will in no wise cast out," says Christ.
>
> But I have no good thing to bring with me, sayest thou.
>
> "I will in no wise cast out," says Christ (1:279-80).

Bunyan insisted that the Gospel be preached to everyone, and everyone be invited, even urged, to come to Jesus. The desire to come, however, he saw as a gift of God. Creatively personifying two words of his text, Bunyan writes, "When *Shall-come*, the absolute promise of God, comes to be fulfilled upon them, then they shall come; because by that promise a cure is provided against the rebellion of their will" (1:256).

Bunyan's catechism, ***Instruction for the Ignorant*** (1675), manifests, comments Richard Greaves, "the evangelical face of Bunyan's Calvinist theology."[12] Bunyan produced his catechism for "the church of Christ in and about Bedford" to put them "again in remembrance of first things" (the title appears, therefore, most inappropriate). He presents the work also "to all those unconverted, old and young, who have been at any time under my preaching, and yet remain in their sins." These people Bunyan entreated to receive the catechism as a token of his love for them and urged them to "read, ponder over, and receive this wholesome medicine prepared for them" (2:675-6).

In ***Saved by Grace*** (1676), Bunyan expounds once again his favorite topic—salvation by grace alone. In it he sets forth both the Reformed doctrine of predestination—the teaching that God chooses some for salvation or, as Bunyan puts it, the fact that God "appointed them their portion and measure of grace, and that before the world began"—and his urgent calling upon sinners to believe and repent. What holds these two apparently contradictory tenets together for Bunyan is God's grace—God's grace in choosing, and God's grace in inviting, the lost to come. In a particularly compelling passage, Bunyan writes:

> O sinner, wilt thou not open? Behold, God the Father and his Son, Jesus Christ, stand both at the door of thy heart, beseeching there for favour from thee, that thou wilt be reconciled to them, with promise, if thou wilt

comply, to forgive thee all thy sins. O grace! O amazing grace! To see a
prince entreat a beggar to receive an alms would be a strange sight; to
see a king entreat the traitor to accept of mercy would be a stranger sight
than that; but to see God entreat a sinner, to hear Christ say, "I stand
at the door and knock," with a heart full and a heaven full of grace to
bestow upon him that opens, this is such a sight as dazzles the eyes of
angels (1:350).

This grace of God that saves the elect and invites the sinner
is, according to Bunyan, the grace of the Trinity—Father, Son,
and Spirit. In writing of the grace of the Son, Bunyan approaches
ecstasy.

Thou Son of the Blessed, what grace was manifest in thy condescension!
Grace brought thee down from heaven, grace stripped thee of thy
glory, grace made thee poor and despicable, grace made thee bear such
burdens of sin, such burdens of sorrow, such burdens of God's curse as
are unspeakable. O Son of God! Grace was in all thy tears, grace came
bubbling out of thy side with thy blood, grace came forth with every
word of thy sweet mouth. Grace came out where the whip smote thee,
where the thorns pricked thee, where the nails and spear pierced thee. O
blessed Son of God! Here is grace indeed! Unsearchable riches of grace!
Unthought-of riches of grace! Grace to make angels wonder, grace to
make sinners happy, grace to astonish devils (1:346).

In addition to *The Life and Death of Mr. Badman* (1680), *The Holy
War* (1682), and *The Pilgrim's Progress, Part II* (1684), the busy pastor
and preacher wrote other books during the last decade of his life,
including the following.

Seasonable Counsel, or Advice to Sufferers (1684) appeared
during a time of renewed persecution of Dissenters. Bunyan states
that Christians should keep themselves "within the bounds of
uprightness and integrity towards both God and man" (2:692). But
we should not think "that our innocent lives will exempt us from
sufferings, or that troubles shall do us such harm. For verily it is for
our present and future good that our God doth send them upon us"
(2:693). Bunyan makes clear that in times of persecution the saints

can do no more than patiently suffer and pray for deliverance. In fact, Bunyan urges Christians to suffer actively for righteousness by willingly embracing affliction. He writes, "To overcome evil with good is a hard task. To rail it down, to cry it down, to pray kings, and parliaments, and men in authority to put it down, this is easier than to . . . endeavour to overcome it with good" (2:719).

A Book for Boys and Girls (1686) shows Bunyan's lifelong love for children. He writes "to the reader" that ministers have failed to communicate with children because they do not get down on their level. Bunyan is not ashamed to do that, he says, "although I think some may call me a baby, 'cause I with them play" (3:748).[13] His *Book for Boys and Girls* contains a series of little pictures familiar to children, to which he gives moral and religious meanings. For example:

> The water is the fish's element;
> Leave her but there, and she is well content.
> So's he, who in the path of life doth plod,
> Take all, says he, let me but have my God (3:750-1).

> This pretty bird, O! how she flies and sings,
> But could she do so if she had not wings?
> Her wings bespeak my faith, her songs my peace;
> When I believe and sing my doubtings cease (3:751).

> Poor silly mole, that thou should'st love to be
> Where thou nor sun, nor moon, nor stars can see.
> But O! how silly's he who doth not care
> So he gets earth, to have of heaven a share! (3:755)

This book shows Bunyan "at his best and most adventurous as a poet, and expresses more completely the many sides of his personality," such as his love for children, his gentleness, his country ways and keen observation of animals and plants. Richard Greaves comments: "Given the fact that it includes poetic versions of the Ten Commandments, the Lord's Prayer, and the [Apostles'] Creed as well as poems on the sacraments, Christ's love, the spouse of Christ, and human nature, *A Book for Boys and Girls* served almost as a catechism in verse."[14]

Bunyan's long years in prison gave him firsthand knowledge of the legal system, which he used to good effect in **The Work of Jesus Christ as an Advocate** (1688). In this treatise he powerfully depicts Christ as an advocate at court who will "stand up and plead" for his people before God the supreme judge and secure for them "a right to the heavenly kingdom" (1:152).

Also in 1688, the year of Bunyan's death, **The Water of Life** appeared. John Bunyan preached and published the good news of God's grace to the very end. As Greaves aptly puts it: "In 1688, when the minds of so many Englishmen were on the political failings of the monarch, Bunyan's message was of free grace for the vilest of sinners and divine intercession in the celestial court of the saints."[15]

Bunyan left more than a dozen treatises unpublished at his death. In 1689 **The Jerusalem Sinner Saved, or Good News for the Vilest of Men**, and **The Acceptable Sacrifice** appeared. In the former, "an evangelical work in the tradition of *Come & Welcome* and *The Water of Life*," Bunyan "explores God's offer of grace and mercy to the greatest offenders—the Jerusalem sinners—first. **The Acceptable Sacrifice** was an expanded sermon on Psalm 51:17—"The sacrifices of God are a broken spirit; a broken and contrite heart, O God, thou wilt not despise." In the preface of the book published in 1689 the London minister George Cokayn wrote that *The Acceptable Sacrifice* is "but a transcript out of [Bunyan's] own heart; for God . . . was still hewing and hammering him by his Word, and sometimes also by more than ordinary temptations and desertions" (1:686).

Other works published posthumously included **Paul's Departure and Crown, Christ a Complete Saviour**, and **The Saints' Privilege and Profit**, all published in 1692. In the first Bunyan exhorted the godly to stand firm in the Gospel. "The great and chief design of God in sending us into the world, especially in converting us and possessing our souls with gifts and graces," Bunyan wrote, is "that we might be to the glory of his grace." (1:729). No work of Bunyan's is more directed to his fellow ministers than this one. He exhorts them to "a diligent watchfulness" and "a diligent preaching [of] the word of the Lord" (1:722). *Christ a Complete Saviour* and *The Saints' Privilege and Profit* are companion volumes based on Hebrews 7:25

and 4:16. Both are books for the persecuted, written in 1686—a time of trouble for noncomformists. Bunyan develops the idea of the throne of grace as a place where saints can take refuge from the fury of their enemies. "As there is mercy to be obtained by us at the throne of grace, for the pardon [of all our sins]," Bunyan writes, "so there is also grace to be found that strengthens us more, to all good walking and living before him" (1:680).

Footnotes

[1] Charles Doe, "A Catalogue-Table of Mr. Bunyan's Books" (3:763). See also Greaves, *Glimpses of Glory*, appendix, 637-41, for a list of Bunyan's works, with date of composition and publication date.

[2] Ola Elizabeth Winslow, *John Bunyan* (New York: Macmillan, 1961), 164.

[3] Talon, *John Bunyan*, 119-20.

[4] Theological words and ideas in Bunyan's thought will be explained more fully in chapter 7.

[5] Greaves, *Glimpses of Glory*, 77.

[6] Lewis, "The Vision of John Bunyan," 152.

[7] Marcus L. Loane, *Makers of Puritan History* (Grand Rapids: Baker Book House, 1961), 158.

[8] Hill, *John Bunyan*, 266.

[9] Greaves, *Glimpses of Glory*, 160.

[10] One of the "dying sayings" attributed to Bunyan was: "When thou prayest, rather let thy heart be without words than thy words without a heart" (1:65).

[11] Greaves, *Glimpses of Glory*, 189.

[12] Greaves, *Glimpses of Glory*, 323.

[13] In *The Saints' Privilege and Profit* Bunyan tells how he enjoyed playing with children, virtually acting like a child himself. "I love to play the child with little children," Bunyan wrote, "and have learned something by so doing" (1:674).

[14] Greaves, *Glimpses of Glory*, 539, 542.

[15] Quoted by Mullett, *John Bunyan*, 284.

The Pilgrim's Progress ... *is, in my conviction, incomparably the best Summa Theologicae Evangelicae ever produced by a writer not miraculously inspired. . . . It is composed in the lowest style of English, without slang or false grammar. If you were to polish it, you would at once destroy the reality of the vision. . . . This wonderful book is one of the few books which may be read repeatedly, at different times, and each time with a new and different pleasure. I read it once as a theologian, and let me assure you that there is great theological acumen in the work; once with devotional feeling; and once as a poet. I could not have believed beforehand that Calvinism could be painted in such exquisitely delightful colours.*

Samuel Taylor Coleridge[1]

Bunyan's Theology

In the conclusion to Part I of **The Pilgrim's Progress** John Bunyan writes:"Take heed also, that thou be not extreme, in playing with the outside of my dream . . . . Do thou the substance of my matter see"(3:167). Literary critics have attempted to understand Bunyan's book through various analytical treatments—including socialist, psychoanalytical, feminist, poststructural, and reader-response. Galen Johnson comments, "These methods are each ultimately self-limiting when they do not sufficiently consider Bunyan's theology as both the inspiration and the aspiration of his works. . . . Even as two characters in **The Pilgrim's Progress** get lost around the Hill Difficulty because they do not enter the Way through the Wicket-gate, one wonders if Bunyan's readers too might lose their direction in his works if they never enter through the door of his theology."[2]

Some have tried to present Bunyan as a champion of individual rights and an encourager of the spiritual quest but have ignored his specific theology. "Thus . . . Bunyan has stood for that in our national tradition which has impelled individuals to uphold what they believe to be right, regardless of consequences to themselves. He has also . . . helped countless readers, latterly all over the world, in that spiritual pilgrimage which, whether or not it is conscious and articulate, we must all make."[3] Yet Bunyan's writings, like Bunyan's life, have one goal—to present as clearly as possible the Christian Gospel. When he could, Bunyan preached it; when he could not preach it, he wrote it. Like the Apostle Paul, he could say, "Woe to me if I do not preach the Gospel!" (1 Corinthians 9:16)

Unlike most other seventeenth-century writers of theological works, Bunyan did not study theology at Oxford or Cambridge. In fact, "Bunyan is the first major English writer who was neither London-based nor university-educated."[4] John Burton of Bedford wrote in his preface to John Bunyan's first book, *Gospel Truths Opened* (published in 1656 when Bunyan was twenty-eight): "This man is not chosen out of an earthly but out of the heavenly university, the Church of Christ. . . . He hath, through grace, taken these three heavenly degrees, to wit, union with Christ, the anointing of the Spirit, and experiences of the temptations of Satan, which do more fit a man for that mighty work of preaching the Gospel than all university learning and degrees that can be had" (2:141). Bunyan was, however, well informed about theology, law, and current events; he was what we would call "a self-educated man."

John Bunyan always maintained that he drew his theology directly from the Bible. In his writings he carefully built up and supported his arguments on the basis of biblical texts. He quoted the older Geneva Bible as well as the Authorized (King James) Version of 1611. Late in life Bunyan writes: "My Bible and concordance are my only library in my writings" (3:464). He was in fact an avid learner from books.[5] In *Grace Abounding* he tells about three books of special significance to him: Luther's commentary on Galatians and books by Calvinists Arthur Dent and Lewis Bayly. Bunyan, however, "for reasons of piety and practicality," stressed his devotion to the Bible. He wanted to appeal to those who would follow the Bible's teachings rather than the words of human authors.[6]

Richard Greaves describes the three strands of Bunyan's theology: "His foundation principles were basically Lutheran, but much of his theology was in full accord with the orthodox Calvinism of the period. His doctrine of the church and sacraments was neither Calvinist nor Lutheran but a heritage from the Independent-Baptist tradition."[7] Another word can be used to describe Bunyan and that is "Puritan." Bunyan had little use for any of these labels. He held to a strict Protestant (and Calvinistic) doctrinal orthodoxy, but he came to dislike greatly a party spirit and an overemphasis on nonessentials.

"I never cared to meddle with things that were controverted and in dispute amongst the saints," he writes, "especially things of the lowest nature" (1:43).

LUTHERAN

After his discovery of Martin Luther's commentary on Galatians, Bunyan saw Luther as a supreme expositor of Scripture and a safe spiritual guide. He felt that apart from the Bible, Luther's book was "most fit for a wounded conscience" like Bunyan's own (1:22). John Bunyan was especially helped and influenced by Luther's teaching that the doctrine of grace can by no means stand with the doctrine of the law. The law, or the covenant of works, condemns because fallen man cannot keep it. Bunyan writes: "Though thou shouldst fulfil this covenant, or law, even all of it, for a long time, ten, twenty, forty, fifty, or threescore years, yet if thou do chance to slip and break one of them but once before thou die, thou art also gone and lost by that covenant" (1:501). The law condemns, but grace saves the sinner. This became the thesis of Bunyan's main theological book, *The Doctrine of the Law and Grace Unfolded*, and the underlying theme of all his works. "Bunyan was too much a Calvinist to espouse ignorance of the law," according to Richard Greaves, "but he firmly believed that salvation was solely a matter of grace, not law."[8]

For Bunyan, as for Luther, the Christian is freed from the law. "Whenever thou who believest in Jesus dost hear the law in its thundering and lightning fits, as if it would burn up heaven and earth," Bunyan advised Christians, "then say thou, I am freed from this law; these thunderings have nothing to do with my soul. . . . When this law with its thundering threatenings doth attempt to lay hold on thy conscience, shut it out with a promise of grace; cry, the inn is [taken] up already, the Lord Jesus is here entertained, and here is no room for the law" (2:388). Bunyan's frequent celebration of the Christian's freedom from the law caused some to accuse him of antinomianism, that is, a rejection of the idea that the Christian's life need be governed by the moral law. Bunyan's fellow Puritan Richard Baxter stated that Bunyan's *Doctrine of the Law and Grace Unfolded* "ignorantly subverted the Gospel of Christ."[9]

John Bunyan, however, stressed, especially in his later works, that the law is for the Christian a guide that is "holy, just, and good." We should thank God for it and obey it, remembering that he who gives it to us is "merciful, gracious, long-suffering, and abundant in goodness and truth" (2:388).

PURITAN

As a Puritan, Bunyan was committed to the regulative principle (sometimes called the Puritan principle): in worship and doctrine we cannot go beyond what is written in the Bible. Bunyan told his accusers when he was imprisoned that the use of the Book of Common Prayer "was not commanded in the Word of God, and therefore I could not use it" (1:55). Charles Doe once asked Bunyan his opinion about a certain point and presented some arguments in favor of it. Bunyan answered, Doe wrote, "that where the Scripture is silent we ought to forbear our opinions; and so he forbore to affirm either for or against, the Scripture being altogether silent in this point" (3:767).

Like most of the Puritans, Bunyan appreciated the good things of life as gifts of God.[10] His pilgrims ate special delicacies and drank wines and spirits (no doubt, in moderation). At the feasts that Emmanuel gave for Mansoul there were "brave entertainment," wines, and a succession of exotic dishes. Bunyan gave up bell ringing (whether because he thought it was sinful in itself or only sinful on the Sabbath is not clear). But his delight in ringing bells appears in both *The Pilgrim's Progress* and *The Holy War*. He also gave up dancing, but Christian and Hopeful danced when they escaped from Giant Despair's prison. There is more celebratory dancing in Part II of *The Pilgrim's Progress*, as well as in *The Holy War*.[11]

CALVINIST

Most English Puritans were Calvinists, and Bunyan was no exception. Richard Greaves describes Bunyan's *Confession of My Faith* (1672) as "a relatively straightforward articulation of Calvinist principles."[12] Someone has called *The Pilgrim's Progress* "the Westminster Confession of Faith with people in it."[13] Indeed there are many points of correspondence between the then—recently completed Puritan confession (1646) and Bunyan's works.

Grace

As Richard Greaves states it, Bunyan's theology was, at its core, "a living, vibrant awareness of divine grace."[14]

Like the Apostle Paul and St. Augustine, Bunyan dramatically experienced God's grace in his own life. One who was utterly unworthy was given the gift of grace that was utterly free. Bunyan never got over it. In his treatise *Saved by Grace* Bunyan speaks of "grace to make angels wonder, grace to make sinners happy, grace to astonish devils" (1:346). Shortly before his death Bunyan wrote, "There is nothing in heaven or earth that can so awe the heart as the grace of God" (3:546). Bunyan found the message of grace throughout the Bible and experienced it dramatically in his own life. And so it filled his books—as it filled his heart and mind.

In *The Pilgrim's Progress*, after Christiana and Mercy are delivered from the two "ill-favoured ones," Mercy sums up what happened (and Bunyan's view of grace) with these words: "Our Lord has taken occasion . . . to make manifest the riches of his grace; for he, as we see, has followed us with unasked kindness, and has delivered us from their hands that were stronger than we, of his mere good pleasure" (3:183).

The Covenant of Grace[15]

Bunyan defined a covenant as a contract with reciprocal conditions. The covenant of works as a means of attaining eternal life was lost to all their descendants by the sin of Adam and Eve. Salvation now can come only through the covenant of grace. The covenant of grace was established in eternity between the Father and the Son,[16] in Bunyan's view, not between God and believers. "This covenant was not made with God and the creature," wrote Bunyan, "not with another poor Adam"; but this covenant was made "with the Second Person, with the Eternal Word of God" (1:522). In fact, "the covenant itself was Christ, as given of God unto us, with all his good conditions, merit and worth" (2:491). All the conditions of the covenant, therefore, are already fulfilled for us by Jesus Christ. "Though there be a condition commanded in the gospel," Bunyan explained, "yet he that commands the condition doth not leave his children to their own natural abilities, that in their own strength they should fulfil them, as the law doth; but the same God that doth command that the condition be fulfilled, even he doth help his children by his Holy Spirit to fulfil the same condition" (1:519).

Predestination

In his *Confession of My Faith* Bunyan described predestination (or election) as "free and permanent, being founded in grace, and the unchangeable will of God." "This decree, choice or election," Bunyan affirmed, "was before the foundation of the world" (2:598). Bunyan's view of predestination is infralapsarian,[17] for God knew of the fall, "having all things present to, and in his wisdom, (before) he made his choice" of whom to save and whom not (2:598).

It is by grace that election "layeth hold of men," Bunyan states (1:355). "The Father by his grace hath bound up them that shall go to heaven in an eternal decree of election," and apart from this election of grace there is no salvation (1:343-4). Grace is even personalized by Bunyan: in *The Saints' Privilege and Profit* he wrote, "'Tis Grace that chooses" (1:653).

For Bunyan the doctrine of election defends and sets forth both the sovereignty of God and the freeness of grace. Therefore, the rejection of the doctrine of election is a serious matter. It is tantamount to rejecting the omniscience, omnipotence, and will of God and to making salvation depend upon works rather than upon grace.

Because God is God, he does what he chooses. Not only does he choose some for eternal life, but for his own holy purpose he blinds the eyes and hardens the hearts of reprobates so that they cannot repent. (See *Mr. Badman* and the end of Part I of *Pilgrim's Progress*.) At the same time, Bunyan insists that the responsibility for eternal damnation is entirely man's. The reprobate is damned because of his sin. Reprobation (God's decision to foreordain some to everlasting death) as distinct from damnation, however, is caused not by sin but by the fact that "only so many are brought home to God as Grace is pleased to bring home to him" (1:356). "Marks" of reprobation include "dallying" with God (1:639) and procrastination (for it is "the hard hap of the reprobate to do all things too late" [3:567]), but the one infallible mark is the sin of final impenitence.

Predestination for Bunyan, as for Calvin, is not a dark and mysterious teaching that causes melancholic introspection over one's salvation, but is itself an integral part of the good news by which men and women are saved. It is the source of comfort in the knowledge that eternal life is from and for all eternity through Christ alone. This doctrine humbles the Christian and gives glory to God in maintaining the sovereignty of God's will over any attempt by sinners to achieve salvation for themselves. Bunyan's predestination is simply synonymous with salvation by grace alone. For Bunyan, to believe in grace, to really believe in grace, is to believe in God's predestination of his chosen ones to eternal salvation.

John Bunyan emphasized both God's election and the necessity for sinners to turn to God. In *The Water of Life*, Bunyan writes that men and women, "though elect, though purchased by the blood of Christ, are dead, and must be dead, until the Spirit of life from God and his throne shall enter into them; until they shall drink it in by vehement thirst, as the parched ground drinks in the rain" (3:552). Although true faith can only come as a divine gift, John Bunyan the pastor always calls on the unconverted to "fly in all haste to Jesus Christ," being persuaded that he "is willing, yea, heartily willing, to present thee before the presence of the glory of God and among the innumerable company of angels with exceeding joy" (1:495).

Bunyan's insistence on both predestination and evangelism puzzles some commentators. Richard Greaves affirms Bunyan's doctrine of predestination but refers to his "pastoral Arminianism" in freely offering the Gospel to sinners and inviting, even urging, them to come to Christ. A better description of Bunyan's practice would be "pastoral Calvinism," because Bunyan, like John Calvin and most Calvinists, affirmed both God's election and the free offer of the Gospel. Michael Davies writes that one should read Bunyan's narratives "through a doctrine of grace which is far from harsh and inhumane, and through a theology which aims to comfort and give hope to anyone, like Christian [in *The Pilgrim's Progress*], burdened by guilt over sin."[18]

Atonement

The *satisfaction* or *Anselmic* view of the atonement is clearly expressed in Bunyan's writings.[19] God could not extend his grace to sinners in a way contrary to his justice. So there had to be a redeemer who was able to satisfy divine justice. But only God himself could do that. At the same time, man had to suffer the consequences of his sin. Therefore, the redeemer had to be both God and man. Christ came as man to take the place of sinful people and provide satisfaction to God for their sins against his law. Sufficient satisfaction demanded that Christ not only suffer the death required of sinners (sometimes called his passive obedience), but also perfectly fulfill the law in his earthly life (his active obedience). Bunyan sums it up: "The righteousness and redemption by which we that believe stand just before God, as saved from the curse of the law, is the righteousness and redemption that consists in the personal acts and performances of . . . this God-man, the Lord's Christ: it consisteth, I say, in his personal fulfilling the law for us to the utmost requirement of the justice of God" (2:595).

Bunyan did not confine his thinking on the atonement to the satisfaction view alone; he also embraced the idea that Christ's atonement was victory over the devil and the powers of darkness (sometimes called the *Christus victor* view). Bunyan wrote: "And forasmuch as, in man's redemption, the undertaker must have respect, not only to the paying of a price but also to the getting of a victory; for there is not only justice to satisfy, but death, devil, hell, and the grave to conquer; therefore hath [Christ] also by himself gotten the victory over these" (1:402).

It was God's grace that "moved him to give Christ a ransom for sinners," Bunyan writes (1:520). As the Father's sending was of grace, so Christ's coming was of grace. Bunyan writes of Christ: "Grace brought thee down from heaven, grace stripped thee of thy glory, grace made thee poor and despicable, grace made thee bear such burdens of sin, such burdens of sorrow, such burdens of God's curse as are unspeakable . . . . Grace was in all thy tears, grace came bubbling out of thy side with thy blood" (1:346).

Most of Bunyan's statements indicate that he believed in a limited or particular atonement, the view that Christ's atoning death was only for the elect, as opposed to general atonement, which taught that Christ died for all; but he did not want to battle over it. He writes: Christ "as a propitiation" is not for our sins only, but also "for the sins of the whole world, to be sure, for the elect throughout the world; and they that will extend it further, let them" (1:170).

Free Will

Bunyan held that man has a free will and that fallen people may do some "good" things. But they can do nothing that is meritorious in the sight of God. They cannot earn their salvation by good works, and they cannot in themselves even want to come to God for salvation. Because of their sinful natures they have to be made willing by divine grace to come to God. The reprobate, Bunyan states, cannot object that divine grace did not work in such manner in their wills, for "God did not determine to bring them to heaven against their hearts and wills, and the love that they had to their sins" (2:123).

In *The Pilgrim's Progress*, Christian is revealed as one of the elect the moment Good-will (Grace) pulls him through the wicket gate; those who enter by other routes are not elect and do not persevere to the end of the journey (3:96-7). However, Bunyan's Christian makes free choices all the time. The journey itself is a matter of choice. And Christian has to do a great deal of knocking at both the wicket gate and the Interpreter's House before either is opened to him.

Can a person refuse God's grace? According to Bunyan, the gift of grace cannot be refused, no more than Lazarus could have refused to come out of the grave at the word of Jesus. That word to Lazarus and God's calling of the sinner to salvation, Bunyan believed, is "a word attended with an arm that [is] omnipotent" (2:599). God's Grace, for Bunyan, is efficacious. It cannot be defeated. It will accomplish God's purpose. It will save all the elect.

Faith

Faith may be understood as "a gift of God" or "an act of ours," Bunyan says. Faith is "not the first nor the second cause of our salvation, but the third, and that but instrumentally—that is, it only layeth hold of and applieth to us that which saveth us, which is the love of God, through the merits of Christ, which are the two main causes of our salvation, without which all other things are nothing, whether it be faith, hope, love or whatever can be done by us" (1:519). There is the necessity of faith but, as we have already seen, it is God's grace that enables the sinner to believe. The elect are not saved because they believe; they believe because they are saved.

Bunyan regarded faith as the instrumental cause of justification; the justification of the elect follows faith. Later he argued that justification precedes faith: "Righteousness by imputation must be first, because . . . faith, which is a part, yea, a great part, of that which is called a principle of grace in the soul, will have nothing to fix itself upon, nor a motive to work by. . . . Faith is like the dove, that found no rest anywhere in all the world until it returned to Noah in the ark" (2:250). Faith now became, for Bunyan, the sign of justification rather than an instrument in God's hands to convey it. In *The Pharisee and the Publican*, from which the above quotation is taken, Bunyan endeavors to show that the Pharisee's human efforts to earn God's acceptance by his "faith" and "good deeds" are futile because they are not the activities of a justified man. Bunyan's earlier view —that faith is the instrumental cause of justification —is more scriptural ("Therefore being justified by faith, we have peace with God through our Lord Jesus Christ" [Romans 5:1]) and more in keeping with standard Christian theology.

Repentance

Repentance, for Bunyan, is "a turning of the heart to God in Christ: a turning of it from sin, the devil, and darkness; to the goodness, grace, and holiness that is in him" (2:600). Repentance, like faith, is dependent on divine grace. It is bestowed on the sinner by God himself, for without grace no one can truly repent, and with God's grace the sinner cannot fail to repent. "For when a man hath heaven and hell before his eyes (as he will have if he be under the power of effectual calling)[20] or when a man hath a revelation of the mercy and justice of God, with a heart-drawing invitation to lay hold on the tender forgiveness of sins; and being made also to behold the goodly beauty of holiness; it must needs be, that repentance appears" (2:600).

Repentance for Bunyan is not a once-for-all act but a continuing, lifelong attitude. He compares the stairs leading to the chambers of Solomon's temple to a "type of a two-fold repentance": "that by which we turn from nature to grace, and that by which we turn from the imperfections which attend a state of grace to glory. Hence true repentance, or the right going up these turning stairs, is called repentance to salvation; for true repentance stoppeth not at the reception of grace; for that is but a going up these stairs to the middle chambers" (3:482).

Justification

The justification of the sinner is accomplished solely by the imputation of Christ's righteousness, that is, God's declaring the sinner righteous on the basis of the righteousness of Christ. We do not contribute to our justification in any way. For Bunyan, as for Luther and Calvin, justification is by faith *alone*, which means that it is simply received. Bunyan rebukes those who say "I will labor to do what I can, and what I cannot do Christ will do for me." This is wrong, he says, "for this is to make Christ but a piece of a Saviour."[21]

Free Offer of the Gospel

With all his emphasis on election, Bunyan does not minimize the importance of the free offer of the Gospel or the necessity for human action. Even though Christian in *The Pilgrim's Progress* could not open the wicket gate for himself, he knocked at the gate "more than once or twice" and said:

> *May I now enter here? Will he within*
> *Open to sorry me, though I have been*
> *An undeserving rebel? Then shall I*
> *Not fail to sing his lasting praise on high (3:96).*

In all of his sixty books Bunyan offers Christ to sinners, pleads with them to repent, answers their objections, and motivates them by threats of judgment and promises of eternal joy. He urges them to read the Bible, especially the Mosaic law, to discover their need and spiritual uncleanness and then to come to Christ for cleansing. As

Greaves expresses it in a memorable metaphor, "The grace of God is like a flowing river, and the would-be saint must do his utmost to place himself in the river's path."[22]

Sanctification

Bunyan was just as fervent in his emphasis on sanctification as he was in preaching justification. He refers to the moral law as "a rule or directory" (or sometimes as a "new law") for those in the covenant of grace. In contrast to the Antinomians (those who believe that the law has no place in a Christian's life) he grants to the law—particularly to the "matter" of it—a place in the lives of believers. The Ten Commandments are a guide for the saints, a rule for the Christian life. But they are only a guide, not a savior or a judge.

Not only is the Christian justified by grace, but there is a sense in which he or she also is sanctified by grace. Bunyan wrote, "As water is that element in which the fish liveth; so grace is that which is the life of the saint . . . . Rivers yield continually fresh and new water. . . . And thus it is with the River of God, which is full of water; it yieldeth continually fresh supplies, fresh and new supplies of grace to those that have business in these waters." (3:544). It is by the continual gift of God's grace that believers are enabled to make progress on their way to the Celestial City.

We find many illustrations of sanctifying grace in the life of Christian in *The Pilgrim's Progress*. In Part I, when Christian comes to Interpreter's House he is shown a fireplace in which a fire is burning higher and hotter, even though a certain one (the devil) is pouring in water to quench it. Christian asks what this means. Interpreter takes him behind the wall and he sees "a man with a vessel of oil in his hand, of the which he [does] also continually cast, but secretly, into the fire." Interpreter explains, "This is Christ, who continually, with the oil of his grace, maintains the work already begun in the heart: by the means of which, notwithstanding what the devil can do, the souls of his people prove gracious still" (3:100). In Part II, before they leave Interpreter's House, Christiana, her sons, and Mercy bathe in the garden to be cleansed "from the soil which they have gathered by traveling." They come out of that "bath of sanctification" (Bunyan's marginal note) "not only sweet and clean, but also much enlivened and strengthened in their joints." Interpreter then sets his seal between their eyes that "they might be known in the places whither they [are] yet to go." The seal "greatly [adds] to their beauty, for it [is] an ornament to their faces. It also [adds] to their gravity and [makes] their countenance more like [that] of angels." "Fine linen white and clean" is brought and the women dress themselves in it. When they are "thus adorned, they seem to be a terror one to the other; for that they [cannot] see that glory each one on herself, which they [can] see in each other" (3:189-90). Thus Bunyan describes the work of God's grace in sanctification and the wonder of it in the life of the Christian.

Perseverance

The perseverance of the believer is "absolutely necessary to the complete saving of the soul," Bunyan maintains. "He that goeth to sea with a purpose to arrive at Spain," he writes, "cannot arrive there if he be drowned by the way; wherefore perseverance is absolutely necessary to the saving of the soul, and therefore it is included in the complete saving of us" (1:339). The perseverance of the saints is assured because of the unchangeable purpose of God. After all, as Bunyan points out, the door of the ark was shut by God, not Noah, and "if God shuts in or out, who can alter it?" (2:472) "The safe state of the saints," Bunyan wrote, "as touching their perseverance," guarantees that "they shall stand though hell rages, though the devil roareth, and all the world endeavoureth the ruin of the saints of God" (1:565).

Those who are "effectually in Christ," Bunyan asserts, can never lose him—nor can they be lost by him. There are, of course, many stumblings and fallings in the Christian life, but "so many times as the soul backslides, so many times God brings him again" (1:353). Bunyan writes: "The law of grace has provided that the children shall not for their sin lose their inheritance in heaven forever." Nothing can make Christ "let go his hold that he hath of you of heaven" (1:187). Again and again Bunyan celebrates this truth. "O it is a blessed thing for God to be our God and our guide even unto death, and then for his angels to conduct us safely to glory; this is saving indeed" (1:341).

Because of the divine nature of the parties to the covenant, nothing could be more certain than the salvation of the elect. Jesus Christ is "bound as a surety and [stands] engaged upon oath to see that all the conditions of the covenant . . . should . . . be accomplished by him" (1:525). Nevertheless Bunyan urges the Christian to press forward strenuously. "It is an easy matter for a man to run hard for a spurt, for a furlong, for a mile or two: O but to hold out for a hundred, for a thousand, for ten thousand miles" (3:387).

Assurance

How can a person know that she or he is elect and so have assurance of salvation? This was the great struggle that Bunyan himself experienced, which he described with agonizing thoroughness in *Grace Abounding*. Bunyan came to realize, however, that the person sincerely seeking Christ already has some evidence of his election. For "coming to Christ is by the gift, promise, and drawing of the Father" (1:275). "Thou shalt not know thy election," Bunyan writes, "by thy giving credit to [God's] promises, and records which he hath given of Jesus Christ's blood and righteousness, together with the rest of his merits—that is, before thou canst know whether thou art elected, thou must believe in Jesus Christ" (1:571). God has two further ways "to show to his children their election": by "testimony of the Spirit, and "by consequence"—that is, by the evidence of the work of the Holy Spirit in their lives.

There is no way for the covenant of grace to be broken, Bunyan maintains. The reason is simple. Fulfillment of the conditions of the covenant have been undertaken by the Son for the elect. Nothing people can do can alter what the Son has already accomplished.

Eschatology[23]

Bunyan's eschatological interests were pronounced but moderate. *Of Antichrist and his Ruin* shows that the Bunyan of the late 1680s, "far from being a political or social revolutionary," was "essentially a conservative, orthodox Christian, and his millenarianism a progressive, hopeful, peaceable view of human history."[24] Bunyan defended a future millennium (a period of a thousand years of blessing and prosperity for the church) during which doctrine and worship will be restored to their apostolic purity. Apart from hoping and believing that the millennium would soon come, Bunyan eschewed any attempt to predict dates. At some point during the millennium, he believed, Antichrist (whom Bunyan identified with the papacy) would fall. Then Jesus will return, in his physical body, to meet his elect—those who had died physically being resurrected from their graves. Bunyan was a postmillennialist; he believed that Christ will return following the thousand-year millennium. The final judgment will then follow.

BAPTIST

In *The Heavenly Footman* Bunyan states that "there is a great running [of Christians] to and fro" but that much of this activity is misdirected. One runs after "the Baptism, and another after the Independency. Here is one for free-will, and another for Presbytery." Bunyan counsels people "to mistrust thy own strength, and throw it away" and get "down on thy knees in prayer to the Lord for the spirit of truth; search his word for direction" and "keep company with the soundest Christians, that have most experience of Christ" (3:383). He warns people against Quakers, Ranters, and Freewillers, and even "too much company with some Anabaptists," though, he adds, "I go under that name myself" (3:383).

Although Bunyan was uneasy with the label "Baptist" (because of his concern for evangelical unity and, no doubt in part, because of his unhappiness about the rigidity of the Baptists concerning baptism), he is rightly described in his seventeenth-century context as a Baptist, or an Independent, because of his views of church polity. When the Bedford church took out its license in 1672, it was as a "Congregational" rather than as a "Baptist" church. Bunyan could be described as an "open-membership, open-communion" Baptist. He believed that true churches should include everyone who shared orthodox Christian teaching, lived as a visible saint, and accepted all like-minded people in the bonds of Christian fellowship. Richard Greaves comments that "this presumably covered much of the spectrum of mainline Protestant Nonconformity."[25]

Church

Like many other Puritans, Bunyan viewed the church as a voluntary company of "visible saints." The invisible universal church is made up of God's elect; the visible particular congregation is made up of professing Christians who are members of a local church. God saves sinners through preaching and other means and then places them in the church for growth. They are "planted in the church of God," Bunyan writes, "as plants before prepared" (2:424).

Church members are required to declare their willingness to subject themselves to the laws and government of Christ in his church. Church discipline is necessary and sometimes leads to excommunication so as to protect the holiness of the church. Bunyan writes:

> Let the churches love their pastors, hear their pastors, be ruled by their pastors, and suffer themselves to be watched over, and to be exhorted, counseled, and, if need be, reproved and rebuked by their pastors. And let the ministers not sleep but be watchful, and look to the ordinances, to the souls of the saints, and the gates of the churches (3:478).

As a Baptist or Independent, Bunyan believed that the congregation of believers has the right to call its own minister. The work of the minister is to exalt Christ by his preaching and example and to make sinners fit for the house of God. The minister is preeminently a servant, a servant of Christ and of his congregation. Bunyan expresses it beautifully: "For ministers, as to their gifts and office, are called stars of God, and are said to be in the hand of Christ" (3:481).

More and more, Bunyan urged that the church unite on essential teachings and allow liberty on nonessentials. In one of his last works, *A Discourse of the Building, Nature, Excellency and Government of the House of God* (1688), he returns again to the theme that the broad fellowship of the church must not be disrupted for the sake of private opinions: "For those that have private opinions too we must make room, or shall the church undo" (2:589). George Whitefield wrote that his "catholic spirit" particularly endeared Bunyan to him. "And I am persuaded," Whitefield went on to say, "that if, like him, we were more deeply and experimentally baptized into the benign and gracious influences of the blessed Spirit, we should be less baptized into the waters of strife about circumstantials and nonessentials."[26]

In *A Holy Life the Beauty of Christianity* (1684) Bunyan complained that "men are wedded to their own opinions, beyond what the law of grace and love will admit." "Here is a Presbyter, here is an Independent, and a Baptist, so joined each man to his own opinion, that they cannot have that communion one with another, as by the testament of the Lord Jesus they are commanded, and enjoined." Bunyan urges Christians to be "sensible to the imperfections that cleave to thy best performances, be clothed with humility, and prefer thy brother before thyself; and know that Christianity lieth not in small matters" (2:538).

John Bunyan's vision of unifying the visible saints, a goal shared in some form by other Dissenters in the late seventeenth century, came to naught, blocked by the harsh opposition of traditional Baptists, the fierceness of whose attack he would find especially painful.

Sacraments

Protestants had reduced the number of sacraments from seven to two—baptism and the Lord's Supper. Bunyan minimized the significance even of the two "ordinances" (as Bunyan and many Puritans preferred to call them). They are "mysteries divine" that "by God's appointment" bring benefit to the believer. They are "helps to our faith." But they are not saving ordinances. Bunyan warned people to rely not on them but on faith. "It is possible to commit idolatry," he wrote, "even with God's own appointments" (2:604). Bunyan feared that many people depended upon outward things, even good things such as baptism and the Lord's Supper, for their salvation. In this way the devil pulled people under the covenant of works.

Although baptism and the Lord's supper are but "shadowish, or figurative, ordinances," they are, Bunyan insisted, "of excellent use to the church in this world; they being to us representations of the death and resurrection of Christ, and are, as God shall make them, helps to our faith therein" (2:604).

Bunyan did not give the Lord's Supper the status that it had in the Church of England, but he affirmed his "reverent esteem" for it

(2:604). In the first part of *The Pilgrim's Progress* he beautifully depicts the Lord's Supper in Christian's meal at the Palace Beautiful, taken at the Lord of the Hill's table, "an obvious allusion to the Lord's table, in the separatist tradition."[27] Two of Bunyan's colleagues in the ministry stated that he was "a son of thunder" when preaching to "secure and dead sinners," but when administering the Lord's Supper he wept.[28]

Bunyan was baptized (or re-baptized as an adult) when he was admitted to the Bedford church in 1655; but as early as *The Doctrine of Law and Grace Unfolded* (1659), he declared that it was the spirit of blasphemy to say that there was no ground for assurance of salvation, or for church membership, unless one was baptized. The decision of the founding members of the Bedford congregation not to require baptism for membership was accepted—and eloquently defended—by Bunyan. In 1673 he set forth his views about baptism in *Differences in Judgment about Water Baptism, No Bar to Communion*. He wanted the church open to all true believers, whether or not they were baptized as adults or even baptized at all. He believed that love must prevail over differing opinions on this issue. Baptism is an "outward thing," he argued (2:626). It is a duty of the believer to be baptized, but even so, he held, it is neither an essential part of the Gospel nor a necessary requirement for church membership.

For Bunyan, the heart of baptism is baptism by the Spirit. This, unlike the external practice, is essential. Baptism by water is not an infallible sign of baptism by the Spirit. It cannot, therefore, be insisted on as an initiating ordinance into Christian fellowship. It is important, however, for its essential prerequisite is visible sainthood. Membership in Bunyan's church at Bedford mandated only "faith in Christ and holiness of life"; but water baptism encouraged (2:605-6). Bunyan believed that those who relied solely on Spirit baptism and rejected water baptism altogether were deficient in light, but should not be excluded from the church.

Bunyan held to "believer's baptism." Only those who have received Christ and demonstrate it by their lives are to receive baptism. Infants, therefore, are not proper subjects for baptism. Bunyan, however, was willing to receive those who held to infant baptism. "[We are] commanded," he wrote, "to bear with the infirmities of

each other." He challenged his stricter Baptist brethren: "If you be
without infirmity, do you first throw a stone at them. They keep their
faith in that to themselves, and trouble not their brethren therewith.
We believe that God hath received them; they do not want to us a
proof of their sonship with God; neither hath he made water a wall
of division between us, and therefore we do receive them" (2:631).
However, Bunyan considered that "when persons can be baptized to
their edification, they have the liberty" (2:630). It is puzzling that
John Bunyan had his own children baptized as infants. It could be
that he considered that baptism in the church of England amounted
"to little more than the registration of a birth."[29]

Bunyan wrote *A Confession of My Faith*, and *A Reason of My Practice
in Worship* (1672) to explain "with whom I dare not hold communion"
and "with whom I dare" (2:602). He followed this with *Differences in
Judgment about Water Baptism, No Bar to Communion* (1673). *Peaceable
Principles* (1674) repeated John Bunyan's convictions—the primacy
of love over baptism, and the absence of any biblical teaching
excluding visible saints from church membership if they lacked
believer's (or any) baptism. For a time Bunyan had a considerable
following in his open view of baptism, but in the end both Baptists
and Congregationalists repudiated his views.

Footnotes

[1] Samuel Taylor Coleridge, *Coleridge on the Seventeenth Century*, ed. Roberta
Florence Brinkley (Durham, North Carolina: Duke University Press, 1955),
475-6.

[2] Johnson, "Reading John Bunyan," 447, 448, 460.

[3] Joyce Godber, *John Bunyan of Bedfordshire*, 9.

[4] Hill, *John Bunyan*, 346. Hill adds, "In his later years, after *The Pilgrim's Progress*,
he visited London frequently as a preacher in demand. But Bedford remained
his home; the army had been his school, and prison his university."

[5] Richard Greaves discusses Bunyan's reading in *Glimpses of Glory*, 603-606.
Greaves states: "Although much of what Bunyan read cannot be identified
with certainty, he was clearly an ardent reader as well as a prolific author"
(606).

[6] Greaves, "Introduction," to Bunyan's *The Doctrine of the Law and Grace Unfolded*
and *I will Pray with the Spirit*, xvii.

Grace Abounding

[7] Richard L. Greaves, *John Bunyan* (Grand Rapids: Wm. B. Eerdmans Publishing Co., 1969), 159.

[8] Greaves, *Glimpses of Glory*, 108.

[9] Greaves, *Glimpses of Glory*, 109. Baxter later wrote that Bunyan's "last preachings" gave him hope that "he repented of his errors." Greaves, *Glimpses of Glory*, 286.

[10] For a balanced account of Puritan convictions and practices, see Leland Ryken, *Worldly Saints: The Puritans As They Really Were* (Grand Rapids: Zondervan Publishing House, 1986).

[11] See examples in *The Pilgrim's Progress* (3:111; 188-9; 197; 204; 219) and *The Holy War* (3:324; 308).

[12] Greaves, *Glimpses of Glory*, 272.

[13] The Westminster Confession of Faith was one of the documents produced by the Westminster Assembly, a gathering of ministers and others appointed by the Puritan Long Parliament and charged with the task of making proposals for the reform of the Church of England to make it "more agreeable to the Word of God."

[14] Greaves, *John Bunyan*, 11.

[15] Hill states that "the most likely single influence" of Puritan covenant theology in Bunyan's thought, "in his later life at least," was his friend John Owen. Hill, *John Bunyan*, 157.

[16] Bunyan declares the unity of justice and love in God by asserting that God, as father, insists on satisfaction for sin and at the same time sacrifices himself, as son, to provide that satisfaction.

[17] *Infralapsarianism* holds that the decree to permit the fall logically preceded that of election. This view is in contrast to that of *supralapsarianism*, which teaches that the decree of election logically preceded the decree to create and to permit the fall.

[18] Michael Davies, *Grace Reading: Theology and Narrative in the Works of John Bunyan* (Oxford: Oxford University Press, 2002), 14.

[19] Anselm (1033-1109), a medieval monk, philosopher, and theologian who became the Archbishop of Canterbury, set forth the classic exposition of the *satisfaction* view of the atonement: the death of Christ was a sacrifice to God in payment of the penalty for the wrong we have done against him.

[20] Effectual calling is God's special working upon the elect so that they respond in faith.

[21] See Hill, *John Bunyan*, 176.

[22] Greaves, "Introduction" to Bunyan's *The Doctrine of the Law and Grace Unfolded* and *I will Pray with the Spirit*, xxxii.

[23] Eschatology is the study of last things.

[24] Aileen M. Ross, "Paradise Regained: The Development of John Bunyan's Millenarianism," in Van Os and Schutte (eds), *Bunyan in England And Abroad*, 73.

[25] Greaves, *Glimpses of Glory*, 580.

[26] George Whitefield, "Recommendatory Preface," *The Works of John Bunyan*, iv.

[27] Greaves, *Glimpses of Glory*, 263.

[28] Greaves, *Glimpses of Glory*, 601.

[29] Mullett, *John Bunyan in Context*, 101. Sons Thomas and Joseph eventually joined the Church of England. Bunyan's oldest son, John, joined the Bedford church but not until 1693.

Bunyan's only weapons were preaching—for which he was sent to jail—and then writing. . . . The tinker's books lasted longer than anyone else's preaching: longer in fact than the British Empire.

Christopher Hill[1]

Preacher, allegorist, Christian humanist, radical—Bunyan remains a cultural phenomenon whose appeal outruns the boundaries of theology, history, psychology, and letters. Perhaps his continued attraction is due in no small measure to the fact that in him, even today, as "in former times men have met with Angels here, have found Pearls here, and have in this place found the words of Life."

James Forrest and Richard Greaves[2]

Conclusion

John Milton and John Bunyan were contemporaries (Milton was twenty years older). They were the two greatest Puritan writers, and indeed two of the greatest English writers, of all time.[3] Milton was a scholar, a poet, and, for a time, a man of importance in state. Bunyan was a simple, self-taught man, who was a prisoner and a preacher. He has been described as "the greatest representative of the common people to find a place in English literature."[4] He did not set out to be a famous author. He was simply a Puritan preacher who wrote when he was prevented by imprisonment from speaking. But "it did not matter that Bunyan had no literary ambition," a modern scholar has written; "in spite of himself he achieved the work of a great writer."[5]

Some scholars and writers have found fault with Bunyan's style, as well as his theology, but others have appreciated the books of the tinker and preacher of Bedford.[6] Augustus Toplady spoke of the "rich fund of heavenly experience, life, and sweetness" of *The Pilgrim's Progress*. Jonathan Swift remarked that he had been more informed and better entertained by a few pages of *The Pilgrim's Progress* than by lengthy discourses on the will and intellect. Samuel Johnson praised Bunyan's allegory for its imagination and style. Benjamin Franklin collected Bunyan's works and acknowledged in his autobiography Bunyan's engaging blend of narrative and dialogue. Sir Walter Scott's works include numerous allusions to Bunyan, and Samuel Taylor Coleridge admired Bunyan's originality. John Ruskin's early criticism of Bunyan gave way to an appreciation for his imaginative teaching, resolute faith, and deep insight into the nature of sin, concluding that in these respects he could be compared with Dante.[7]

Many novelists have been inspired or influenced by Bunyan, including Daniel Defoe, Charles Dickens, Herman Melville, William Makepeace Thackeray, Charlotte Bronte, George Eliot, John Greenleaf Whittier, Walt Whitman, Matthew Arnold, and John Buchan. So profound was the impact of *The Pilgrim's Progress* on the nineteenth-century Indian poet Krishna Pillai that he converted to Christianity. This, I believe, would have pleased Bunyan more than "all the literary accolades."[8]

A portrait of John Bunyan hung in Robert Browning's London study, and *The Pilgrim's Progress* was, Browning said, the object of his "utmost admiration and reverence."[9] Browning's poem "Ned Bratts" tells the story of the trial at Bedford, "one daft Midsummer's Day," of the wicked Ned Bratts and his wife, Tabby. They freely, and even proudly, confessed their numerous crimes to the justices. But they also talked about "the Tinker in our [prison], pulled-up for gospelling twelve years ago," who "scorned to take money he did not earn" and so taught himself to make "laces, tagged and tough." When Tabby later met John Bunyan, intending to rail against him because his blind daughter no longer came to their wicked house to sell laces, she explained to the judges, "His language was not ours: 'Tis my belief God spoke: no tinker has such powers." Bunyan's daughter gave Tabby a copy of *The Pilgrim's Progress*, telling her that it was "the book [her father] wrote: it reads as if he spoke himself." Tabby read the book and pled with her husband:

> *Wicked dear Husband, first despair and then rejoice!*
> *Dear wicked Husband, waste no tick of moment more,*
> *Be saved like me, bald trunk! There's greenness yet at core,*
> *Sap under slough! Read, read!*

Ned read—and he too found salvation. Hearing their story, the people who had gathered to be entertained burst out with shouts of "triumph, joy, and praise." The poem ends: "And happily hanged were they—why lengthen out my tale? Where Bunyan's Statue stands facing where stood his jail."[10]

Rudyard Kipling's poem "The Holy War" attempted to rally England in 1917 to fight the country's enemies in another "Holy

War."[11] Kipling paid tribute to Bunyan with these lines:

> *A tinker out of Bedford,*
> *A vagrant oft in quod [prison],*
> *A private under Fairfax,*
> *A minister of God . . .*
> *A pedlar from a hovel,*
> *The lowest of the low—*
> *The Father of the Novel,*
> *Salvation's first Defoe.*[12]

Robert Louis Stevenson wrote concerning the tiny illustrations in an edition of *The Pilgrim's Progress* that he loved:

> *I have here before me an edition of the **Pilgrim's Progress**, illustrated. Whoever he was, the author of these wonderful little pictures may lay claim to be the best illustrator of Bunyan. . . . The designer also has lain down and dreamed a dream, as literal, as quaint, and almost as apposite as Bunyan's; and text and pictures make but the two sides of the same homespun yet impassioned story.*[13]

Thomas Babington Macaulay wrote:

> *That wonderful book, while it obtains admiration from the most fastidious critics, is loved by those who are too simple to admire it. Doctor Johnson, all whose studies were desultory, and who hated, as he said, to read books through, made an exception in favour of the **Pilgrim's Progress**. That work was one of the two or three works which he wished longer. . . .*
>
> *[It is] the highest miracle of genius that things which are not should be as though they were, that the imaginations of one mind should become the personal recollections of another. And this miracle the tinker has wrought. There is no ascent, no declivity, no resting-place, no turnstile [in **The Pilgrim's Progress**], with which we are not perfectly acquainted.*[14]

George Bernard Shaw regarded John Bunyan as the "greatest English dramatizer of life." In an essay entitled "Better than Shakespeare," he wrote:

All that you miss in Shakespeare you find in Bunyan, to whom the true heroic came quite obviously and naturally. The world was to him a more terrible place than it was to Shakespeare; but he saw through it a path at the end of which a man might look not only forward to the Celestial City, but back on his life and say: "Tho' with great difficulty I am got hither, yet now I do not repent me of all the trouble I have been at to arrive where I am. My sword I give to him that shall succeed me in my pilgrimage, and my courage and skill to him that can get them." The heart vibrates like a bell to such an utterance as this: to turn from it to "Out, out brief candle," and "The rest is silence," and "We are such stuff as dreams are made on; and our little life is rounded by sleep" is to turn from life, strength, resolution, morning air and eternal youth, to the terrors of a drunken nightmare. [15]

C. S. Lewis, as a young Oxford don at the end of 1929, read Bunyan's spiritual autobiography, *Grace Abounding*. He wrote to a friend: "I should like to know in general what you think of all the darker side of religion as we find it in old books. Formerly I regarded it as mere devil-worship based on horrible superstitions. Now that I have found and am still finding more and more the element of truth in the old beliefs, I feel that I cannot dismiss even their dreadful side so cavalierly. There must be something in it: only what?" [16] Before long, Lewis found what was in it. He came to like, and then to love, the message of God's grace that he found in Bunyan. [17]

The astonishing thing about John Bunyan is not merely the esteem of some great writers but the love of the common people and children for his books, especially *The Pilgrim's Progress*. Robert Blatchford described Bunyan as "the friend and teacher of my childhood: *The Pilgrim's Progress* was my first book . . . in my tenth year I knew it almost by heart." Like many other children, he enacted scenes from the book. Equipping himself with a wooden sword and a paper helmet young Blatchford went out "as Greatheart and did deeds of valour and puissance upon [a poodle] who was good enough to double the parts of Giant Grim and the two lions. The stairway to the bedroom was the Hill Difficulty, the dark lobby was the Valley of the Shadow, and often I swam in great fear and peril, and with profuse sputterings, across the black River of Death, which lay between kitchen and scullery."[18]

By 1740, approximately 155 editions of Bunyan's dozen best sellers had been issued, accounting for perhaps 200,000 copies. Twenty-two editions of *The Pilgrim's Progress* had been published by 1700, 70 by 1800, and more than 1,300 by 1938.[19] Until recently the sales of no other book except the Bible have exceeded it. It has followed the Bible to almost every land and has been translated into over two hundred languages.[20] Isabel Hofmeyr's *The Portable Bunyan: A Transnational History of The Pilgrim's Progress* describes how Bunyan's book was translated into eighty African languages during the nineteenth century. In 1986, 200,000 copies of *The Pilgrim's Progress* printed in Chinese by the government of the People's Republic of China as a sample of western literature and culture sold out in three days.

Although the popular appeal of John Bunyan and his great book waned during the twentieth century, scholarly interest quickened. "*The Pilgrim's Progress* has most definitely moved from its secure place in the hearts of Victorian readers to the minds of contemporary scholars of literature and history, from the bookshelves of nineteenth-century homes to the bookshops of most universities," comments Michael Davies.[21] Commencing in 1976, a new, critical edition of Bunyan's works (under the direction of Roger Sharrock) was produced by Oxford University Press. In the last fifty years more than seventy-five doctoral theses have been written on Bunyan and his works. There is an International John Bunyan Society. The tercentenary of Bunyan's birth produced at least twenty biographies in 1927 and 1928. A journal called *Bunyan Studies* began in 1988 as part of the Bunyan Festival, which marked the tercentenary of Bunyan's death. Books on John Bunyan regularly appear from evangelical and secular publishers, including *Graceful Reading: Theology and Narrative in the Works of John Bunyan* by Michael Davies (Oxford University Press, 2002), *Glimpses of Glory: John Bunyan and English Dissent* by Richard L. Greaves (Stanford University Press, 2002), and *The Portable Bunyan: A Transnational History of The Pilgrim's Progress* by Isabel Hofmeyr (Princeton University Press, 2004).

None of this would have impressed John Bunyan. A "servant in the Gospel" was the way he often signed himself. That is all he wanted to be.

Footnotes

[1] Hill, *John Bunyan*, 368.

[2] Forrest and Greaves, *John Bunyan: A Reference Guide*, xvii.

[3] Thomas Babington Macaulay claimed that in the seventeenth century "there were only two minds which possessed the imaginative faculty in a very eminent degree"—Milton's and Bunyan's. Greaves, *Glimpses of Glory*, 626.

[4] Sharrock, *John Bunyan*, 9.

[5] Talon, *John Bunyan*, 134.

[6] Critics of Bunyan have included Edmund Burke, David Hume, Alexander Pope, Samuel Butler, Robert Bridges, and Alfred Noyes.

[7] See Greaves, *Glimpses of Glory*, 624-7.

[8] Greaves, *Glimpses of Glory*, 632.

[9] Hugh Martin, *The Faith of Robert Browning*, Richmond, Virginia: John Knox Press, 13.

[10] Robert Browning, 1065-70.

[11] Rudyard Kipling, *The Complete Verse* (London: Kyle Cathie Ltd., 1990), 234-5.

[12] Daniel Defoe (1660-1731) was a journalist who wrote *Robinson Crusoe*, often viewed as the pioneer English novel. Bunyan's *Life and Death of Mr. Badman*, written about forty years before *Robinson Crusoe*, is considered by some the earliest English novel.

[13] Stevenson, "Introduction," *The Pilgrim's Progress*, v.

[14] Thomas Babington Macaulay, *John Bunyan* (Cambridge: The University Press, 1898), 30-1.

[15] George Bernard Shaw, "Better than Shakespeare," in *Dramatic Opinions and Essays*, 143.

[16] Roger Lancelyn Green and Walter Hooper, *C. S. Lewis: A Biography* (London: Collins, 1974), 98.

[17] Michael W. Price writes that Lewis's writings "demonstrate that Bunyan—particularly *The Pilgrim's Progress*—served as a touchstone for his thinking since his childhood." Lewis read aloud (from his own armchair, no less) his essay on "The Vision of John Bunyan" for broadcast on the BBC on October 16, 1962. That essay, Price states, "climaxes a lifelong passion" of Lewis for the writings of Bunyan. Michael W. Price, "Seventeenth Century," in *Reading the Classics with C. S. Lewis*, ed. Thomas L. Martin (Grand Rapids: Baker Academic, 2000), 151-2.

[18] Hofmeyr, *The Portable Bunyan*, 59-60.

[19] These figures are from Greaves, *Glimpses of Glory*, 611-2.

[20] More than 1300 editions of *The Pilgrim's Progress* had been printed by 1938.

[21] Davies, *Graceful Reading*, 347.

Bibliography

Reference
John Bunyan: A Reference Guide, by James F. Forrest and Richard Lee Greaves (Boston, G. K. Hall & Co., 1982) is an annotated listing of books and articles about Bunyan from 1656 to 1981.

Bunyan's Works
The Works of John Bunyan, edited by George Offor, was published in three volumes in 1854 by W. G. Blackie and Son, Glasgow, and reprinted in 1991 by the Banner of Truth Trust, Edinburgh, and Carlisle, Pennsylvania.

A new edition of *The Miscellaneous Works of John Bunyan* in thirteen volumes, edited by Roger Sharrock, was published by Oxford (Clarendon Press) in 1976-94.

Biographical Studies
Brown, John, *John Bunyan (1628-1688): His Life, Times, and Work.* London: Hulbert Publishing Co., 1928.

Brown's classic biography was revised by Frank Mott Harrison in 1928.

Davies, Gaius, *Genius and Grace: Sketches from a Psychiatrist's Notebook.* London: Hodder & Stoughton, 1992.

One of the chapters of this book is devoted to Bunyan. The author attempts to show from **Grace Abounding** *how ill Bunyan was with a severe obsessive-compulsive disorder. At times (even after he began to preach) he would have such a strong urge to blaspheme that he felt he had to hold his hand over his mouth. Bunyan's serious neurosis took the form of obsessional thoughts, compulsions, illusions, and the hearing of voices. At the same time, he experienced crippling anxiety and frequent bouts of despair and anguish. This struggle, part of Bunyan's intense and prolonged spiritual crisis, enabled him to be a great preacher and counselor. Bunyan experienced both mental and spiritual suffering. "I am not trying to reduce his spiritual experience to a mere illness (however severe)," writes Davies, "but rather am trying to show how the spiritual and psychiatric aspects, though separate, are inevitably intertwined" (64).*

Furlong, Monica, *Puritan's Progress*. New York: Coward, McCann & Geoghegan, 1975.

Furlong presents a more positive view than some other writers in her estimation of Bunyan's female characters in Part II of **The Pilgrim's Progress**, *saying that Christiana "presides over the whole enterprise" and that Mercy acts as "a kind of grown-up sister-figure" (179).*

Greaves, Richard L., *Glimpses of Glory: John Bunyan and English Dissent*. Stanford, California: Stanford University Press, 2002.

Greaves culminates four decades of Bunyan studies with this major work. He presents Bunyan's life with scholarly care and thorough knowledge of primary and secondary sources. Greaves locates Bunyan in historical context and describes his writings chronologically within the biography.

Hill, Christopher, *A Tinker and a Poor Man: John Bunyan and His Church, 1628-1688*. New York: W. W. Norton & Co., 1990.

Hill is particularly interested in political and social themes. He attempts to analyze Bunyan within the social forces of lower-class religious dissent in seventeenth-century England. Hill, however, acknowledges that Bunyan's interests were far from political. "For him the first priority was to be able to worship and preach according to what he believed to be God's will"(15).

Mullett, Michael, *John Bunyan in Context*. Pittsburgh: DuQuesne University Press, 1996.

This book is a scholarly study of Bunyan's historical setting, life, and writings by a competent historian. Unfortunately, Bunyan's biblical and theological ideas (by far the most important to Bunyan) are of secondary concern to Mullett.

Piper, John, *The Hidden Smile of God:The Fruit of Affliction in the Lives of John Bunyan,William Cowper, and David Brainerd*. Wheaton: Crossway Books, 2001.

Piper, the senior pastor of Bethlehem Baptist Church in Minneapolis, treats suffering and service in the life of John Bunyan in a chapter called "To Live Upon God That Is Invisible."

Sharrock, Roger, *John Bunyan*. London: Macmillan, 1968.

*Sharrock, the general editor of **The Miscellaneous Works of John Bunyan**, gives an introduction to Bunyan's life and work that incorporates the findings of modern scholarship. He attempts to do equal justice to Bunyan's spiritual history and to his place in the Puritan literary tradition.*

Talon, Henri, *John Bunyan: The Man and His Works*. Cambridge: Harvard University Press, 1951.

This book is a competent and interesting treatment of Bunyan's life, writings, and thought by a French Catholic scholar. Talon's discussion of Bunyan's theology, however, goes astray because of the author's faulty understanding of Calvinism.

Whyte, Alexander, *Bunyan Characters: Bunyan Himself as Seen in His Grace Abounding*. Edinburgh: Oliphant, Anderson & Ferrier, n.d.

Whyte, a Scottish Presbyterian minister, draws important lessons from Bunyan's life.

Winslow, Ola Elizabeth, *John Bunyan*. New York: Macmillan, 1961.

Winslow has produced a well-written and competent study of Bunyan and his writings.

Literary and Theological Studies

Davies, Michael, *Graceful Reading: Theology and Narrative in the Works of John Bunyan*. Oxford: Oxford University Press, 2002.

Davies correctly centers Bunyan's writings on the doctrine of grace and the free offer of the Gospel to sinners. He does not seem to realize, however, that Bunyan thus represents the mainstream of Calvinist orthodoxy. Davies' literary analysis of Bunyan is highly speculative and leads the reader away from a proper interpretation of Bunyan's thought.

Greaves, Richard L., *John Bunyan*. Grand Rapids: Wm. B. Eerdmans Publishing Company, 1969.

This important book provides a careful study of Bunyan's theological views.

Hofmeyr, Isabel, *The Portable Bunyan: A Transnational History of The Pilgrim's Progress*. Princeton: Princeton University Press, 2004.

*The Portable Bunyan tells the story of how **The Pilgrim's Progress** traveled abroad with the Protestant mission movement, was adapted and reworked by the societies into which it came, and, finally, how its circulation throughout the empire affected Bunyan's standing back in England. Hofmeyr's literary and social theories often overwhelm an appreciative understanding of the real meaning of **The Pilgrim's Progress**.*

Johnson, Galen, "'Be Not Extream': The Limits of Theory in Reading

John Bunyan," in *Christianity and Literature 49* (Summer 2000): 447-64.

> *Johnson provides a useful analysis of various critical treatments of Bunyan, including New Critical, Marxist, psychoanalytical, feminist, poststructural, and reader-response. Johnson concludes that although various factors shaped Bunyan's works, "none was stronger than his Luthero-Puritan religious beliefs"(460).*

Kaufman, U. Milo, "*The Pilgrim's Progress* and *The Pilgrim's Regress:* John Bunyan and C. S. Lewis on the Shape of the Christian Quest," in Bunyan in Our Time, ed. Robert G. Collmer. Kent, Ohio: Kent State University Press, 1989, 186-199.

Kaufman, U. Milo, *"The Pilgrim's Progress" and Traditions in Puritan Meditation.* New Haven: Yale University Press, 1966.

> *Kaufman attempts to place Bunyan in the tradition of "Puritan meditation."*

Kelman, John, *The Road: A Study of John Bunyan's "Pilgrim's Progress."* Port Washington, New York: Kennikat Press, 1970.

> *Kelman's commentary on* **The Pilgrim's Progress** *is sometimes very illuminating, sometimes not.*

Lewis, C. S., "The Vision of John Bunyan," in *Selected Literary Essays* by C. S. Lewis, ed., Walter Hooper. Cambridge: Cambridge University Press, 1969, 146-53.

> *Lewis provides wise words about* **The Pilgrim's Progress** *as literature and theology.*

Loane, Marcus L., *Makers of Puritan History.* Grand Rapids: Baker Book House, 1961.

> *Bunyan is one of four "Puritans" treated in this book by the Archbishop of Sydney and Principal of Moore College.*

Martin, Hugh, *Great Christian Books.* London: S. C. M. Press, 1945.

Whyte, Alexander, *Bunyan Characters in The Pilgrim's Progress* and *Bunyan Characters in The Holy War.* Edinburgh: Oliphant, Anderson & Ferrier, n.d. (reprinted by Wipf and Stock Publishers, 2000).

> *In addition to* **Bunyan Himself as seen in his Grace Abounding** *(see above), Whyte has written three other books on the writings of Bunyan—two on* **The Pilgrim's Progress** *and one on* **The Holy War**. *All four books comprise lectures Whyte gave on Sunday evenings to his Edinburgh congregation. The lectures range far beyond Bunyan writings but often capture the spiritual significance of Bunyan's thought.*

Art, Literature, and Music

Art

Bunyan's works, especially *The Pilgrim's Progress*, have inspired and challenged illustrators and artists.

William Blake, poet and artist, produced twenty-eight watercolors illustrating *The Pilgrim's Progress*. Blake died in 1827 and was buried at Bunhill Fields, not far from the grave of John Bunyan. In the introduction to an edition of *The Pilgrim's Progress* containing twelve of Blake's watercolors are these words:

> *Blake had previously made superb designs for* **Paradise Lost**, *but he was more at home with* **The Pilgrim's Progress**. *For* **The Pilgrim's Progress** *was the poor man's* **Paradise Lost**, *and Blake, like Bunyan, was a poor man save in the things of the spirit.* [1]

The Samuel Bagster edition of *The Pilgrim's Progress* includes numerous small drawings, hardly bigger than one inch by one inch. In an introduction to this edition Robert Louis Stevenson comments:

> *[I cannot] dismiss in any other words than those of gratitude a series*

of pictures which have, to one at least, been the visible embodiment of Bunyan from childhood up, and shown him, through all his years, Greatheart lunging at Giant Maul and Apollyon breathing fire at Christian, and every turn and town along the road to the Celestial City, and that bright place itself, seen as to a stave of music, shining afar off upon the hill-top, the candle of the world.[2]

Artistic depictions of scenes from *The Pilgrim's Progress* are found on the bronze doors at the entrance to Bunyan Meeting, Bedford; and in a number of stained glass windows, including the Abbey Church, Elstow (which also has a window illustrating *The Holy War*); Westminster Abbey, London; and the Princeton University Chapel, Princeton, New Jersey.

Literature

The Pilgrim's Regress: An Allegorical Apology for Christianity, Reason and Romanticism by C. S. Lewis is the most important writing that uses Bunyan's theme and, in this case, an adaptation of Bunyan's famous title. Instead of *Christian*, the central figure is *John*, loosely based on C. S. Lewis himself. He sets out on a journey that takes him off the straight road into deviant paths of arid intellectualism and emotional excesses. John's way is a *regress* rather than a *progress* because he is in fact going away from, rather than towards, the beautiful island that he seeks (which is Lewis's equivalent to the Celestial City of Bunyan). On his journey John encounters characters like *Mr. Enlightenment* from the city of Claptrap and *Media Halfways* from the city of Thrill. Later John is imprisoned by *the Spirit of the Age*, but he is rescued by the tall, blue-clad figure of *Reason*. The hermit *History* and *Mother Kirk* also help him retrace his steps and come at last to his goal. In an afterword to the third edition, Lewis wrote that "on the intellectual side" his own progress had been "from 'popular realism' to Philosophical Idealism; from Idealism to Pantheism; from Pantheism to Theism; and from Theism to Christianity."[3] Lewis's story gives a vivid picture of the intellectual climate of the 1920s and early 1930s.

"The Celestial Railroad," a short story by Nathaniel Hawthorne, mocks the easy salvation of modern "liberal" religion in contrast to the rugged and difficult road of *The Pilgrim's Progress*. *Mr. Smooth it-away* and the other passengers on the Celestial Railroad are the most up-to-date specimens of mid-nineteenth-century thought and are placed in immediate ironic contrast to Bunyan's pilgrims toiling along the old hard way toward the Celestial City. Hawthorne's characters include the *Rev. Mr. Shallow-deep*, the *Rev. Mr. This-to-day*, the *Rev. Mr. That-to-morrow*, and the gentlemen from the town of Shun-repentance. The giants *Pope* and *Pagan* are replaced by *Giant Transcendentalist*, who is, Hawthorne assures us, "German by birth" and whom no one can understand because of the strangeness of his language. Hawthorne begins his story this way:

> *Not a great while ago, passing through the gate of dreams, I visited that region of the earth in which lies the famous City of Destruction. It interested me much to learn that by the public spirit of some of the inhabitants a railroad has recently been established between this populous and flourishing town and the Celestial City.*[4]

Louisa May Alcott's *Little Women* was inspired by Bunyan's *Pilgrim's Progress*. Chapter One, "Playing Pilgrims," includes the following paragraphs:

> *Mrs. March broke the silence that followed Jo's words by saying in her cheery voice, "Do you remember how you used to play Pilgrim's Progress when you were little things? Nothing delighted you more than to have me tie my piece bags on your backs for burdens, give you hats and sticks and rolls of paper, and let you travel through the house from the cellar, which was the City of Destruction, up, up, to the housetop, where you had all the lovely things you could collect to make a Celestial City."*
>
> *"What fun it was, especially going by the lions, fighting Apollyon, and passing through the Valley where the hobgoblins were!" said Jo.*
>
> *"I liked the place where the bundles fell off and tumbled downstairs," said Meg.*
>
> *"My favorite part was when we came out on the flat roof where our flowers and arbors and pretty things were, and all stood and sung for joy up there in the sunshine," said Beth, smiling, as if that pleasant moment had come back to her.*

"I don't remember much about it, except that I was afraid of the cellar and the dark entry, and always liked the cake and milk we had at the top. If I wasn't too old for such things, I'd rather like to play it over again," said Amy, who began to talk of renouncing childish things at the mature age of twelve.

"We never are too old for this, my dear, because it is a play we are playing all the time in one way or another. Our burdens are here, our road is before us, and the longing for goodness and happiness is the guide that leads us through many troubles and mistakes to the peace which is a true Celestial City. Now my little pilgrims, suppose you begin again, not in play, but in earnest, and see how far on you can get before father comes home."

Alcott uses Bunyan's ideas in her famous book but removes his distinctive Christian and Puritan theology. Rather than a book about sin and salvation and heaven at last, it is a book encouraging efforts toward kindness and goodness.

Music

There are some delightful (and spiritually significant) poems in Bunyan's *Prison Meditations* and *Book for Boys and Girls*. Two memorable passages of verse in *The Pilgrim's Progress* have been set to music and appear in various hymnbooks.

One, recorded in Part II, is the *Song of the shepherd's boy* in the Valley of Humiliation:

He that is down needs fear no fall;
He that is low, no pride,
He that is humble, ever shall
Have God to be his guide.

I am content with what I have,
Little be it, or much;
And, Lord, contentment still I crave,
Because thou savest such.

Fulness to such a burden is,

> *That go on pilgrimage;*
> *Here little, and hereafter bliss,*
> *Is best from age to age (3:206).* [5]

The shepherd's boy is "clearly one who can use language with care and attention, using simple monosyllabic words to say complex things."[6] Mr. Great-heart is moved. "Do you hear him?" he asks. "I will dare to say, that this boy lives a merrier life, and wears more of that herb called heart's-ease in his bosom, than he that is clad in silk and velvet" (3:206).

The second hymn is "*the Pilgrim Song*" (sometimes called "*The Tinker's Hymn*") that Bunyan places in Part II after the testimony of the courageous *Valiant-for-Truth*, who tells *Great-heart*: "I believed, and therefore came out, got into the way, fought all that set themselves against me, and, by believing, am come to this place" (3:235).

> *Who would true valor see,*
> *Let him come hither;*
> *One here will constant be,*
> *Come wind, come weather.*
> *There's no discouragement*
> *Shall make him once relent,*
> *His first avow'd intent,*
> *To be a pilgrim.*
>
> *Who so beset him round*
> *With dismal stories,*
> *Do but themselves confound,*
> *His strength the more is;*
> *No lion can him fright,*
> *He'll with a giant fight;*
> *But he will have a right*
> *To be a pilgrim.*
>
> *Hobgoblin nor foul fiend*
> *Can daunt his spirit;*
> *He knows he at the end*
> *Shall life inherit.*

Then fancies fly away,
He'll fear not what men say;
He'll labour night and day
To be a pilgrim (3:235).[7]

Bunyan, who had served in the Parliamentary army, "must have known that it was one thing to volunteer and another to continue to be a good soldier after the first flush of enthusiasm had died away. So constancy is of paramount importance, as *The Pilgrim's Progress* shows: the book is full of characters who set out on the journey, or who join up with the pilgrims from time to time, but who literally fall by the wayside."[8]

Bunyan's words remind us that being a pilgrim is a privilege given by God; it is also an arduous undertaking demanding watchfulness and courage. Bunyan compresses so much of what the Christian life means in the space of three verses. The first verse stresses the need for courage and constancy in the face of discouraging and difficult circumstances that Christian pilgrims encounter along the way to heaven. The second describes the strong, fearless spirit with which the pilgrim meets and defeats his foes. The third points to the goal of the journey: life eternal, the Christian's heavenly inheritance.

Canon C. Winfred Douglas (who wrote the hymn tune "St. Dunstan's" for Bunyan's words) commented, "Bunyan's burly song strikes a new and welcome note. . . . The quaint sincerity of the words stirs us out of our easygoing, dull Christianity to the thrill of great adventure."[9]

Following the armistice ending World War I, the BBC broadcast a musical setting of the first part of *The Pilgrim's Progress* and in 1928 broadcast another adaptation of the text of the book, set to music by Sir Granville Bantock.

Ralph Vaughan Williams knew and loved the writings of Bunyan all his life, and setting Bunyan to music occupied him on and off for over forty years.[10] In 1909 Vaughan Williams's *Pilgrim's Progress* was presented at Reigate Priory. The performance comprised twelve episodes, with Prelude and Epilogue founded on the Roundhead hymn tune "York." Vaughan Williams's *Shepherds of the Delectable Mountains* was first performed at London's Royal College of Music in 1922. The text—skillfully adapted by Vaughan Williams from *The Pilgrim's Progress*—briefly summarizes the story from Christian's meeting the Shepherds to his crossing the River and entering the Celestial City. It was presented as an operatic scene in one short act, with six singing roles (including the off-stage Voice of a Bird singing Psalm 23) and a small chorus. In 1942 there was a BBC production-adaptation of the complete *Pilgrim's Progress* by Edward Sackville-West in thirty-eight episodes, with "incidental" music written by Vaughan Williams. Sir Adrian Boult conducted the BBC Symphony Orchestra and Chorus. As Christian, Sir John Gielgud (who said that the role was one with which he strongly identified) gave one of the outstanding performances of his broadcasting career. The culmination of Vaughan Williams's work on Bunyan, and his last opera, *The Pilgrim's Progress* was performed at the Royal Opera House, Covent Garden, London, as part of the Festival of Britain in 1951 and at Cambridge University in 1954.

Footnotes

[1] John Bunyan, *The Pilgrim's Progress* (New York: The Heritage Press, 1942), xvi. S. Foster Damon writes, "As Bunyan explained his meanings so clearly, and as Blake agreed with them, his illustrations follow the text with his usual detailed precision, and with but a slight symbolic amplification to underscore Bunyan's meaning." S. Foster Damon, *A Blake Dictionary: The Ideas and Symbols of William Blake* (Providence: Brown University Press, 1965), 62. See Gerda S. Norvig, *Dark Figures in the Desired Country: Blake's Illustrations to "The Pilgrim's Progress"* (Berkeley, California: University of California Press, 1993).

[2] Stevenson, "Introduction," *The Pilgrim's Progress*, xv.

[3] C. S. Lewis, *The Pilgrim's Regress: An Allegorical Apology for Christianity, Reason and Romanticism* (Grand Rapids: William B. Eerdmans Publishing Company, 1981), 200.

[4] Nathaniel Hawthorne, *Hawthorne's Short Stories* (New York: Alfred A. Knopf, 1964), 234.

[5] *Hymns Ancient and Modern* (1950).

[6] J. R. Watson, *The English Hymn: A Critical and Historical Study* (Oxford: Clarendon Press, 1999), 123.

[7] *English Hymnal* (1906).

[8] Watson, *The English Hymn*, 127.

[9] From the *Hymnal Companion* (1940). There is another tune that has been used

for Bunyan's "Pilgrim Song."The story goes that in 1904 R. Vaughan Williams heard a ploughman from the village of Monk's Gate, near Horsham, singing an old Sussex folk-song. The words were commonplace but the tune was distinctive, and it occurred to Vaughan Williams that he could adapt it to suit Bunyan's lines. He did this and named it "Monk's Gate."

[10] Sir Edward Elgar planned a symphonic drama of *The Pilgrim's Progress*, but it was never completed.

Had John Bunyan been born a Londoner in 1628 and lived his boy life in and out of crooked streets, crowded tenements, noisy city clamors, and, in Defoe's word, "drawn his breath in sin," there would probably have been in his Dream no wicket gate yonder over the plain, no undiscovered path the other side of the stile, no sound of bells across the valley, no Enchanted Ground, no Delectable Mountains, no castle in the far distance. **Pilgrim's Progress** *is a country book; in fact, a Midland country book.*

Ola Elizabeth Winslow[1]

Appendix 1

Bunyan Sites

ELSTOW

1. Bunyan's birthplace

John Bunyan was born in a cottage at the far eastern end of Elstow Parish, close to Harrowden. The Bunyan family had lived in the area for over four centuries. The cottage is no longer there (its site is marked by a stone placed there in 1951), but a row of Tudor cottages in nearby Elstow has been restored to the way it looked in Bunyan's time.

2. Elstow Abbey

Bunyan was baptized in this Anglican church on November 30, 1628 (as were his parents). The baptismal font and communion table used in Bunyan's day have been preserved, as have the door and wicket gate that were formerly at the church's northern entrance. The door and wicket gate appear in *The Pilgrim's Progress*. The church's detached belfry, in which, as a young man, Bunyan regularly rang the bell, also appears in *Pilgrim's Progress* as the strong castle from which Beelzebub shot arrows at those who approached the wicket gate. Two stained glass windows depict scenes from *The Pilgrim's Progress* and *The Holy War*. Bunyan's mother, father, and sister are buried in the graveyard.

3. Elstow Green

The church overlooks Elstow Green, where young John Bunyan

danced and played games on Sunday. One Sunday, after hearing the vicar preach against breaking the Sabbath by working or playing, Bunyan went as usual to the green to play a game called "tip-cat." He heard a voice from heaven saying, "Wilt thou leave thy sins and go to heaven, or have thy sins and go to hell?"

The remains of a cross mark the site on Elstow Green where the annual May Fair was held, with merchants, jugglers, actors, and rogues of all kinds. This event is pictured in *Pilgrim's Progress* as Vanity Fair.

4. Moot Hall

Elstow Moot Hall (once called Green House) was built in the late fifteenth century for use as a market house in connection with the village fairs. It was the focus of village life. An upper room was used as a school and place of worship and also served as a place for hearing disputes. The annual three-day fair in May occupied the Moot Hall, and the green was covered with booths. There were jugglers, games, and plays. Occupants of nearby houses sold beer. Knaves and thieves worked the crowds, tempted by all the money that was changing hands. John Bunyan was no doubt at the Elstow fair in 1645 when ill feeling between soldiers and people turned to violence. The Moot Hall is now a museum depicting English seventeenth-century life.

BEDFORD

1. St. John's Rectory

St. John's Rectory is adjacent to St. John's Church in St. John's Street, 300 yards south of the river.

In the early 1650s Bunyan met John Gifford, pastor of the Independent congregation that at the time met at St. John's Church. In the rectory Gifford, once a notorious sinner, had long conversations with Bunyan about spiritual matters. Gifford is portrayed in *The Pilgrim's Progress* as Evangelist, who faithfully directed Christian toward the wicket gate and the cross. The rectory appears in *The Pilgrim's Progress* as Interpreter's House, where Christian stopped for help and guidance. ("Then Christian went on till he came to the House of the Interpreter. . . . 'Sir,' said Christian, 'I was told . . . that if I called here you would show me excellent things [that] would be a help to me in my journey.'")

St. John's Rectory is now occupied by St. John Ambulance, but one room, a memorial to the time of Bunyan, is open to the public. A plaque on the wall commemorates the conversations of Bunyan and Gifford.

2. River Great Ouse

In a little backwater that runs off the River Great Ouse, Bunyan was (re)baptized as an adult by John Gifford. Tradition holds that the "gathered church" that used St. John's came the short distance to this inlet of Bedford's river. The traditional site of the baptism is on the south bank of the river between Duck Mill Lane Car Park and the Weir Bridge. A plaque marks the spot.

John Bunyan may refer to the River Great Ouse in this description in *The Pilgrim's Progress*: Christian and Hopeful "went on their way to a pleasant river. . . . On either side of the river was . . . a meadow, curiously beautified with lilies, and it was green all the year long."

3. Town Gaol

A plaque on the present bridge over the River Great Ouse (built in 1813) states that Bunyan's second and shorter imprisonment of 1676 was served in the Town Gaol, which was then part of the main bridge over the river. Stronger evidence now points to Bunyan's having served both his sentences in the County Gaol by the crossroads in Bedford High Street. This structure had six cells and two dungeons and was demolished in 1802. An inscribed slab in the pavement marks the site. A model of the Town Gaol can be seen in the Bunyan Museum in Mill Street.

4. Swan Hotel

In the seventeenth century, the Swan Hotel (on the Embankment close to the Town Bridge) had chambers set aside for judges when the County Assizes were held in town. Here, in August 1661, Bunyan's second wife, Elizabeth, pled for her husband's release. A picture of Elizabeth before the judges can be seen in the Bunyan Museum in Mill Street. The hotel was rebuilt in 1794. The staircase now in use in the Swan Hotel came from Houghton House near Ampthill. (See Ampthill)

5. Chapel of Herne

In January 1661, seven or eight weeks after his arrest for preaching at the hamlet of Samsell, Bunyan was brought before the magistrates of the Bedford Quarter Sessions in an old building known as the Chapel of Herne. (The Town Hall Office Building now stands on the site of the chapel.) Bunyan, who could have been released if he had promised not to preach to a public gathering again, courageously told the authorities, "If I was out of prison today, I would preach the Gospel again tomorrow, by the help of God." Bunyan was sentenced by Sir John Keeling, chairman of the magistrates, to three months in prison and was threatened with exile if he did not conform. (Sir John Keeling was probably the character Bunyan had in mind when he described "Lord Hategood" in the trial of Faithful at Vanity Fair in *The Pilgrim's Progress*.)

6. Bunyan's Statue

The bronze statue of John Bunyan that stands on St. Peter's Green (where according to tradition Bunyan often preached) at the northern end of the High Street was presented to the town in 1874 by the Duke of Bedford. Sir J. E. Boehm's statue is nine feet tall, weighs over three tons, and is made of melted-down guns. Around the pedestal are three bronze panels illustrating scenes from *Pilgrim's Progress*. They depict the minister at the Interpreter's House (with "his eyes . . . lifted up to heaven"), Christian's meeting with Evangelist, and the angels at the cross.

7. County Gaol

A plaque in the pavement at the corner of High and Silver streets marks the location of the County Gaol (which was demolished in 1801). Bunyan probably served both his prison sentences here in this dirty, overcrowded "den." Here Bunyan's blind daughter, Mary, brought him food for his supper. The soup jug she carried and other relics associated with the County Gaol are part of the collection of the Bunyan Museum in Mill Street.

8. Bunyan's Home

A plaque at 17 St. Cuthbert's Street marks the site of the cottage to which Bunyan and his family—his first wife and two daughters, Mary and Elizabet—moved in 1655. (The Bunyans had lived in a house in the center of the village of Elstow when he married in 1649. That house was frequently visited in later years by admirers of Bunyan, and bits of wood were chipped away for souvenirs. The house was demolished in 1968.) The Bedford cottage was Bunyan's home for the rest of his life—thirty-three years. Here he lived with his wife and their four children and, later, his second wife, Elizabeth, and two more children. It was even more humble than the cottage in Elstow. When the cottage was demolished in 1838, Bunyan's Deed of Gift (or will) was found concealed behind a brick in the chimney corner. Following the accession of James II, Bunyan had feared further persecution and the possible seizure of his possessions. He drew up his will in 1685, leaving his very modest estate to Elizabeth, his wife. The document is now on display in the Bunyan Museum.

9. Bunyan Meeting House and Bunyan Museum

Since the Restoration, the Independent congregation that Bunyan served as pastor had met wherever it could find a place. In 1672 Bunyan bought a barn and orchard in Mill Street for the sum of fifty pounds. The barn was converted into a meeting place for the church. In 1707 it was replaced with a meeting house, and in 1849 the present church, known as Bunyan Meeting, was built. The bronze doors at the entrance to the church were presented to Bunyan Meeting House by the Duke of Bedford in 1876. The doors' ten panels depict scenes from *Pilgrim's Progress*, as do the stained glass windows of the church. One of the windows was unveiled by the Archbishop of Canterbury in 1988. The Bunyan Museum, located in the church buildings, contains two hundred editions and translations of *The Pilgrim's Progress*, as well as displays setting forth Bunyan's life and times.

10. Bedford Central Library

In the foyer of the library, located in Harpur Street, is a modern mural sculpture depicting scenes from *The Pilgrim's Progress*. The library possesses an extensive collection of books by and about Bunyan.

11. Bedford Museum
In Castle Lane, the museum has displays of the history (and natural history) of Bedford.

12. The Cecil Higgins Art Gallery
The Art Gallery, in Castle Close, has an embroidered panel called "Bunyan's Dream" on permanent display. It was completed (with over two million stitches) in 1979 to celebrate the tercentenary of *The Pilgrim's Progress* and pictures Bunyan asleep in prison dreaming his great dream.

STEVINGTON

(Follow the A428 from Bedford toward Northampton and turn right a mile past Bromham)

A fourteenth-century cross, which would have been familiar to John Bunyan, stands in the center of the village of Stevington. In *The Pilgrim's Progress* Christian lost his burden at the cross: "He ran . . . till he came at a place somewhat ascending; and upon that place stood a cross, and a little below, in the bottom, a sepulchre. So I saw in my dream that, just as Christian came up with the cross, his burden loosed from off his shoulders, and fell from off his back and began to tumble; and so continued to do till it came to the mouth of the sepulchre, where it fell in, and I saw it no more."

AMPTHILL

Ampthill Hill (*just north of Ampthill on the B530*)
Bunyan worked as a tinker and carried a heavy iron anvil with him on his travels through the district. The steep Ampthill Hill would have been a hard climb for Bunyan and is probably "Hill Difficulty" in *The Pilgrim's Progress*. At the bottom of the hill was a spring from which the pilgrim drank as he began to climb. "I looked then after

Christian, to see him go up the hill, where I perceived [that] he fell from running to going, and from going to clambering upon his hands and knees, because of the steepness of the place."

Houghton House (*follow the B530 from Bedford to Ampthill and turn left down the narrow road at the top of Ampthill Hill*)

An ancient building, Houghton House is probably "House Beautiful," where Christian was refreshed in *The Pilgrim's Progress*: "And many of them meeting him at the threshold of the house said, 'Come in, thou blessed of the Lord; this house was built by the Lord of the Hill on purpose to entertain such pilgrims in.'"

John Bunyan probably visited Houghton House to make and repair cooking utensils. The account books show the entry "Paid the brazier."

Looking south from the visitors' car park at Houghton House, one often can see the Chilterns. These hills, called in *The Pilgrim's Progress* the "Delectable Mountains," were pointed out to Christian on the morning he left "House Beautiful."

The John Bunyan Trail was created by the Ramblers Association (Beds Area) as a contribution to their Sixtieth Jubilee Celebration. There is a 45-mile "Pilgrim's Progress" through the Bedfordshire countryside, as well as a 25-mile trail. Descriptive brochures and maps are available from the Tourist Information Centre, 10 St. Paul's Square, Bedford MK40 ISL, England.

LONDON

Bunhill Fields

Bunyan is buried at Bunhill Fields, located in the southern part of the London Borough of Islington. By the time of Charles II, these four acres had become a burial ground for Dissenters. Today Bunhill Fields is a green, peaceful place, just north of the busy City of London Square Mile. Old plane trees, ash, and English oaks provide shade and beauty around the graves of some of England's greats, including poet-painter William Blake (who produced twenty-nine paintings based on Bunyan's *Pilgrim's Progress*); author Daniel Defoe; theologian John Gill; hymn writer Isaac Watts; Susanna Wesley, the mother of John and Charles Wesley; and Puritan heroes Thomas Goodwin and John Owen. Centrally located is Bunyan's tomb. The recumbent effigy dates from 1862, and the inscription reads: "John Bunyan, Author of Pilgrim's Progress, Ob. 31st August, 1688, Aet. 60. Restored by public subscription under the presidency of the Right Hon. the Earl of Shaftesbury. May 1862." Bas-reliefs on the tomb show Christian weighed down by his burden of sin and losing his burden at the foot of the cross.

Footnotes

[1] Winslow, *John Bunyan*, 11.

Appendix 2

Children's Versions Of The Pilgrim's Progress

In commenting on *The Pilgrim's Progress*, Robert Lawson wrote in 1939 that many children, "finding Bunyan's original wordiness a veritable Slough of Despond, have, like Pliable, given up and gone home." Recommending an abridged version of the classic by Mary Godolphin, Lawson stated that with the "excess wordage removed, Pilgrim really makes Progress and his journey to the Promised Land becomes a fast-moving story of adventure, with giants, dragons and excitements galore." Two comments are called for. To begin with, Bunyan's *Pilgrim's Progress* is not beyond many older children. It would be a mistake for them to settle for an abridged form of the story, missing the fullness of the original. The long conversations, reduced or altogether left out of the shorter forms, are an important part of Bunyan's book. If only the action remains in the retelling, much of the meaning is lost. Having said that, the abridgments can serve to introduce younger children to Bunyan's masterpiece and prepare them for reading the full story later.

A survey of four "children's versions" of *The Pilgrim's Progress* follows, with comments on the texts and—an important part of any book for children—the illustrations. The first is a book for very young children; the other three are designed for older children and perhaps early teens.

The Evergreen Wood (Thomas Nelson, 1992) is skillfully written and beautifully illustrated by Linda and Alan Parry, who drew inspiration for their text and pictures from their country home in the heart of England. Their pilgrim, Christopher Mouse—dressed in Puritan garb—flees "the Dark Wood", which is scheduled to be destroyed by developers, to go to "the Evergreen Wood", a place where all creatures are promised peace and safety. After falling into a great miry swamp, Christopher comes to "Badger's House," where he is encouraged on his way. His upward path leads him to the Lamb with a shepherd's staff. His burden slips off his back and rolls away, and he is given a book, a key, and a new suit of clothes. Christopher climbs up "the Steep Hill" and comes to the safety of the Great Oak Tree, where he receives armor for all but his back. "The Black Valley" brings an encounter with a fearsome Wildcat and a surprise meeting with another pilgrim, Woodley Woodmouse. Woodley gives Christopher a letter from Christina, Christopher's wife, stating that she and the children are planning to follow him as soon as the Knight who is to serve as their guide arrives. At "Rat Fair," Christopher and Woodley are arrested for disturbing the peace. Christopher is released, but Woodley is sentenced to six months of hard labor. Bunyan's account of Faithful's execution at Vanity Fair was no doubt judged too traumatic for little children. Christopher and a new friend, Heathley—a young black rat—are caught sleeping by a Fox and thrown into his lair. They dig their way out and escape. After many more adventures, the two "pilgrims" pass safely over the Enchanted Ground, swim a river, and are welcomed to the Evergreen Wood. They are told the good news that Woodley has been released and is on his way and that the Knight, with Christina and her children, is expected soon. "My happiness," says Christopher, "is almost complete." (I wonder what is meant by "almost.")

The Evergreen Wood is an adaptation of Bunyan's *Pilgrim's Progress* that might appeal to very little children. It tells an exciting story but does not explicitly set forth Bunyan's Christian message. It will be the task of the reader to explain the meaning of the story in words that children can understand. A few times the author of *The Evergreen Wood* alters the thrust of Bunyan's theology, as when she writes that Christopher and Heathley dig themselves out of the Fox's lair. In contrast, Bunyan's Christian and Hopeful escape Giant Despair's dungeon only when Christian remembers that he has "a key called Promise." Another change, justifiable in a book for very young children, has to do with the man in the iron cage in Interpreter's House. In *The Pilgrim's Progress* Christian learns that the man in the cage was once, as he thought, bound for the Celestial City but now he is "a man of Despair." He had failed "to watch and be sober" and had "sinned against the Light of the Word and the Goodness of God." He had so hardened his heart, he told Christian, that he could not now repent. In *The Evergreen Wood*, however, Christopher sees in one corner of a room in the Badger's House, near the warmth of the fire, a cage where a little dormouse lives. "Why is Dormouse in a cage?" asked Christopher. "Dormouse set off on the journey to The Evergreen Wood," explains Brockley the Badger, "but he was too fearful to continue, so I allow him to live here until he can find enough courage to go on." A similar change comes at the very end of the book. In *The Pilgrim's Progress*, Ignorance follows Christian and Hopeful across the river in a ferry operated by Vain-Hope. He comes to the gate of the city, but when he can produce no certificate, two angels bind him and take him to the door in the side of the hill and put him in. "Then I saw that there was a Way to Hell," writes Bunyan, "even from the Gates of Heaven, as well as from the City of Destruction." This incident in *The Evergreen Wood* portrays the mole Shady discovering an old flat-bottomed boat. "Shady loved boats. He leapt onto it, poled it free of the reeds, and glided off down the river. Christopher and Heathley saw him go. Shady seemed to have forgotten all about them and the Evergreen Wood." These changes are understandable in a book for small children. They do not present wrong ideas, but there will come a time for the sterner theology of Bunyan.

Pilgrim's Progress "retold and shortened for modern readers" by Mary Godolphin (1884) and illustrated by Robert Lawson (1939) is an excellent abridgment of Bunyan's masterpiece (J. B. Lippincott, 1884, 1939). Godolphin's text, which reduces the book to less than one-fifth of its original length, manages to include almost all of the major events, and accurate summaries of many of the conversations—in words usually taken directly from Bunyan. Godolphin omits entirely the man in the iron cage in Interpreter's House, the two giants, Pope and Pagan, and the fate of Ignorance. The death of Faithful at Vanity Fair, however, is included and is described as "the worst death that could be thought of." According to Robert Lawson, who wrote the foreword to the 1939 edition, it became apparent that Mary Godolphin had done "an almost perfect job, and it was decided to use her text exactly as it stood" rather than create another abridgment.[1] Concerning the illustrations, Lawson wrote, "I have tried more than anything else to make the characters living and real, with fairly accurate costumes and surroundings of Bunyan's time." His pictures strike me, however, as more medieval than seventeenth-century.

One of the strengths of Godolphin's abridgment is her inclusion of Christiana's journey. Fifty pages of her text treat Part I, and forty pages, Part II. (Part II in Bunyan's original is slightly shorter than Part I). Great-Heart appears prominently in Godolphin's story, as he does in Bunyan's original, but another memorable character of Part II, Valiant-for-Truth, is missing.

Dangerous Journey (Marshall Morgan and Scott/Eerdmans, 1985), with text by Oliver Hunkin and illustrations by Alan Parry, was produced for Channel Four Television and Yorkshire Television Limited. The title (which was included in the subtitle of the first edition of *Pilgrim's Progress*) captures the essence of only part of Bunyan's story. The journey from the City of Destruction to the Celestial City was indeed filled with enemies and dangers, but there were also times of joy, pleasure, rest, good food, dancing—and plenty of excellent conversation. Hunkin's text comprises a greatly shortened version of *Pilgrim's Progress*, but it is generally faithful to Bunyan and often in Bunyan's words. Alan Parry (who illustrated *The Evergreen Wood*) uses a fairly elaborate cartoon style to produce lively pictures of seventeenth-century English people and scenes. The "bad" people, giants, and dangerous animals are all depicted as grossly ugly and evil. The best pictures are of landscapes and buildings.

Hunkin's text remains close to Bunyan's story. When Christian comes to Interpreter's House, he asks the man in the iron cage what he has done to bring himself to that condition. The man replies:

I failed to keep watch. I followed the pleasures of this world, which promised me all manners of delights. But they proved to be an empty

bubble. *And now I am shut up in this iron cage—a man of despair who*
can't get out.

Then follow the words: "No further explanations were given.
No one said who put him there. But the Interpreter whispered to
Christian: 'Bear well in mind what you have seen.'"

At the end of the Valley of the Shadow of Death, at the place of
the "pile of skulls and mangled bones" of former pilgrims, is the
home of two giants. *Dangerous Journey* explains, "But one had now
been dead for many years," and the other, "whose name was Pagan,
though he was still alive, was, by reason of his age, grown too stiff in
his joints to venture far." In Bunyan's story, however, it is Pagan who
has been dead many days. Bunyan, in his time, saw raw paganism
as no longer a threat to England. The other giant, named Pope, is
still alive but old and stiff and not now a danger to pilgrims. When
Bunyan wrote Part I of *Pilgrim's Progress*, it appeared that Roman
Catholicism had lost its power in England.

As in Bunyan's account, Faithful in *Dangerous Journey* is put to
death at Vanity Fair. He is carried to heaven in a chariot to the sound
of trumpets. And so he arrives first at the Celestial City, and, "having
been Faithful unto death, the King would give him a crown of life."

At the end of *Dangerous Journey*, when all heaven is welcoming
Christian and Hopeful, Ignorance arrives and is refused entrance
because he does not have a "parchment-roll." He "sorrowfully
turned back," and that is the last they see of Ignorance. No mention
is made of his having been bound and put in the door in the side of
the hill—the way to hell.

The last chapter of *Dangerous Journey* is a short summary of Part
II of *Pilgrim's Progress*, the story of Christiana's journey. It is told
too briefly, however, to capture the charm and significance of the
original.

John Bunyan's *Pilgrim's Progress* (William B. Eerdmans, 1994)
is "retold" by Gary D. Schmidt, professor of English at Calvin
College, and illustrated by Barry Moser. The first of Moser's fifty
watercolors is a portrait of Bunyan and the last a drawing of the
Celestial City. In between are wonderful depictions of scenes from
Bunyan's book, set in different historical eras. Christian is pictured

as a contemporary young man, burdened with a backpack piled high, walking through a field of wheat that looks as if it could be in Kansas, and reading a book. Later scenes of hills and mountains resemble the Rocky Mountains of the American West. My favorite sketch is of Evangelist—who is pictured as a distinguished black man, with white hair and beard, wearing a white suit, red tie, and red handkerchief. (This is especially important because in Bunyan's book it is Flatterer, "a false apostle that hath transformed himself into an angel of light," who is described, unfortunately, as "a black man, clothed in white.")

Schmidt's text, as he explains in the preface, is "not . . . *Pilgrim's Progress* with the language simplified or the lengthy discussions cut out." In his book, Schmidt tries "to stay close to Bunyan's original," but he attempts to tell his story to a contemporary audience— "which is, after all, what [Bunyan] did." Schmidt usually follows very closely Bunyan's own account. Occasionally he adds an engaging new thought or incident. For example, after Christian left home, Christiana, in Schmidt's story, looked out of the window when she heard the jeering and laughing at Pliable's pitiful return after he fell in the Slough of Despond. Christiana

> turned when her youngest child, David, held out his hands to be picked up. "Such a little one," she cooed as she carried him away from the window, but he had not been interested in the street at all. He pointed to a window that looked over fields to the east. "Light," he said, pointing with a fist. "Light." But she did not see it.

In Schmidt's text, at the end of the Valley of the Shadow of Death, Christian encountered only one giant—Pagan. In Bunyan's account Pagan was dead, and Pope, the other enemy of Christian pilgrims, was so weakened that he was unable to continue his assault on them. Schmidt does not mention Giant Pope.

An appealing addition to the story occurs at the end when Christian and Hopeful crossed the river. According to Schmidt,

> when they came out of the waters, they felt that their bodies had changed. They were light and new and strong. All that was mortal had

been washed away in the river. And Christian's armor had floated back
to the other shore, where it was being reverently gathered by fair hands
so that it might be carried to the Armory of the Palace Beautiful, where
at this moment a new banner was being hung, with a story as new and
as old as all the world.

Schmidt adds a surprise ending to Bunyan's account of the man in the iron cage in Interpreter's House. The man said to Christian, "Leave me alone. Must you plague me with your possibilities? I am Despair, and I am lost." Christian and the Interpreter left the room quietly and not a little sadly. "Is there no hope for him?" asked Christian. "One," said the Interpreter. (In Bunyan's account, Interpreter's final word is a warning to Christian.) Schmidt's Interpreter did not explain, but at the end of the story, when Christian and Hopeful reached the gates of the Celestial City, the bells rang and a cry went up "so loud and so joyous that it woke Despair back in the Interpreter's House. He looked up and, with shaking hand, reached for the door of his cage."

Schmidt's retelling does not include Bunyan's Part II—the story of Christiana—but his account ends with Christian looking back through the gates of the Celestial City just before they closed. He saw the whole landscape of his journey, all the way down to the City of Destruction, "and even his own house, where the door had just opened and Christiana had stepped out, shepherding their four children toward the path that would lead them to the Shining Gate."

Footnotes

[1] Mary Godolphin's text, with the language modernized "to some degree" and the story expanded by nearly a third, was reprinted in 1999 by Christian Family Publications as an "edition written in words of one syllable" for "both children and adults." It is not strictly a book of words of one syllable; Bunyan's original is mainly a book of words of one syllable. Other recent modernized texts of *Pilgrim's Progress* include *Pilgrim's Progress in Today's English* retold by James H. Thomas (Chicago: Moody Press, 1964), *The New Pilgrim's Progress* updated by Judith E. Markham (Grand Rapids: Discovery House Publishers, 1989), and *Little Pilgrim's Progress* by Helen L. Taylor (Chicago: Moody Press, n.d.).

Christian Focus Publications
publishes books for all ages

Our mission statement —

STAYING FAITHFUL
In dependence upon God we seek to help make His infallible Word, the Bible, relevant. Our aim is to ensure that the Lord Jesus Christ is presented as the only hope to obtain forgiveness of sin, live a useful life and look forward to heaven with Him.

REACHING OUT
Christ's last command requires us to reach out to our world with His gospel. We seek to help fulfill that by publishing books that point people towards Jesus and help them develop a Christ-like maturity. We aim to equip all levels of readers for life, work, ministry and mission.

Books in our adult range are published in three imprints.

Christian Focus contains popular works including biographies, commentaries, basic doctrine and Christian living. Our children's books are also published in this imprint.

Mentor focuses on books written at a level suitable for Bible College and seminary students, pastors, and other serious readers. The imprint includes commentaries, doctrinal studies, examination of current issues and church history.

Christian Heritage contains classic writings from the past.

Christian Focus Publications, Ltd
Geanies House, Fearn,
Ross-shire, IV20 1TW, Scotland, United Kingdom
info@christianfocus.com